Text
Rice

Freedom of Association

CHARLES E. RICE

Freedom of Association

Foreword by Robert B. McKay

New York University Press — 1962

Library of Congress Catalog Card Number: 62–16636

Manufactured in the United States of America

Publication of this work was made possible by a partial subsidy from THE FORD FOUNDATION, to whom the publishers make grateful acknowledgment.

To my mother and my wife, whose encouragement and assistance have been indispensable.

Acknowledgments

I wish to acknowledge gratefully the counsel and recommendations of Professors Robert B. McKay and Edmond Cahn of the New York University School of Law. The assistance of Mr. Francis C. Suarino in verifying the accuracy of the manuscript was essential and excellently rendered. Mrs. Michael Suchy and Mrs. Adrian C. Wyker contributed substantially through the reliability of the clerical tasks that they performed.

Foreword

During the Constitutional Convention in 1787, Alexander Hamilton and others argued that a Bill of Rights was not essential because the proposed government, which was to have only limited powers, could not restrict the liberty of citizens without express authority. Although that view prevailed at the time, some states demanded, as the price of ratification of the basic Constitution, a promise that a Bill of Rights would be proposed at the first opportunity. Few would now doubt the wisdom of their insistence that the essential liberties be guaranteed in unmistakable terms. In that original charter of American liberty, the First Amendment was of crucial importance, and the centrality of its role has, if anything, increased over the years.

With this background in mind, a person reading the First Amendment for the first time might expect to find there the grand passion of the Declaration of Independence, or at least the serene eloquence of the Preamble of the Constitution. Instead, the enumerated proscriptions upon Congressional action, although strikingly absolute in character, provide a different, but also compelling authority in the very matter-of-factness of their statement. The explanation for this seemingly relaxed approach to beliefs deeply held probably lies in the fact that all the ratifying states apparently shared these views without reservation. Accordingly, it was natural that the language should be imperative ("Congress shall make no law. . . ."); and the specified freedoms seemed at the time as all-inclusive and as precise as language permitted. Although stated as prohibitions, the enumerated categories in sum should be regarded as affirmative guarantees relating to the central theme of free belief and expression. The six rights or freedoms thus assured include four that are familiar to all—separation of Church and State, free exercise of religion, freedom of speech, and freedom of the press—as well as two that are less well known—freedom of assembly, and the right of petition.

Doubtless in 1791, when the First Amendment was ratified, this statement of rights seemed altogether adequate to assure freedom of belief and expression against intrusion by the national government. In fact, no one suggested for more than a century and a half that the list was less than all-inclusive. Specifically, it was not until 1958 that a further freedom was discovered in the First Amendment. In *NAACP v. Alabama,* Mr. Justice Harlan stated for a unanimous Court (357 U.S. 449, 460): "It is beyond debate that freedom to engage in association for the advancement of beliefs and ideas is an inseparable aspect of the 'liberty' assured by the Due Process Clause of the Fourteenth Amendment, which embraces freedom of speech." Thus, almost casually, was freedom of association written into the First and Fourteenth Amendments as a limitation on the national and state governments respectively.

It is of course not accurate to think of this modern enunciation of freedom of association as judicial amendment of the Constitution. Although a literal reading of the First Amendment discloses no reference to freedom of association as such, no one can doubt, once the question is raised, that where freedom of speech and assembly are found, there also must reside freedom of association. To be sure, association is not quite the same as either speech or assembly. A person may associate himself with others without ever meeting in person with those with whom he seeks common cause; and he may not speak at all beyond whatever few words may be required in the act of joining. But clearly the reason for which he associates himself is to encourage assembly for the shaping of common goals and to permit speech by or in the name of the group.

Such interstitial elaboration of the bare bones of a constitution is of course a proper judicial function for a constitutional court. Fortunately, in this instance the development was easy because the principle stated was readily understandable—and because it was agreed upon by a unanimous Court. It is even possible, with the advantage of hindsight, to speculate that the formulation of freedom of association as a basic right could have been predicted by the careful observer. Mr. Justice Rutledge, speaking for the Court in 1944 in *Thomas v. Collins* (323 U.S. 516, 530), had said:

It is therefore in our tradition to allow the widest room for discussion, the narrowest range for its restriction, particularly when this right is exercised in conjunction with peaceable assembly. It was not by accident that the rights to freedom in speech and press were coupled in a single guaranty with the rights of the people peaceably to assemble and to petition for redress of grievances.

Similarly, in January 1958, only a few months before the decision in *NAACP v. Alabama,* the Court held invalid on its face a municipal ordinance that made it an offense to "solicit" citizens of that community to become members of any "organization, union or society." Although decision in that case, *Staub v. City of Baxley* (355 U.S. 321), was grounded on freedom of speech, the right protected had a dual aspect. Not only was the solicitor assured of his right to seek members, but potential members as well were protected in their right to learn about—and to join if so inclined—the organization in question.

It was not a very long step from such rulings to the decision that Alabama, in the particular context of racial hostility, could not compel the NAACP to disclose the names of its members within the state, that result being based on freedom of association guaranteed by the First and Fourteenth Amendments. Accordingly, it is demonstrable that *NAACP v. Alabama* is merely the culminating episode and that its antecedents lie deep in the jurisprudence and history of American traditions of liberty. Charles E. Rice, assistant professor of law at Fordham University, has told the complete story in this volume, which he appropriately calls *Freedom of Association.* Not only does Professor Rice demonstrate convincingly the inevitable logic of this development, but he has as well explored and illuminated the significance for the future of the concept of freedom of association. He argues persuasively that freedom of association is not simply another and essentially distinct freedom within the framework of the First and Fourteenth Amendments. More significantly, the recognition of freedom of association as a separately cognizable right provides a new perspective with which to understand freedoms long articulated, and to strengthen further the liberties they are meant to safeguard.

Take a single example. Professor Rice suggests how the freedom-of-association concept can strengthen the establishment and free-exercise clauses of the First Amendment, which have regularly been subject to "unsatisfactory and contradictory analyses." He says:

For example, the free-exercise and establishment arguments against most indirect public subventions of religion are weakened by the facts that there usually is no substantial impairment of the dissenting taxpayer's right to exercise his own religion and that the treatment of indirect aid as an "establishment of religion" involves a considerable stretching of that concept. When the taxpayer objects, however, that he is being compelled to associate with others in their religious endeavors, his objection carries a greater plausibility even though he still must surmount the hurdles created by the nonabsolute character of freedom of association and the *de minimis* nature of his interest in most such public subsidies.

In his exploration of the potentialities of freedom of association for the further strengthening of notions of individual liberty, Professor Rice has chosen an effective organizational frame. Perhaps he took his lead from Mr. Justice Harlan's comment in *NAACP v. Alabama* (357 U.S. at 460–61): "Of course, it is immaterial whether the beliefs sought to be advanced by association pertain to political, economic, religious or cultural matters. . . ." In similar spirit, Professor Rice has chosen four important areas as the background of his study.

Religious, political, and subversive associations have been chosen here because they present most clearly the problem of freedom to associate for the purpose of promulgating ideas, which is a central constitutional issue of our time and which was the type of freedom of association expressly sanctioned in *NAACP v. Alabama*, above. Our fourth category, the association regulating livelihood, includes the right to associate, or not, in labor unions, and the intriguing incidence of similar problems in professional associations. These associations, which regulate or directly affect the livelihood of their members, are pertinent because they are ones in which both the right to join and the right not to join have been squarely and exhaustively challenged.

The particular value of this study—in its original form a dissertation submitted as part of the requirements for a J.S.D. at the New York University School of Law—is that it offers new insight into the familiar, yet always controversial, area of First Amendment freedoms. Probably it is unnecessary to remind the reader that, because the subject of the volume is the First Amendment, there will inevitably be disagreement over interpretation. The important thing is that the relevant arguments have been made, clearly and calmly. Professor Rice has made a real contribution to understanding in the area by indicating unmistakably the points on which discussion of the pertinent issues should center. Freedom of speech itself will be furthered to the extent that this volume stimulates, as it should, rational discussion and new comprehension of the concept of freedom of association.

ROBERT B. MCKAY
Professor of Law, New York University

New York City
August 1962

Contents

Introduction

In 1958, the following language was figuratively engrafted upon the Constitution of the United States:

> . . . It is beyond debate that freedom to engage in association for the advancement of beliefs and ideas is an inseparable aspect of the "liberty" assured by the Due Process Clause of the Fourteenth Amendment, which embraces freedom of speech.[1]

This rule of law, so precisely enunciated by the Supreme Court, was not expressly avowed in any of the decisions cited in its support.[2] In fact, what the court did in the NAACP decision was to recognize and proclaim, for the first time in unequivocal terms,[3] a freedom which had been latent in many years of constitutional development. Nowhere in the Constitution is freedom of association, or the right to associate, mentioned. But, as the language of the court implies, freedom of association is nothing new. The right to associate for the advancement of ideas has been recognized im-

[1] NAACP v. Alabama, 357 U.S. 449, 460 (1958).

[2] Gitlow v. New York, 268 U.S. 652, 666 (1925); Palko v. Connecticut, 302 U.S. 319, 324 (1937); Cantwell v. Connecticut, 310 U.S. 296, 303 (1940); Staub v. Baxley, 355 U.S. 313, 321 (1958).

[3] Compare Article 20 of the Universal Declaration of Human Rights: "(1) Everyone has the right to freedom of peaceful assembly and association. (2) No one may be compelled to belong to an association." Compare also the language of Georges Gurvitch's Draft Declaration of Social Rights, Art. LVIII: "Le Pluralisme des groupes, et des ensembles autonomes et equivalents se servant réciproquement de contrepoids est proclamé une des garanties fondamentales de la liberté humaine et des droits sociaux de l'homme. Le droit à ce pluralisme commun à l'homme, au producteur, au consommateur et au citoyen, sera protégé par tous les moyens dont dispose la Nation, s'affirmant comme unité immanente dans la pluralité des groupes." Gurvitch, La Déclaration des droits sociaux (New York, 1944).

plicitly in the past, and it has underlain important decisions which have been formally ascribed to the application of other freedoms.

Indeed, it seems reasonable to conclude, from a study of the past developments and present situation, that the right to associate is not limited, as were the facts in the NAACP case itself, to association for the spread of ideas, but rather includes association for other purposes as well.[4] It is in the area of groups for the advancement of ideas, however, that the right of association has sustained its heaviest attacks and received its clearest definition.

The purpose here is to examine this newly articulated freedom of association, with particular emphasis upon the right, and sometimes the duty, of the individual to associate, and his correlative right or duty not to associate. Only incidentally, and as far as necessary to the central inquiry, will the rights and duties of associations themselves be discussed. It is necessary to distinguish between the right to associate for a purpose, and the right as an individual, without associating, to act for the same purpose as the organization. Often these two rights coincide, but sometimes they diverge. It frequently happens that vindications of the right to associate for a particular purpose are merely vindications of a right to do something the person could do as an individual; for instance, the right to associate with others for the purpose of offering religious worship. Such examples, therefore, are not solely referable to a right of association. There are situations, however, in which an individual's right to do, or not to do, a particular thing becomes greater or less when he acts in association with others. A person who conscientiously objects to military service has a clearer immunity to service if his objection is a tenet of a religious group to which he belongs; at least the governing statutes recognize this to be so. Conversely, a person's individual right to oppose the government decreases when he does so in association with others in such a way as to subject himself to the strictures validly imposed upon members of subversive groups. In these and other instances, the right to associate for some purposes is accorded higher standing than the right to associate for others. The right to join together for religious purposes is therefore, as we shall see, accorded a higher standing than the right

[4] See Schlesinger, Biography of a Nation of Joiners, 50 Am. Hist. Rev. 1 (1944). But see Note, Freedom of Association: Constitutional Right or Judicial Technique?, 46 Va. L. Rev. 730 (1960), asserting that freedom of association is merely a judicial technique for dealing with certain types of cases rather than an independent constitutional right.

to associate for subversive ends. Out of such varied situations, there can be developed a freedom of association which is not simply coextensive with individual civil liberties in general.

The elevation of freedom of association to the rank of a fundamental liberty was but the culmination of converging past developments. This newly recognized freedom is raised upon propositions of long standing. In tracing its outlines, we must examine those situations in which its underlying norms have been formulated. Those general principles, and their application, can be discerned in four instances in which men have sought to exercise their right of association. Men have sought to form and join religious groups, associations regulating livelihood, political parties and pressure groups, and what, for various reasons, have been called subversive associations. Other types of associations could have been selected for analysis, e.g., commercial corporations and partnerships,[5] trade associations,[6] and fraternal organizations.[7] But religious, political, and subversive associations have been chosen here because they present most clearly the problem of freedom to associate for the purpose of promulgating ideas, which is a central constitutional issue of our time and which was the type of freedom of association expressly sanctioned in *NAACP v. Alabama,* above. Our fourth category, the association regulating livelihood, includes the right to associate, or not, in labor unions, and the intriguing incidence of similar problems in professional associations. These organizations, which regulate or directly affect the livelihood of their members, are pertinent because they are ones in which both the right to join and the right not to join have been squarely and exhaustively challenged. The issues raised by those challenges are pertinent to the other associations we shall discuss and to freedom of association in general.

The task, then, is to identify the constituent principles of freedom of association, to catalogue its past development and to indicate its position and durability in the hierarchy of fundamental liberties.

[5] See Davis, Essays in the Earlier History of American Corporations (Cambridge, 1917); Mason, The Corporation in Modern Society (Cambridge, 1959); Hammond, Banks and Politics in America (Princeton, 1957).

[6] See Jones, Trade Associations and the Law (New York, 1922).

[7] See Ferguson, Fifty Million Brothers (New York, 1937).

to associate for adversative ends. Out of such varied situations, there can be developed a freedom of association which is not simply coextensive with individual civil liberties in general.

The elevation of freedom of association to the rank of a fundamental liberty was but the culmination of converging past developments. The newly recognized freedom is raised upon propositions of long standing. In tracing its origins we must examine those situations in which its underlying norms have been formulated. These general principles and their application are documented in four [illegible] association. [illegible] groups [illegible] Other types of associations could have been selected for analysis, [illegible] corporations, and partnerships, [illegible] and fraternal organizations. But religious, political, and subversive associations have been chosen here because they [illegible] freedom to associate [illegible] is a central constitutional [illegible] freedom of association [illegible] above. The fourth category [illegible] includes [illegible]

Freedom of Association

I. *Jurisprudential Background*

It is essential to realize, in probing this new, but yet old, freedom, that it has deep philosophical roots. The roster of intellectual history is studded with scholars who have examined the right of the individual to combine with others and to form, as it were, voluntary subgovernments directed toward private ends. If the right of the individual to combine be denied, we have obviously restricted his freedom. But if we acknowledge the right of combination, the resultant group may, by the force inherent in unity and cooperation, possess powers which curtail the freedoms of nonmembers.[1] Indeed, if partial societies are to be encouraged, they may reach a point at which their pretensions to authority will rival that of the state itself.[2] It is this prospect which conjures up the familiar disputations between monists and pluralists. The monist postulates a single source of comprehensive and theoretically unlimited authority, i.e., of sovereignty in society. The pluralist envisions a society without such a hierarchical centralization of political will, but rather with authority and power divided and apportioned among coordinate bodies.[3] The issue of pluralism is relevant to our thesis only insofar as it illuminates the importance, and far-reaching effects, of the right of association. We are primarily concerned here with the right or duty to join an association, and not with the function of associations themselves as alternative, i.e., pluralistic, centers of political and social authority.

[1] Dicey, Law and Public Opinion in England 154–55 (London, 1926).
[2] See Sutherland, Private Government and Public Policy, 41 Yale Rev. 407 (1952)
[3] On the question of pluralism generally, see Hsiao, Political Pluralism 3–8 passim (New York, 1927).

The question of the individual's right to associate has attracted philosophers from the earliest days. Moreover, some of those who pondered the issue were familiar to the men who wrought the Constitution of the United States. We ought, therefore, in order to understand freedom of association and its importance in America, to scan the philosophers. Some we will discuss because their positions on the right of association were apparently known to the Founding Fathers. Others are relevant because, even though the reliance of the framers upon them is not verifiable, their speculations are important to a general understanding of the subject. We cannot here essay a survey of all who have written on the question. Nor can we hope to treat intensively those whom we do mention. Rather, we can show merely that the architects of jurisprudence have not been silent on the right to associate, that the framers could not have been ignorant of the issue, and that the presently operative principles have a more enduring basis than might otherwise appear.

PHILOSOPHERS PRIOR TO SEVENTEENTH AND EIGHTEENTH CENTURIES

Many of the natural-law theories of the Founding Fathers have been traced back to earlier writers such as Aristotle, Aquinas and others.[4] It is, therefore, relevant to note briefly the ideas of some of those earlier thinkers who adverted to the right of association.

Plato (427–347 B.C.), for example, demanded that the individual should identify himself with no lower order than the State, and he continually extolled the virtues of family-like unity in the State.[5] His ultraorganic conception of the State, reminiscent of Sparta, did not recognize the right of intermediate associations to exist.[6] Despite some amelioration of his strict views in his progression from the *Republic* through the *Statesman* to the *Laws*,[7] Plato held throughout to the theory that the State is the paramount agency for the satisfaction of the needs of the individual, and that to it

[4] Dumbauld, The Declaration of Independence & What It Means Today 37, 42 (Norman, 1950).

[5] Republic, Bks. V and X Statesman; see Plato, The Dialogues of Plato, III, 156, 157 and IV, 453 (Jowett transl.) (Oxford, 1892).

[6] Barker, Greek Political Theory 234 (London, 1951); Del Vecchio, Philosophy of Law (Martin transl.) 31 (Washington, 1953).

[7] Barker, Greek Political Theory 206, 282, 318 et seq. (London, 1951); Field, The Philosophy of Plato 77 (Oxford, 1949).

the individual owes an undivided loyalty undistracted by partial allegiances.[8]

Aristotle (384–322 B.C.) was Plato's pupil, but he rejected his master's total unification of the State.[9] Although conceding the necessity of the State, and its priority in the body politic,[10] Aristotle explicitly recognized a pluralistic feature of society and a right in the citizen to form and join "partial limited associations" which are "parts of the grand association which is the body politic." [11] Where Plato implied a necessary submergence of the individual under the direct influence of the total State, Aristotle advanced the right of association as a protection against a universal conformity, while recognizing the role of the citizen as an integral part of the overall society.[12] Mirrored in this conflict between the great master and his pupil we can see a basic constitutional and legal tension of our own day. Indeed, lest we congratulate ourselves on having discovered, in 1958, a new freedom, we ought to recall that Theophrastus, Aristotle's successor as head of the Lyceum, was expelled from his post by a decree which was later declared unconstitutional as an infringement on the right of association.[13]

From Aristotle we proceed to Augustine (354–430), who is pertinent because he traced, albeit somewhat vaguely, a theory of the relation between religious associations and the State. In Augustine's view, the Church and the temporal city do find a *modus communiter vivendi,* in which Christians "obey the laws of the earthly city, whereby the things necessary for the maintenance of this mortal life are administered." [14] Although Christians are to participate

[8] See The Laws, Bk. IX; Plato, The Dialogues of Plato, V, 259–60 (Jowett transl.) (Oxford, 1892).

[9] Politics, II, 5; Hamburger, Morals and Law; the Growth of Aristotle's Legal Theory 169–70 (New Haven, 1951); The Great Legal Philosophers (Morris ed.) 33 (Philadelphia, 1959).

[10] See Politics, VIII, 1; Hamburger, Morals and Law; the Growth of Aristotle's Legal Theory 170 (New Haven, 1951); Del Vecchio, Philosophy of Law (Martin transl.) 34 (Washington, 1953).

[11] Nicomachean Ethics, Bk. 8, Ch. 9; Aristotle, The Nicomachean Ethics (Thomson transl.) 219–20 (London, 1959).

[12] See Politics, VIII, 1; Hamburger, Morals and Law; the Growth of Aristotle's Legal Theory 170 (New Haven, 1951).

[13] See Cahn, The Predicament of Democratic Man 99 (New York, 1961).

[14] De Civitate Dei, XIX, 17; St. Augustine, The City of God (Dods transl.) 696 (Modern Library, New York, 1950); see Versfeld, A Guide to the City of God 89–90 (New York, 1958).

in the life and culture of the civil community,[15] they must not repose ultimate trust in the earthly city and must be prepared to stand on conscience.[16] Indeed, Augustine insisted that no genuine community could exist without a common religious allegiance.[17] He argued also for the use by the State of force to induce the common religious adherence.[18] From this, it is but a short step to religious domination over the State; for, if the State is to extirpate heresy, the Church must lend its expert advice, and ultimately direction, as to what is heresy.[19] In later times, this idea underlay the organic view of a united society, with the ecclesiastical function being superior to the civil.[20] It is an idea which was rejected in the Protestant Reformation,[21] scorned by the philosophers of the Enlightenment,[22] and obviously considered by the framers of the United States Constitution as inimical to the religious freedom they sought to achieve.

As an exponent of natural law, Thomas Aquinas (1225–1274) has influenced all succeeding generations, including, to an uncertain degree, those of eighteenth-century England and America.[23] Aquinas recognized the right to associate and form partial communities within the State.[24] However, he considered the State to be the highest community and an essential product of the social nature of man.[25] He did not regard the right of association, rooted in man's nature though it is, to be absolutely inalienable.[26] Aquinas formulated a theory of the relation between Church and State, whereby the temporal power is supreme in matters which concern the civil welfare, and the spiritual power rules in matters affecting the salva-

[15] See De Civitate Dei, XIX, 23; St. Augustine, The City of God (Dods transl.) 701–706 (Modern Library, New York, 1950); Versfeld, A Guide to the City of God 90 (New York, 1958).

[16] Versfeld, ibid.

[17] De Civitate Dei, XIX, 23; St. Augustine, The City of God (Dods transl.) 705–706 (Modern Library, New York, 1950).

[18] Figgis, The Political Aspects of St. Augustine's "City of God" 78 (London, 1921).

[19] Id. at 79–80.

[20] Figgis, Political Thought from Gerson to Gratius, 1414–1625 57 (New York, 1960); Versfeld, A Guide to the City of God 93 (New York, 1958).

[21] Id. at 89–90.

[22] See generally, Martin, French Liberal Thought in the Eighteenth Century 136 passim (London, 1939).

[23] Dumbauld, The Declaration of Independence & What It Means Today 37 (Norman, 1950).

[24] Commentary on the Politics of Aristotle, Bk. 1, Intro.; Aquinas: Selected Political Writings (D'Entreves ed.; Dawson transl.) 197 (Oxford, 1948).

[25] See De Regimine Principum, Bk. 1, Ch. 1 (D'Entreves ed.) id. at 3.

[26] Id. at xxx.

tion of the soul.[27] In the implied sanction he gave to the right of revolution, based upon his opinion that a human law deflecting from the law of nature is no law but rather a perversion of law and not obligatory, Aquinas was in accord with the philosophy of the American Revolution and the Constitution.[28] In Aquinas can be found a source of much later thought which accepted, perhaps unconsciously, his notions of rationality and the common good,[29] including their application to the right of association, while rejecting the overtones of ecclesiastical superiority which are instinct in his thought.

Other philosophers prior to the seventeenth century could be adduced to show the more remote jurisprudential sources of the right of association in the Constitution. For example, Marsilius of Padua (1290–1343), in expounding the virtues of the nonclerical State, urged that religious associations ought to be purely voluntary.[30] The Erastian effect of Lutheranism, tending toward an aggrandizement of State power, is also significant.[31] The cause of religious toleration was championed, although somewhat hesitantly, by the Politiques of the sixteenth century, such as Bodin and L'Hospital.[32] Some of the associational questions of today were foreshadowed by Roman law, with its exaltation of the State in some stages of its public law, and the rather atomistic character of its private law.[33] However, the purpose of this work, of indicating merely the existence and some characteristics of early speculation on the right of association, renders unnecessary a broader or deeper treatment of the subject. It was in the seventeenth and eighteenth centuries that definition, and disputation, of the right of association began in earnest, and it was those centuries which proximately influenced American institutions.

[27] Sum. Theolog., Qu. 147, Art. 3, Concl. (D'Entreves ed.) id. at 167. Commentary on the Sentences of Peter Lombard, Dist. 44, Qu. 3, Art. 4 (D'Entreves ed.) 187.

[28] McLaughlin, A Constitutional History of the United States 96 (New York, 1933).

[29] See Sum. Theolog., Qu. 90, Art. 2; The Great Legal Philosophers (Morris ed.) 58–59 (Philadelphia, 1959).

[30] Figgis, Political Thought from Gerson to Grotius, 1414–1625, 33–34 (New York, 1960).

[31] Id. at 89–90.

[32] Id. at 130–32.

[33] Lewis, The Genossenschaft-Theory of Otto von Gierke 47 (Madison, 1935); Walsh, A History of Anglo-American Law 377–88 (Indianapolis, 1932).

HOBBES

From the recognition by Aristotle and Aquinas of a natural, albeit not absolute, right of man to associate, we turn first to Thomas Hobbes (1588–1679), who ruled that subordinate associations lawfully exist only by permission of the sovereign. The sovereign he defines as ". . . One Person, of whose Acts a great Multitude, by mutual Covenants one with another, have made themselves every one the Author, to the end he may use the strength and means of them all, as he shall think expedient, for their Peace and Common Defence."[34] "The great Leviathan," Hobbes tells us, "is that mortal god to which we owe, under the immortal God, our peace and defence."[35]

In Chapter 22 of his major work, *Leviathan,* Hobbes classified systems (i.e., groups or associations) as regular (i.e., organized) and irregular (i.e., unorganized, such as a mass meeting or mob).[36] Of regular systems, only Commonwealths are absolute and independent, i.e., "subject to none but their own Representative."[37] Other regular systems are dependent or subordinate. Of subordinate regular systems, some are political, i.e., "made by authority from the Sovereign Power of the Common-wealth."[38] The main "politicall" subordinate regular systems are the municipal corporation and the business corporation, i.e., the company of merchants. The remaining subordinate regular systems are private, i.e., "constituted by Subjects among themselves, or by authority from a stranger."[39] Of such private subordinate regular systems, the only ones which are lawful are those allowed to continue by the Sovereign,[40] e.g., the family unit. All other private bodies are unlawful.[41] Included in that unlawful category are groups of beggars, thieves, and gypsies "and the Corporations of men, that by authority from any forraign Person, unite themselves in another's Dominion, for the easier propagation of Doctrines, and for making a party, against the Power of the

[34] Leviathan, Ch. 17; Hobbes, Leviathan 90 (Ernest Rhys, ed., London); see also The Great Legal Philosophers (Morris ed.) 120 (Philadelphia, 1959).

[35] Leviathan, Ch. 17; see Stephen, Hobbes 182 (London, 1904).

[36] Horn, Groups and the Constitution 5–6 (Stanford, 1956).

[37] Leviathan, Ch. 22; Hobbes, Leviathan 117–18 (Rhys ed.).

[38] Leviathan, Ch. 22.

[39] Leviathan, Ch. 22.

[40] Hobbes, Leviathan 117–118 (Ernest Rhys ed., London).

[41] Id. at 124.

Common-wealth." [42] The latter is an obvious reference to the Church of Rome.

Irregular systems are lawful if not forbidden by the Sovereign and if not formed with evil design or intent. Factions and conspiracies are considered "unnecessary to the maintaining of Peace and Justice" [43] and unlawful:

> Factions for Government of Religion, as of Papists, Protestants, etc. or of State, as Patricians, and Plebeians of old time in Rome, and of Aristocraticalls and Democraticalls of old time in Greece, are unjust, as being contrary to the peace and safety of the people, and a taking of the Sword out of the hand of the Sovereign.[44]

Hobbes here is condemning independent religious groups, aristocracies, political parties and pressure groups.

An irregular system, i.e., a mere assembly, may be unlawful and seditious because of its purpose and size:

> It may be lawfull for a thousand men, to joyn in a Petition to be delivered to a Judge or Magistrate: yet if a thousand men come to present it, it is a tumultuous assembly; because there needs but one or two for that purpose. But in such cases as these, it is not a set number that makes the Assembly Unlawfull, but such a number, as the present Officers are not able to suppresse, and bring to Justice.[45]

Sedition, and seditious combination, are unlawful, at least as long as the Sovereign performs his function of providing security.[46] Hobbes described as "a Sedition" an "Assembly, whereof men can give no just account." Such is a breach of the obligation owed by all men to the Sovereign. No subject can transfer his allegiance without the consent of the Sovereign.[47] The will of the Sovereign is the will of all; he is under no obligation of allegiance to his subjects, but is the object of their obligation.[48] It is, moreover, the duty of the Sovereign to suppress even murmurs of discontent, and the ventilation of seditious opinions. For the diseases which bring about the "dissolution of Common-wealths are seditious opinions." [49]

[42] Leviathan, Ch. 22; Hobbes, Leviathan, id. at 124.
[43] Ibid.
[44] Leviathan, Ch. 22; Hobbes, Leviathan, id. at 125–26.
[45] Leviathan, Ch. 22; Hobbes, id. at 125.
[46] See Leviathan, Ch. 29; The Great Legal Philosophers (Morris ed.) 130–31 (Philadelphia, 1959).
[47] See Stephen, Hobbes 196 (London, 1904).
[48] Id. at 195.
[49] Id. at 221.

Of all seditions, perhaps the most iniquitous, in Hobbes's view, is that of an independent Church. Since the Sovereign, in the interest of the preservation of peace, has the sole right to decide what opinions may be voiced in the Commonwealth, Hobbes would necessarily forbid any division between the civil and the spiritual power.[50] In *Leviathan,* Hobbes was wont to refer to such a Church with independent pretensions as "the kingdom of darkness." [51] Indeed, half of *Leviathan* [52] is devoted to his argument against the separation of spiritual and temporal authority. He contends that the Sovereign must be supreme in both fields because the Church (especially the Church of Rome) has no claim to authority and is merely the pretending heir of the defunct Roman Empire:

> And if a man consider the originall of this great Ecclesiasticall Dominion, he will easily perceive, that the Papacy, is no other than the Ghost of the deceased Romane Empire, sitting crowned upon the grave thereof: For so did the Papacy start up on a Sudden out of the ruines of that Heathen Power.[53]

In dedicating his work, *Seven Problems,* to Charles II, Hobbes remarked, "Religion is not philosophy but law." [54] When the Sovereign authorizes or prohibits the preaching of particular doctrines, he does so not on the basis of truth or falsity, but on the basis of whether the doctrine in question is conducive to peace or discord. Correspondingly, when a subject professes his faith in the religion established or authorized by the Sovereign, he does so not from theological conviction but from obedience to the proper political authority of the Sovereign.[55] In practical effect, then, Hobbes would permit the existence only of such religious associations as would be compatible with the political design of the Sovereign. Any Church permitted to exist would be fused with the State, but with the ecclesiastical authority in a position of subjection rather than one of theocratic domination. Hobbes's design for an omnipotent State exerted considerable influence on the succeeding generations and presented an alternative, rejected by his and the following century, to the more benign conceptions of Locke.[56]

[50] Taylor, Thomas Hobbes 116 (London, 1908).
[51] Id. at 121–22.
[52] The third part, "Of a Christian Common-wealth" and the fourth, "Of the Kingdom of Darkness."
[53] Leviathan, Ch. 47; Hobbes, Leviathan 381 (Ernest Rhys, ed., London).
[54] Stephen, Hobbes 231 (London, 1904).
[55] Taylor, Thomas Hobbes 117 (London, 1908).
[56] Plucknett, A Concise History of the Common Law 61–62 (Boston, 1956).

LOCKE

John Locke (1632–1704) believed that man has a natural and inalienable right to associate, which is subject only to clearly necessary limitation. Locke did not construct a general theory of association. Rather, his principles must be abstracted largely from his thorough discussion of Church-State relations.[57] Fundamentally, Locke postulated a separation of functions between the Church and the State. He described the State as ". . . a society of men constituted only for the procuring, preserving and advancing of their own civil interests . . . life, liberty, health, and indolency of body; and the possession of outward things . . . the whole jurisdiction of the magistrate reaches only to these civil commitments . . . it neither can nor ought in any manner to be extended to the salvation of souls. . . ."[58]

A Church Locke considered to be a manmade voluntary institution:

> . . . a voluntary society of men, joining themselves together of their own accord in order to the public worshipping of God in such manner as they judge acceptable to him, and effectual to the salvation of their souls . . . All discipline ought therefore to tend to that end, and all ecclesiastical laws to be thereunto confined.[59]

On the boundaries between these two human institutions, Locke observed:

> . . . the church itself is a thing absolutely separate and distinct from the commonwealth. The boundaries on both sides are fixed and immovable. He jumbles heaven and earth together, the things most remote and opposite, who mixes these two societies, which are in their original end, business, and in everything perfectly distinct and infinitely different from each other.[60]

Locke believed that the State can reasonably regulate outward religious rites when they impinge upon the peace and order of society, but cannot impose discriminatory restrictions upon the observances of the Church:

[57] See Horn, Groups and the Constitution 7–8 (Stanford, 1956).
[58] Letter on Toleration; quoted in Horn, id. at 24–27.
[59] Ibid.
[60] Ibid.

Whatsoever is lawful in the commonwealth can not be prohibited by the magistrate in the church. Whatsoever is permitted unto any of his subjects for their ordinary use, neither can nor ought to be forbidden by him to any sect of people for their religious uses.

Those religious practices which are dangerous to the members of the sect or to others (as polygamy would be) ". . . are not lawful in the ordinary course of life, nor in any private house; and therefore neither are they so in the worship of God, or in any religious meeting. . . . Only it is to be observed that, in this case, the law is not made about a religious, but a political matter." [61]

Presumably, Locke would have the State decide whether a question is a religious or a political matter, but the State is to be governed in this decision by the spirit of tolerance.[62] Purely speculative articles of faith, those which are required only to be believed,[63] are deemed wholly beyond the power of the State.[64] On this invulnerability of belief, Locke agrees with Hobbes, who said,

> . . . belief and unbelief never follow men's commands. Faith is a gift of God, which man can neither give, nor take away by promises of rewards, or menaces of torture.[65]

When we turn to practical religious beliefs, which influence conduct, Locke does recognize a competence in the state to intervene:

> A good life, in which consists not the least part of religion and true piety, concerns also the civil government; and in it lies the safety both of men's souls and of the commonwealth. Moral actions belong therefore to the jurisdiction both of the outward and inward court . . . both of the magistrate and conscience.[66]

[61] Letter on Toleration; quoted in Horn, Groups and the Constitution 24–27 (Stanford, 1956).

[62] See Horn, ibid.

[63] See Horn, id. at 27.

[64] Locke helped in drafting the Carolina Charter of 1669, which provided that "No person whatsoever shall disturb, molest, or persecute another for his speculative opinions in religion, or his way of worship." The Federal and State Constitutions, Colonial Charters, and Other Organic Laws (Thorpe ed.) 5 2785 (Washington, 1909); Perry, Sources of Our Liberties 166–67 (Chicago, 1959). Note the similar language of a proposal by Senators who supported established churches, in the Congress in 1789, that the First Amendment, then being drafted, should begin, "Congress shall make no law establishing articles of faith or a mode of worship or prohibiting the free exercise of religion." See discussion in Cahn, The "Establishment of Religion" Puzzle, 36 N.Y.U.L. Rev. 1274, 1280 (1961).

[65] Leviathan, Ch. 22, "Of Power Ecclesiastical"; Horn, Groups and the Constitution 26 (Stanford, 1956).

[66] Letter on Toleration; quoted in Horn, Groups and the Constitution 24–27 (Stanford, 1956).

However, the general rule remains toleration of religious doctrine, with three exceptions:

> First, No opinions contrary to human society, or to those moral rules which are necessary to the preservation of civil society, are to be tolerated by the magistrate. . . .
>
> Again: That church can have no right to be tolerated by the magistrate, which is constituted upon such a bottom, that all those who enter into it, do thereby ipso facto, deliver themselves up to the protection and service of another prince. For by this means the magistrate would give way to the settling of a foreign jurisdiction in his own country, and suffer his own people to be listed, as it were, for soldiers against his own government. . . .
>
> Lastly, those are not to be tolerated who deny the being of a God. Promises, covenants, and oaths, which are the bonds of human society, can have no hold upon an atheist. The taking away of God, tho' but even in thought, dissolves all. Besides also, those that by their atheism undermine and destroy all religion, can have no pretense of religion whereupon to challenge the privilege of a toleration.[67]

Locke, as American history attests, was a philosopher of revolution in that he recognized a limited right of revolt, and apparently of association for that purpose, against a seriously usurping government. In his *Treatise on Government,* he stated that whenever the legislators or executive:

> . . . endeavour to take away and destroy the property of the people, or to reduce them to slavery under arbitrary power, they put themselves into a state of war with the people, who are thereupon absolved from any farther obedience, and are left to the common refuge which God hath provided for all men against force and violence.[68]

The influence of Locke on the framers of the Constitution was pervasive.[69] His application of natural-law thinking to the problem of religious associations, and his concept of limited government in general, were accepted in the Colonies, and the Founding Fathers

[67] Letter on Toleration, 58–60; quoted in 1 Stokes, Church and State in the United States 145 (New York, 1950). James Madison later went beyond Locke's advocacy of mere toleration of nonadherents of the established church, and assaulted the very foundations of the establishment idea; see the discussion in Cahn, The "Establishment of Religion" Puzzle, 36 N.Y.U.L. Rev. 1274, 1277, 1283 (1961).

[68] Locke, Of Civil Government 229 (Everyman's Library, London, 1924).

[69] See MacIver, "European Doctrine and the Constitution," in The Constitution Reconsidered (Read ed.) 151–52 (New York, 1938); Dumbauld, The Declaration of Independence & What It Means Today 74–82 (Norman, 1950).

sought to put them into practical operation.[70] It is a reasonable assumption that Locke's intimation of a benevolent attitude toward the right of association in general was also favorably received by many of his readers in the Colonies.

HARRINGTON AND OTHERS

James Harrington (1611–1677) ranks next to Locke among the English writers who had influence in colonial America.[71] John Adams especially was influenced by him.[72] Harrington's popularity was widespread among the colonial intellectuals from the publication of his *Oceana* in 1656 through and beyond the American Revolution.[73]

Harrington is best remembered for his advocacy of a threefold division of governmental powers, embodying the monarchical, aristocratic, and democratic principles.[74] He does not appear to have explored the right of association in general although, as with Locke, an indication of his attitude may be seen in his treatment of religious associations. One is reminded of some American colonial establishments of religion by Harrington's advocacy of a national religion in his ideal commonwealth of Oceana,[75] with his insistence that membership in the national religion be "voluntary" and that no "gathered congregation" ("being neither Jewish nor idolatrous") shall be molested in their worship.[76]

The attitude of the framers toward the right of association was influenced by other English scholars as well. Blackstone, in postulating a concession theory of corporate personality, impliedly recognized a right in the individual to join voluntary unincorporated asso-

[70] See Rogge, The First & the Fifth 229–30 (New York, 1960); Dumbauld, id., 42. That Madison went further and rejected Locke's sanction of an established church is verified in Cahn, The "Establishment of Religion" Puzzle, 34 N.Y.U.L. Rev. 1274, 1277, 1283 (1961).

[71] See Dwight, "Harrington and His Influence upon American Political Institutions," 2 Pol. Sci. Q. 1 (1887); MacIver, "European Doctrine and the Constitution," in The Constitution Reconsidered (Read ed.) 54 (New York, 1938).

[72] Schneider, Philosophical Differences between the Constitution and the Bill of Rights, in The Constitution Reconsidered (Read ed.) 155 (New York, 1938).

[73] See generally, Smith, Harrington and His Oceana 152–200 (Cambridge, 1914).

[74] See Rogge, The First & the Fifth 229–30 (New York, 1960); Pargellis, The Theory of Balanced Government, in The Constitution Reconsidered (Read ed.) 39 (New York, 1938).

[75] Oceana, Pts. I and III; Ideal Commonwealth (Morley ed.) 210, 245 (London, 1901).

[76] Oceana, Pt. III; Morley, id. at 291.

ciations.[77] The problem of seditious associations was variously attacked. Bacon (1561–1626) opposed the suppression of discussion as a means of curbing seditions, which he ascribed to poverty and discontentment; but he did sanction measures to restrict combinations among seditious factions.[78] Similar views were expressed on the Continent by Spinoza (1632–1677).[79] John Milton's impassioned plea against censorship of heretical and seditious pamphlets is familiar to all.[80] The inevitability of political parties was convincingly argued by Edmund Burke in 1770,[81] a view to which even John Adams was to become ultimately resigned.[82]

ROUSSEAU AND OTHERS

The Constitution of the United States was a product of the eighteenth-century Enlightenment, the Age of Reason, as well as of the constitutional development of seventeenth-century England.[83] The men of the Enlightenment believed implicitly in natural law, in the undeniable Rights of Man, and in the infallibility of human reason as the means of discovering those rights.[84]

Jean Jacques Rousseau (1712–1778) immediately comes to mind as an exponent of the French Enlightenment. He is important for

[77] Commentaries, Bk. 1, Ch. 18; Blackstone, Commentaries on the Laws of England (Chase ed.) 184–86 (New York, 1936).

[78] 3 Bacon, Of Seditions and Troubles (Eliot ed.) 38–39, 43 (The Harvard Classics, New York, 1909). Bacon strongly influenced Jefferson; MacIver, European Doctrine and the Constitution, in The Constitution Reconsidered (Read ed.) 52 (New York, 1938).

[79] Spinoza, Tractatus Politicus, pref.; Durant, The Story of Philosophy 212 (New York, 1938).

[80] "And though the winds of doctrine were let loose to play upon the earth, so Truth be in the field, we do injuriously by licensing and prohibiting to misdoubt her strength. Let her and Falsehood grapple; who ever knew Truth put to the worse, in a free and open encounter." 3 Milton, Areopagitica (Eliot ed.) 239 (The Harvard Classics, New York, 1909); see Rogge, The First & the Fifth 17–18 (New York, 1960).

[81] Burke, Thoughts on the Cause of the Present Discontents (London, 1770); see Pargellis, The Theory of Balanced Government, in The Constitution Reconsidered (Read ed.) 49 (New York, 1938).

[82] Cahn, The Predicament of Democratic Man 100–101 (New York, 1961).

[83] The former element seems to have predominated in the Virginia Declaration of Rights of 1776 and the Virginia Constitution; and the latter in the United States Constitution itself. See Schneider, Philosophical Differences between the Constitution and the Bill of Rights, in The Constitution Reconsidered (Read ed.) 155 (New York, 1938).

[84] See generally, Becker, Heavenly City of the Eighteenth-Century Philosophers (New Haven, 1932); Martin, French Liberal Thought in the Eighteenth Century (London, 1929).

us, also, because he attempted to articulate a theory of the relation of the voluntary association to the State, and of the right to associate in general. Like Hobbes, Rousseau regarded unfavorably the growth of numerous secondary associations. That attitude stemmed from his belief that sovereignty, founded on the social contract, is vested in the people as a whole, and that law ought to be an expression of their general will.[85] While Rousseau's State would be democratic and observant of legal forms, the unlimited power accorded to the general will does not differ radically from the power conferred upon the total and aristocratic State of Plato.[86]

Rousseau's attitude toward the right of association is epitomized in the following passage from *The Social Contract:*

> If, when the people, being furnished with adequate information, held its deliberations, the citizens had not communication one with another, the grand total of the small differences would always give the general will, and the decision would always be good. But when factions arise, and partial associations are formed at the expense of the great association, the will of each of these associations becomes general in relation to its members, while it remains particular in relation to the State: it may then be said that there are no longer as many votes as there are men, but only as many as there are associations. The differences become less numerous and give a less general result. Lastly, when one of these associations is so great as to prevail over all the rest, the result is no longer a sum of small differences, but a single difference; in this case there is no longer a general will, and the opinion which prevails is purely particular.
>
> It is therefore essential, if the general will is to be able to express itself, that there should be no partial society within the State, and that each citizen should think only his own thoughts: which was indeed the sublime and unique system established by the great Lycurgus. But if there are partial societies, it is best to have as many as possible and to prevent them from being unequal. These precautions are the only ones that can guarantee that the general will shall be always enlightened, and that the people shall in no way deceive itself.[87]

The evident antipathy of Rousseau to the pressure group and the faction doubtless endeared him to the architects of the United

[85] See The Social Contract, Bk. 1, Ch. 6; The Great Legal Philosophers (Morris ed.) 218 (Philadelphia, 1959).

[86] See Barker, Greek Political Theory 389 (London, 1951).

[87] The Social Contract, Bk. 2, Ch. 3; Rousseau, Social Contract, and Other Works (Cole transl.) 25–26 (Oxford, 1913); see The Great Legal Philosophers (Morris ed.) 221 (Philadelphia, 1959).

States Constitution.[88] A note of resigned practicality is apparent also in his recognition that it may be impossible to prevent the multiplication of such divisive associations, in which event the general interest will best be served by making such groups so numerous that each will be individually less able to distort the expression of the general will.[89]

On the relation between religious groups and the State, Rousseau advocated a civil religion, voluntary in nature and social in creed, but apostasy from which would be a capital crime, equivalent to treason. Rousseau's religion would be established by the State, not from motives of faith, but for the reason that religious motivations are conducive to the development of the high public spirit which is necessary for the good of the State.[90]

Rousseau's ideas, particularly his *Social Contract,* influenced, at least indirectly, the Encyclopedists and other philosophers of eighteenth-century France.[91] Insofar as those others reflected on the right of association, they appear to have been hostile to it. Generally, they championed an individualistic "liberty," by which they meant a liberation from the Church, the mercantilist system, including especially the guilds, and from censorship in general.[92] Condorcet (1743–1794), for example, bitterly attacked the monopolistic guilds and corporations, and perpetual monastic associations, which he regarded as excrescences of the feudal system which recognized men only as members of a group or class.[93] The hostility of the philosophers to that all-pervading compulsory association, the Church, is famous. Voltaire (1694–1778), who had the admiration and friendship of Franklin and other American leaders,[94] attacked the compulsory and privileged Church in his *Treatise on Toleration* in 1763 and in other works.[95] His assaults were matched in purpose,

[88] See The Federalist, No. 10.

[89] The Social Contract, Bk. 2, Ch. 3; The Great Legal Philosophers (Morris ed.) 221 (Philadelphia, 1959).

[90] The Social Contract, Bk. 4, Ch. 8; id. at 235–36; see Wright, The Meaning of Rousseau 88–89 (Oxford, 1929).

[91] Del Vecchio, Philosophy of Law (Martin transl.) 102 (Washington, 1953).

[92] Schapiro, Condorcet and the Rise of Liberalism 59 (New York, 1934).

[93] See id. at 113, 160, 185.

[94] See Barr, Voltaire in America (1744–1800) 56, 114–15 (Baltimore, 1941). James Madison followed Voltaire in advocating a multiplicity of sects as a safeguard of religious freedom. See Cahn, The "Establishment of Religion" Puzzle, 34 N.Y.U.L. Rev. 1274, 1287 (1961); Brant, Madison: On the Separation of Church and State, 8 William & Mary Q. 12 (1951).

[95] See Durant, The Story of Philosophy 259 (New York, 1938); Barr, id. at 104.

if not in stridency, by his contemporaries of the Enlightenment.[96] Their hostility to associations in general, and their similarity therein to Rousseau, is seen in the fact that when the Revolutionary intellectuals found the National Assembly at their disposal, one of their early actions, in 1789, was to dissolve at a stroke all trade guilds, corporations and unions.[97] In the *Loi Chapelier*[98] the Revolution prohibited, with personal sanctions, the formation of any corporate bodies, professional associations, trade unions and the like.[99] This Revolutionary antagonism was later codified in the *Code Pénal* of 1810 (Articles 291, 292) which punished criminally all associations (except mercantile partnerships) of more than twenty persons unless specifically authorized by the government.[100]

OTHER JURISPRUDENTIAL ASPECTS

If this were a discourse only upon the philosophical wellsprings of freedom of association, it would be profitable to expand our study of the jurisprudential background. The many varieties of speculation on the right of association have hardly been intimated here because our purpose has been only to place in perspective the relevant provisions, or lack of them, in the Constitution, and the likely attitudes of the framers toward the right of association. We have seen that the Social-contract school, relying upon natural law and predominant in eighteenth-century France and America, appealed to the individual as the basis of State authority, with, in most cases, little room for intermediate organizations. Different is the approach of some modern natural-law scholars. Jacques Maritain, for example, states that the basic political reality is not the State, but the entire "body politic with its multifarious institutions, the multiple communities which it involves, and the moral community which grows out of it."[101] Indeed, Maritain recognizes a real necessity for intermediate associations in the modern pluralistic society.[102]

[96] Martin, French Liberal Thought in the Eighteenth Century 113 (London, 1929).
[97] See Dicey, Law and Public Opinion in England 469 (London, 1926).
[98] June 14–17, 1791.
[99] Duguit, Law in the Modern State (Frida & Harold Laski transls.) 111 (New York, 1919); Cahn, The Predicament of Democratic Man 100 (New York, 1961); Dicey, Law and Public Opinion in England 469 (London, 1926).
[100] See ibid.
[101] Maritain, Man and the State 202 (Chicago, 1951).
[102] Id. at 11.

In any detailed treatment, mention would also be made of anarchistic approaches to the problem of associations, often involving a reliance upon voluntary groups of one sort or another to perform the tasks now executed by compulsory government. Pyotr A. Kropotkin, for example, held that without government, every normal individual would join some association; where some individuals would be inclined toward antisocial acts, fear of ostracism would furnish a sufficient deterrent.[103] Of greater modern significance is the work of the Syndicalists, who proposed, as a substitute for the State machinery, control by autonomous units of organized workers. Typified by Georges Sorel,[104] they postulated a duty, and not merely a right, of workers to join such organizations,[105] and they proposed direct, and often violent, action to attain their ends.[106]

The right to join and form associations was carried to an apparently logical conclusion by the German, Otto von Gierke (1841–1921), who attributed to the voluntary organization a personality all its own.[107] He treated the association as an organic entity, which is not merely represented by its members but rather acts through them as the human body acts through its members.[108] The State also is an association, but it is the "sovereign" association in a structured hierarchy, and is charged with the duty of persuading or even coercing subordinates to implement the general will of which it is the oracle.[109]

The rules and regulations of a voluntary association have been said, by Duguit for example, to be genuine laws, binding the members beyond the obligations of contract.[110] The idea of the partition of sovereignty among coordinate entities, erected upon a basis of function, has been supported by Laski,[111] who regarded "the power

[103] Coker, Recent Political Thought 212 (New York, 1934); see Kropotkin, Mutual Aid, Ch. 8 (New York, 1919).

[104] See Sorel, Reflections on Violence (Hulme transl.) (New York, 1914).

[105] See Coker, Recent Political Thought Ch. 8 (New York, 1934).

[106] See Brissenden, The I.W.W. (New York, 1919).

[107] Lewis, The Genossenschaft-Theory of Otto von Gierke, 56 (Madison, 1935).

[108] See id. at 57–58; Del Vecchio, Philosophy of Law (Martin transl.) 347–48 (Washington, 1953).

[109] See Laski, Authority in the Modern State 65 (New Haven, 1919); Horn, Groups and the Constitution, 10, 13 (Stanford, 1956); Lewis, The Genossenschaft-Theory of Otto von Gierke 65 (Madison, 1935); Laski, The Foundations of Sovereignty 157 (New York, 1921).

[110] Duguit, Law in the Modern State (Frida & Harold Laski transls.) 113–14 (New York, 1919).

[111] Laski, The Foundations of Sovereignty 240–41 (New York, 1921); see also Hsiao, Political Pluralism 166, 168 (New York, 1927).

to combine for social effort" as a natural right "integral to citizenship."[112]

Many more objects of inquiry in this area could be enumerated. However, considerations of space and purpose impel us to leave the jurisprudential background of freedom of association with this treatment, cursory though it may be. The aim has been to demonstrate, by selection of a few examples, that the problems of association have occupied the minds of thoughtful men for many centuries. Thereby we may realize more readily that the basic legal and constitutional questions in this field are not wholly ones of first impression. It is to those constitutional and legal questions, and their immediate backdrop, that we ought now to direct our attention.

[112] Id. at 245–46; see also Laski, Authority in the Modern State (New Haven, 1919).

II. American Background of Freedom of Association

No real understanding of the present status of freedom of association in the United States can be had without a consideration of the pre-Revolutionary conditions and institutions from which our present forms have sprung. Even in those colonial days, there were embryonic forms of voluntary organizations—religious, political, labor, and, after a fashion, subversive.[1] A brief reference to them will set the stage for a more detailed consideration of the later developments. For clarity, the American background of freedom of association is here divided analytically into three periods of time. The developments before the Revolution, both proximate to and remote from that event, must be surveyed to appreciate the changes that followed. The changes wrought by the birth of the new nation have been divided into those between the start of the Revolution and the Constitutional Convention of 1787, and those which resulted from the charter produced in that Convention. Especially in the field of religious associations were the years between 1775 and 1787 of importance. But for the other types of organizations as well, the pre-Convention developments provide the immediate backdrop for the treatment, or rather the lack of it, of freedom of association by the framers of the Constitution.

[1] As will be discussed later herein, the subversive association is to be distinguished usually from the political party and pressure group by the fundamental hostility of the former to the basic values of the contemporary society and by its general disregard for legal forms and standards. The line between the subversive and the nonsubversive is, to say the least, difficult to draw with finality.

PRE-REVOLUTIONARY SITUATION

1. Established Churches

Magna Carta included the ringing pledge, "That the Church of England shall be free, and enjoy her whole rights and privileges inviolate."[2] This religious guarantee was something new in English constitutional history. It is common learning that this and other provisions of the great charter were overlooked or spurned in centuries following 1215.[3] However, in the seventeenth century, Magna Carta was resurrected as a defense of liberty against the arbitrary government of the Stuarts.[4] The Petition of Right in 1628, the Bill of Rights in 1689, and the Act of Toleration in 1689 are well-recognized milestones on the road to religious and political freedom.[5] They reflected an attitude which came to cherish those freedoms, an attitude which was carried by the colonists to the New World.[6]

The British government originally intended to make the Anglican the established Colonial Church, at least in all the royal colonies,[7] but this design was frustrated by events.[8] Apart from the passing establishment of the Dutch Reformed Church in New Netherland,[9] there were both Anglican and Congregational tax-supported, established churches in the colonies.[10] The Congregational Church was introduced in the Plymouth settlement by the Pilgrims in 1620.[11] Thence it spread throughout New England and became the State Church in each colony in the region except Rhode Island.[12] In

[2] 1 Stokes, Church and State in the United States 130 (New York, 1950).

[3] Id. at 130–32.

[4] Hayes, Baldwin & Cole, History of Europe 578–80 (New York, 1949).

[5] Palmer, A History of the Modern World 153 (New York, 1959); Hayes, Baldwin & Cole, id. at 581, 587.

[6] See 1 Stokes, Church and State in the United States 130–32 (New York, 1950).

[7] Massachusetts, New Hampshire, New York, New Jersey, Georgia, North Carolina, South Carolina, and Virginia were the royal colonies at the end of the colonial era; Connecticut and Rhode Island were charter colonies; Pennsylvania, Delaware, and Maryland were proprietary; Hicks & Mowry, A Short History of American Democracy 56 (Boston, 1956).

[8] 1 Chitwood & Owsley, A Short History of the American People 156–57 (New York, 1951).

[9] Hicks & Mowry, A Short History of American Democracy 38–39 (Boston, 1956).

[10] 1 Chitwood & Owsley, A Short History of the American People 155 (New York, 1951).

[11] Id. at 157.

[12] See 1 Harlow, The Growth of the United States 30–33 (New York, 1943); Chitwood & Owsley, id. at 157.

Rhode Island, there never was an established Church.[13] The Congregational establishments in Massachusetts, New Hampshire, and Connecticut endured until after the end of the Colonial period.[14] In New Netherland, the Dutch Reformed was the State Church until it was supplanted in 1664 by a technical establishment of the Anglican religion in the newly named colony of New York.[15] But that was really an establishment in name only, and, with the exception of some tax support and official recognition of the Anglican as one of the legitimate Protestant religions, freedom of choice and from coercion were well extended in colonial New York.[16]

By 1775, the Anglican Church was established by law also in Maryland,[17] Virginia, North Carolina, and Georgia. In all of these, the Anglican Church was supported by the government and was guaranteed its income from tax revenues. Often, however, the arrangement proved to be a disadvantage to the Church, owing to the frequent inadequacy of the tax-paid support and the disaffection which it engendered.[18]

In 1775, there were no establishments in New Jersey, Pennsylvania,[19] and Delaware, in addition, of course, to Rhode Island. But even these colonies, except for Rhode Island, had laws unfavorable to Catholics and non-Christians.[20]

[13] Chitwood & Owsley, ibid.; Pfeffer, Church, State and Freedom 75 (Boston, 1953).

[14] Beth, The American Theory of Church and State 59–60 (Gainesville, Florida, 1958); Chitwood & Owsley, id. at 158; Adams, The Epic of America 158 (New York, 1931).

[15] See Hicks & Mowry, A Short History of American Democracy 38–39 (Boston, 1956).

[16] See 1 Chitwood & Owsley, A Short History of the American People 156–57 (New York, 1951); 1 Harlow, The Growth of the United States 72 (New York, 1943).

[17] Maryland granted toleration to all Trinitarian Christians in the Toleration Act of 1649. For a discussion of this Act and the later progression to an Anglican establishment, see American State Papers on Freedom in Religion 43–47 (Washington, Religious Liberty Association, 1949).

[18] 1 Chitwood & Owsley, A Short History of the American People 156–57 (New York, 1951); Beth, The American Theory of Church and State 59–60 (Gainesville, Florida, 1958); Harvard University, Center for the Study of the History of Liberty in America, The Dimensions of Liberty 195 (Cambridge, prepublication draft, March 15, 1961).

[19] See Greene, Religion and the State 57–58 (New York, 1941); 1 Beard, Chas. A. & Mary R., The Rise of American Civilization 72 (New York, 1947).

[20] Beth, The American Theory of Church and State 59–60 (Gainesville, Florida, 1958).

2. *Position of Labor*

It was not until the era of the Industrial Revolution that the evolution of the employment relation brought into existence combinations of workmen for the purpose of securing better conditions of work or payment.[21] It was the factory system in England which crystallized the felt need of the wage earners for concerted action, and which generated those primitive, but genuine, labor associations which sought to rectify the imbalances in power and bargaining position which then existed between employer and employee.[22]

English common law, by the end of the eighteenth century, had anathematized most forms of concerted economic action to raise prices or wages as criminal conspiracies.[23] There are varying opinions about the origin of that attitude. Some trace it to a statement by Hawkins, "There can be no doubt, but that all confederacies whatsoever, wrongfully to prejudice a third person are highly criminal at common law." [24] Most observers, however, ascribe the inclusion of acts in restraint of trade within the classification of criminal conspiracy to such inclusion by the Court of Star Chamber in the early seventeenth century, and assert that the precedent was followed by the King's Bench upon its absorption of the jurisdiction of the Court of Star Chamber.[25]

Regardless of its origin, the treatment of most concerted labor action as criminal conspiracy was carried over to the American colonies.[26] In fact, even before the Industrial Revolution, many colonies had emulated the mother country by enacting stern labor measures.[27] Compulsory labor statutes and laws penalizing idleness were usual, both in Elizabethan England and in the colonies.[28] The workhouse system was also introduced into the colonies as a remedy

[21] See Gregory, Labor and the Law 13–14 (New York, 1958).

[22] Palmer, A History of the Modern World 426–29 (New York, 1958).

[23] See Morris, Criminal Conspiracy and Early Labor Organizations, Pol. Sci. Q. 52–57 (1937).

[24] Hawkins, Bk. 1, Ch. 72, A Treatise of the Pleas of the Crown (London, 1716); Morris, Government and Labor in Early America 137–38 (New York, 1946).

[25] 2 Pollock & Maitland, The History of English Law 539 (Cambridge, 1923).

[26] See Gregory, Labor and the Law 22 (New York, 1958); Morris, Government and Labor in Early America 137–38 (New York, 1946).

[27] Adams, The Epic of America 37–38 (New York, 1931).

[28] 39, 40 Eliz. c. 4; Plymouth Col. Rec., XI, 32, 90 (1639), 143, 144 (1658), 206 (1661–1663); Rhode Island Col. Rec., III, 452 (1702); Conn. Pub. Rec., I, 528 (1650), VI, 82 (1718); No. Car. Laws of 1755, c. 4; New York Col. Laws, II, 56 (1721).

for poverty and unemployment.[29] Such forced labor was even at times made available to private businessmen.[30]

There were various early forms of combination among wage earners and other workers in Colonial America. Guilds were sometimes recognized by law, and master craftsmen occasionally banded together to control markets and fix prices and wages.[31] Such guilds and similar societies of master workmen were infrequently found outside of New England.[32] Workers in licensed trades—that is, in those endowed with a public interest—occasionally joined together to compel the local government authorities to grant them higher wages or prices.[33] Organization of the medical and legal professions, for example, was quite advanced by the end of the Colonial period.[34]

Indentured servants, mostly in the Southern colonies, frequently formed conspiracies to flee from their labor or strike for better working conditions.[35] Free white workmen also banded together at times to exclude competition from the free Negroes, or Negro slaves, who could and would work for lower wages.[36] Sometimes such groups succeeded in obtaining legislation imposing a duty on the importation of slaves, although such legislation was generally disallowed by the King in council.[37]

Combinations of employers for purposes of trade monopoly and wage and price fixing were more common in the colonies than associations of journeymen, and were generally undisturbed by the law.[38] Moreover, collective action by journeymen workers in the colonies to raise wages or improve working conditions was rather rare, although there are records of strikes and slowdowns.[39]

[29] Pa. Stat. at Large (Mitchell and Flanders), V, 84, 85 (1749), VII, 15 (1766), 85–88 (1767); Plymouth Col. Rec., XI, 120 (1658); See 1 Labaree, Royal Instructions to Colonial Governors 342–43 (New York, 1935).

[30] See New Haven Col. Rec., 1638–1639, at 143.

[31] On the guilds in Massachusetts, see Mass. Col. Laws. 1660–1672, Intro. at 72; Hazard, The Organization of the Boot and Shoe Industry in Massachusetts before 1875 9 (Cambridge, 1921).

[32] Morris, Government and Labor in Early America 141, 146 (New York, 1946).

[33] Id. at 156.

[34] See Packard, History of Medicine in the United States 167 (New York, 1931); Shafer, The American Medical Profession, 1783–1850, 206 (New York, 1936); Hamlin, Legal Education in Colonial New York 35, 96, 158, 159 (New York, 1940)

[35] Morris, Government and Labor in Early America 167 (New York, 1946).

[36] Id. at 182.

[37] Id. at 186.

[38] Id. at 193–94.

[39] See id. at 195, for a discussion of a strike of Maine fishery workers in 1636; on the journeymen tailors' strike in New York in 1768, see id. at 196; for other examples, see Faulkner, American Economic History 311–15 (New York, 1949).

The principal kind of permanent association of workers to rise in the Colonial period was the philanthropic type of craftsmen's association. These "friendly societies" usually included masters as well as journeymen, although the maritime groups appear to have been confined to masters. As benevolent mutual-aid societies, they seem to have been strongest in New England. They do not appear to have undertaken direct action for improved wages, prices or working conditions, although they probably did engage in some such activity at times.[40] It should be noted that the existence of such associations does not demonstrate the existence of bona-fide labor unions in the modern sense of the term.[41] The rise of genuine labor associations for unrestricted purposes was to await a later era.

3. *Political Parties and Pressure Groups*

In America the government goes for less than in Europe, the parties count for more. The great moving forces are the parties.[42]

So wrote an astute observer of the American scene and system. The present-day institutionalization of the political party as a primary organ of governmental and societal control is a phenomenon with historical roots. In the treatment later in this work of political associations and pressure groups, examination will be made in some detail of them and of their regulation. At this point, however, it will be instructive to scan the Colonial period and note the existence, even then, of genuine, albeit embryonic, parties and interest groups. Perhaps of greater importance is the practical absence at that time of regulatory legislation.

During the Colonial period, there were no party organizations and machinery as we know them today. What political groups existed corresponded roughly to the party divisions in England between Whigs (or Liberals) and Tories (or Conservatives).[43] The bases of division between the two elements were economic, political, and social, with more of the economically successful and large rural landowners apparently inclining toward the Tories and a greater acknowledgement of the prerogatives of the Crown.[44]

[40] See Morris, Government and Labor in Early America 198–99 (New York, 1946).
[41] See Rayback, A History of American Labor 54 et seq. (New York, 1959).
[42] 2 Bryce, The American Commonwealth 5 (London, 1907).
[43] Woodburn, Political Parties and Party Problems in the United States 4 (New York & London, 1924).
[44] Id. at 7, 9.

With the application of stricter controls by the British government in the 1760's, the party divisions in the colonies were sharpened.[45] Both elements thereafter generally recognized the unfairness of at least some of the British impositions. The Tories, however, emphasized the advantages to the colonies of affiliation with the Empire and sought conciliation more ardently than the Whigs, who were determined not to yield to the Parliamentary intrusions.[46] This division is, of course, an oversimplification, since both groups were further divided into their own extreme and moderate elements, although, as the time of decision approached, the undecided were forced to cast their lots with one side or the other.[47] It has been estimated that one-third of the populace remained loyal to the mother country throughout the conflict.[48]

The political party in the colonies was complemented by the pressure group, with the latter often gaining a greater stature than the former. The inter-colonial committees of correspondence, initiated by Samuel Adams in 1772, were effective in providing inspiration and liaison, and led to the establishment of a network of radical groups prepared to exert appropriate pressure on short notice.[49] A more formidable, and practically official, instrument of pressure was the Continental Association, formed by the First Continental Congress in 1774 and designed to implement a policy of nonimportation of British goods.[50] This association, which operated through local, popularly elected committees, was very effective.[51] Other unofficial pressure groups were formed from time to time, sometimes on occupational lines, sometimes on geographical or other bases, which exerted *ad hoc* pressure against what they conceived to be oppressive measures.[52] Merchants' committees, mechanics' committees and insurrectionary associations such as the Sons of Liberty were some of these. So effective were the combined efforts of all these pressure groups that a Tory was driven to complain

[45] 1 Chitwood & Owsley, A Short History of the American People 197 (New York, 1951).

[46] Hicks & Mowry, A Short History of American Democracy 74 (Boston, 1956).

[47] 1 Chitwood & Owsley, A Short History of the American People 197–98 (New York, 1951); Hicks & Mowry, id. at 75–76.

[48] Chitwood & Owsley, id. at 75–76

[49] Hicks & Mowry, id. at 73; Schlesinger, Biography of a Nation of Joiners, 50 Am. Hist. Rev. 4–5 (1944).

[50] 1 Harlow, The Growth of the United States 152–53 (New York, 1943).

[51] Hicks & Mowry, A Short History of American Democracy 75 (Boston, 1956).

[52] Schlesinger, Biography of a Nation of Joiners, 50 Am. Hist. Rev. 4–5 (1944).

that the network "takes the Government out of the hands of the Governour, Council and General Assembly; and the execution of the laws out of the hands of the Civil Magistrates and the Juries." [53]

It is worthy of note that there was lacking, throughout the colonial period, the sort of regulation of the internal affairs of parties and pressure groups to which we are accustomed today.[54]

4. Insurrectionary Associations

In a search for "subversive" associations in our colonial period, one is struck by their scarcity. Agitational groups there were, and insurrection was often the aim as well as the result of the disruptive activity.[55] But it would be greatly stretching the point to find in that period an association which was subversive in the usual modern sense of the term—that is, which was marked principally by implacable opposition to the very foundations of society.[56] It is difficult to distinguish, in the pre-Revolutionary period, between the pressure groups and the groups which showed much less regard for the bounds of the law in expressing their protests and inciting opposition to the Crown. Because of the frequency with which their activities took on a frankly illegal and usually clandestine cast, the latter associations are here termed insurrectionary, to distinguish them from the contemporary lawful pressure groups, and from the subversive groups of the modern day which nurture a deeper hostility to the basic norms of society. The first group which comes to mind in this regard is the Sons of Liberty, formed more or less spontaneously to demonstrate opposition to the hated Grenville legislation, which included the Stamp Act of 1765.[57] Indeed, the name of the society seems to have been drawn from the language of a Member of Parliament, one Isaac Barré, who, in opposing the Stamp Act, referred to the colonial agitators as "sons of Liberty." [58] The name was first used in the colonies in Connecti-

[53] New York Gazeteer, Feb. 16, 1775; quoted in Schlesinger, ibid.

[54] See Morse, Parties and Party Leaders xxviii-xxix (Boston, 1923).

[55] See Scott, The Slave Insurrection in New York in 1712, 45 N.Y. Hist. Soc. Q. 43 (1961).

[56] See Harvard University, Center for the Study of the History of Liberty in America, The Dimensions of Liberty 247–48 (Cambridge, prepublication draft, March 15, 1961).

[57] 1 Chitwood & Owsley, A Short History of the American People 184 (New York, 1951).

[58] Hart, Epochs of American History (Formation of the Union, 1750–1829) 56 (New York, 1925).

cut, whence it spread through the other colonies, with a formal society of that name being formed in New York in January of 1766.[59]

Throughout its activity, the Sons of Liberty had a rather indefinite structure, which varied from colony to colony. Many and varied protesting groups appear to have arrogated the name to themselves, and the membership of the genuine group seems to have been not very stable.[60] Originally, professional men, small businessmen, and merchants exercised considerable influence in the groups,[61] but control soon gravitated into the hands of poorer members of the populace,[62] although this pattern was by no means uniform in all the colonies. The purpose of the Sons of Liberty appears to have been the fusion into a single political organization of all the opponents of the newly restrictive British colonial policy. That purpose they failed to achieve, but they did galvanize the spirit of resistance which finally did prevail.[63]

Between the imposition of stricter British regulations on the colonies in 1763 and the start of the military Revolution in 1775, many loose and *ad hoc* combinations were formed, among masters and journeymen as well as mechanics and laborers, for the purpose of protesting the British policies.[64] Such groups were hardly associations in any meaningful sense of the word. Moreover, control of their activities gradually devolved upon the more radical working-class element, which generally seized the initiative in promoting nonimportation agreements and coercing the observance of them, in creating inflammatory incidents and in staging demonstrations, activities which also came to be characteristic of the Sons of Liberty.[65] Especially prominent in such movements were the seamen and maritime workers.[66] In New York they adopted the name of Sons of Neptune, and their organization appears to have been a model for the later organization and tactics of the Sons of Liberty in that state.[67]

While the agitations of the Sons of Liberty and minor groups

[59] 1 Harlow, The Growth of the United States 130 (New York, 1943).
[60] Van Tyne, The Causes of the War of Independence 169–71 (New York, 1951).
[61] The Constitution of the United States of America (Corwin ed.) 165 (Washington, Government Printing Office, 1953).
[62] See Morris, Government and Labor in Early America 189 (New York, 1946).
[63] See 1 Harlow, The Growth of the United States 130 (New York, 1943).
[64] Morris, Government and Labor in Early America 188 (New York, 1946).
[65] Id. at 188–89.
[66] Id. at 189.
[67] See Dawson, The Sons of Liberty in New York 51 et seq. (Poughkeepsie, 1859).

included breaches of the peace and other unlawful conduct, efforts against them appear to have been made by the colonial governments through existing forms of control and prosecution,[68] without the sort of special legislation employed against the anarchists, syndicalists and other disruptive groups of later years.[69]

B. CHANGES EFFECTED BY REVOLUTION

The treatment, or lack of it, of freedom of association by the Constitutional Convention of 1787 is better understood against the background of the years intervening since the start of the Revolution. In the ferment of those formative years, the associational structure of colonial life was not exempt from change.

1. Disestablishment of Churches and Extension of Religious Freedom

Even before the Declaration of Independence, the colonies had begun to form state governments and adopt constitutions.[70] By the spring of 1777, every colony had organized an independent government, with eleven proclaiming new constitutions, and Connecticut and Rhode Island continuing to operate under the framework of their liberal colonial charters.[71] As we have noted already, at the start of the Revolution there were established churches, of varying degrees of effectiveness, in nine colonies. The Anglican Church was quickly disestablished in New York, Maryland, North Carolina, South Carolina, and Georgia.[72] Disestablishment proved more difficult in Virginia and New England, where it finally came in New Hampshire in 1817, in Connecticut in 1818 and in Massachusetts in 1833.[73]

Developments in Virginia were determinative and descriptive of

[68] See Harvard University, Center for the Study of the History of Liberty in America, The Dimensions of Liberty 140 (Cambridge, prepublication draft, March 15, 1961).

[69] See Van Tyne, The Causes of the War of Independence 169–71 (New York, 1951).

[70] Dumbauld, The Bill of Rights and What It Means Today 3 et seq. (Norman, 1957).

[71] 1 Chitwood & Owsley, A Short History of the American People 223 (New York, 1951).

[72] Id. at 231.

[73] Adams, The Epic of America 158 (New York, 1931); Chitwood & Owsley, ibid.

the future course of religious establishment in the nation. The drama of religious freedom of choice in that state was played out between 1776 and 1786, from the adoption of the Declaration of Rights to the enactment of the Statute for Religious Freedom. The Virginia Declaration of Rights, in 1776, did not reject the Anglican establishment,[74] but Article 16 thereof, coauthored by James Madison and George Mason, proclaimed "that Religion or the duty which we owe to our Creator and the Manner of discharging it, can be directed only by reason and conviction, not by force or violence."[75]

In the General Assembly of 1779, Thomas Jefferson introduced his Bill for Establishing Religious Freedom. When Jefferson left for Europe in 1784, Madison became the chief sponsor of the measure until its enactment in 1786.[76] The climax in the affair came in 1784 and 1785, with the struggle over the Assessment Bill, entitled "A Bill for Establishing a Provision for Teachers of the Christian Religion."[77] That bill provided an assessment for the support of Christian education, with the taxpayer having the privilege of designating which Church would receive his money.[78] Madison vehemently opposed the bill.[79] In 1785, he issued his *Memorial and Remonstrance* against it.[80] Madison attacked the proposed assessment as an establishment of Christianity, and asked:

> Who does not see that the same authority which can establish Christianity, in exclusion of all other Religions, may establish with the same ease any particular sect of Christians, in exclusion of all other Sects? That the same authority which can force a citizen to contribute three pence only of his property for the support of any one establishment, may force him to conform to any other establishment in all cases whatsoever?[81]

Madison declared in the *Memorial and Remonstrance* that "Religion is wholly exempt" from the "cognizance" of civil society.[82]

The *Remonstrance* generated a flood of petitions to the General Assembly, thereby contributing to the final defeat in committee of

[74] Brant, James Madison, The Virginia Revolutionist 245–46 (Indianapolis, 1941).
[75] See Appendix to dissent by Rutledge, J., in Everson v. Board of Education, 330 U.S. 1, 64 (1947).
[76] See 1 Randall, The Life of Thomas Jefferson 220 (New York, 1858).
[77] Appendix to Rutledge dissent, supra note 75, 330 U.S. at 72.
[78] Eckenrode, Separation of Church and State in Virginia 86 (1910).
[79] Id. at 100.
[80] For text, see Appendix to Rutledge dissent, supra note 75, 330 U.S. at 63.
[81] Id. 330 U.S. at 65–66.
[82] Id. 330 U.S. at 64–65.

the Assessment Bill in December, 1785.[83] Thereupon, Madison succeeded in achieving the passage, in January, 1786, of Jefferson's long-pending Bill for Establishing Religious Freedom, terminating the establishment of the Anglican Church.[84] As a practical matter, it has been said that the establishment in Virginia came to an end as early as 1777, with the suspension of the compulsory payment of tithes for the support of the Anglican Church, which suspension proved to be permanent.[85] However, the events of 1785, and the final triumph of Jefferson's bill, provided a clarion call for religious liberty and, as we shall see, exerted a considerable influence in the formulation of the Bill of Rights of the Constitution of the United States.[86]

Mention ought to be made of the Northwest Ordinance, adopted by Congress on July 13, 1787, while the Constitutional Convention was in session, for the government of the Northwest Territory.[87] Article 1 provided that:

> No person, demeaning himself in a peaceable and orderly manner, shall ever be molested on account of his mode of worship or religious sentiments, in the said territory.[88]

In addition to this prototype of the free-exercise clause of the First Amendment, Article 3 of the ordinance proclaimed:

> Religion, morality, and knowledge being necessary to good government and the happiness of mankind, schools and the means of education shall forever be encouraged.[89]

Article 3, with its apparent sanction of a benevolent promotion by the state of religious education, seems to reflect a different philosophy from some interpretations of the First Amendment, in our time, which posit a theoretically strict incapacity of government to aid any or all religions.[90] The Northwest Ordinance has been

[83] See Eckenrode, Separation of Church and State in Virginia, Ch. 5 (1910).

[84] 1 Chitwood & Owsley, A Short History of the American People 231 (New York, 1951).

[85] Eckenrode, Separation of Church and State in Virginia 53 (1910).

[86] For a statistical analysis of the status of religious freedoms in the original state constitutions, see Pfeffer, Church, State and Freedom 106 (Boston, 1953); see also Beth, The American Theory of Church and State 59–60 (Gainesville, Florida, 1958).

[87] The Constitution of the United States of America (Corwin ed.) 749 (Washington, Government Printing Office, 1953).

[88] 1 Stat. 51 n.

[89] Ibid.

[90] See, for example, Everson v. Board of Education, 330 U.S. 1, 15, 16 (1947).

called the foremost achievement of the Congress under the Articles of Confederation.[91] But its significance transcends that distinction. It provided the pattern for future territorial organization, and made explicit the postulates of religious and political freedom which underlay the American system.[92]

2. *Development of Labor Associations*

With the end of the Revolution, the economic and regional groupings of the people became more sharp. Moreover, the conservative-rural and radical-urban groupings were taking on a political character, with journeymen undertaking political action, usually in conjunction with the more radical political groups.[93] During the post-Revolutionary period, employers continued to enter into trade associations to protect their markets and economic positions and to secure government protection for commerce.[94] With the decline of the apprenticeship system, the rise of the factory system, and the narrowing of the door through which workers had entered easily into the ranks of employers, the trade union began to develop as an independent, viable institution.[95] Even before 1800, skilled workers such as the New York typographers, carpenters, masons, and coopers had set up effective trade unions.[96] Union activity in Philadelphia was even more widespread.[97] These beginnings foreshadowed the serious commencement of the labor movement in the nineteenth century.[98]

It is significant that, although the law continued to regard most concerted labor action as unlawful, there appears to have been virtually no infliction of criminal penalties upon such action in the

[91] 1 Chitwood & Owsley, A Short History of the American People 246–47 (New York, 1951).

[92] 1 Harlow, The Growth of the United States 208–209 (New York, 1943); Swarthout & Bartley, Principles and Problems of American National Government 46–47 (New York, 1955).

[93] See Jensen, The Articles of Confederation: An Interpretation of Social-Constitutional History of the American Revolution, 1774–1781 (Madison, 1940).

[94] Morris, Government and Labor in Early America 201 (New York, 1946).

[95] Id. at 200.

[96] Ibid. For other examples see Faulkner, American Economic History 311–15 (New York, 1949); Rayback, A History of American Labor 54 et seq. (New York, 1959).

[97] For a discussion of the activity of the cordwainers in that city, see Wright, The Battles of Labor 77–78 (Philadelphia, 1906).

[98] See 1 Chitwood & Owsley, A Short History of the American People 538 (New York, 1951).

post-Revolutionary period, whether masters or journeymen were involved.[99]

3. Political Parties and Pressure Groups

The triumph of the Revolution worked the destruction of the Tory Party in America and the complete victory of the Whigs.[100] In a manner of speaking, everyone had become a Whig. Strictly considered, there were no parties in the post-Revolutionary period but, as events were to prove, the material was there from which new parties would be formed upon the presentation of a divisive issue.[101]

In the Constitutional Convention of 1787, we may discern the real beginning of permanent political alignment in the United States. In that body, the Large State element, led by Madison of Virginia, Wilson of Pennsylvania and King of Massachusetts, worked for a genuine national government, while the Small State group, led by Martin of Maryland, Patterson of New Jersey and Ellsworth and Johnson of Connecticut, sought a confederate form of government.[102] After the establishment of the new government, the Large State party took the name of Federalist, while the Small State group was known, for the time being, as Anti-Federal.[103] Actually, even in that time, and surely during the interim between the Revolution and 1787, these so-called parties were not really such, but were merely representative of the two main opposing tendencies.[104]

4. Insurrectionary Associations

As the Revolution drew to a close, the agitational ferment which had succeeded so well against the mother country was diverted into economic and social channels.[105]

[99] Morris, Government and Labor in Early America 205–206 (New York, 1946); Faulkner, American Economic History 312–13 (New York, 1949).

[100] Woodburn, Political Parties and Party Problems in the United States 10 (New York & London, 1924).

[101] 1 Harlow, Growth of the United States 258–59 (New York, 1943).

[102] Woodburn, Political Parties and Party Problems in the United States 10–11 (New York & London, 1924).

[103] Adams, The Epic of America 110–13 (New York, 1931).

[104] Woodburn, Political Parties and Party Problems in the United States 12–13 (New York & London, 1924); Swarthout & Bartley, Principles and Problems of American National Government 223 (New York, 1955).

[105] Hart, Epochs of American History (Formation of the Union 1750–1829) 123 (New York, 1925).

By 1783, the national currency was "not worth a Continental."[106] Commerce was conducted on what was essentially a specie basis. When the purchases of foreign goods rose immediately after the war, the nation was drained of the specie required for currency.[107] The result was deflation, a phenomenon injurious to debtors and beneficial to creditors.[108] Agitation for the issuance of paper money by the states followed, and it was successful in seven states, notably in Rhode Island.[109] Inevitably, the popular discontent which resulted from the deflation generated insurrectionary pressures.[110] Shays' Rebellion, a populist-agrarian effort to seize control of the Massachusetts government in 1786, was the principal such disorder.[111] There were lesser disturbances of a similar character in other states.[112]

In none of these insurrectionary movements can we detect any sort of permanent or stable organization.[113] Rather, they were generally loosely knit groups, sufficient for the occasion but hardly qualifying as real associations in the modern sense of the term.[114] Nor were they the targets of specific legislation stigmatizing them as subversive associations. Rather, such disturbances as were created were suppressed within the framework of existing statutory and common law.[115]

[106] 1 Chitwood & Owsley, A Short History of the American People 242 (New York, 1951).

[107] Id. at 242–44.

[108] Faulkner, American Economic History 149–50 (New York, 1949).

[109] 1 Chitwood & Owsley, A Short History of the American People 242–44 (New York, 1951).

[110] 1 Harlow, The Growth of the United States 222–25 (New York, 1943); Swarthout & Bartley, Principles and Problems of American National Government 141 (New York, 1955).

[111] Beard, Chas. A. & Mary R., The Rise of American Civilization 307 (New York, 1930); Hicks & Mowry, A Short History of American Democracy 104 (Boston, 1956).

[112] 1 Chitwood & Owsley, A Short History of the American People 242–44 (New York, 1951); Faulkner, American Economic History 149–50 (New York, 1949); 1 Harlow, The Growth of the United States 220–26 (New York, 1943).

[113] See Hicks & Mowry, A Short History of American Democracy 104 (Boston, 1956).

[114] 1 Chitwood & Owsley, A Short History of the American People 244 (New York, 1951).

[115] See 1 Harlow, The Growth of the United States 222–25 (New York, 1943).

C. MEANING AND EFFECT OF THE ADOPTION OF THE UNITED STATES CONSTITUTION

1. Constitutional Convention

When the delegates to the Constitutional Convention met in May of 1787, they had many problems with which to deal. In view of this, and in view of the fact that the right of association was still in its embryonic stage as a political freedom, it is not surprising that freedom of association was not explicitly discussed during the deliberations of the Convention.

There were references to the danger of faction, as in Mr. Gerry's warning, on July 25th, that popular election of the Executive would leave the way open for a "set of men," such as the "respectable, United, and influential" Order of the Cincinnati, to influence unduly the decision of the people.[116] There was also a brief discussion of the desirability of expressly prohibiting a religious test for public office under the new government, an issue which relates to the question of religious association.[117] On two occasions, proposals seeking a guaranty of liberty of the press were advanced, but without success.[118]

Other than these few collateral references, the right of association was not a subject of discussion in the Convention. Interestingly, a motion was made [119] on September 12, 1787, "to appoint a Committee to prepare a Bill of Rights," but it was defeated by a vote of ten to none.[120] The reasoning of those who opposed the adoption of a Bill of Rights was epitomized by Hamilton in Number 84 of *The Federalist:*

> "Bills of Rights" would contain various exceptions to powers not granted; and on this very account, would afford a considerable pre-

[116] Documents Illustrative of the Formation of the Union of the American States 454 (Washington, Government Printing Office, 1927); see Walsh, The Political Science of John Adams 130 (New York, 1915).

[117] See debates of August 20th and August 30th, reported in Documents Illustrative of the Formation of the Union of the American States 576, 647 (Washington, Government Printing Office, 1927).

[118] 2 Records of the Federal Convention of 1787 (Farrand ed.) 334, 341, 617 (New Haven, 1937).

[119] Introduced by Gerry of Massachusetts, and seconded by Mason of Virginia.

[120] 2 Records of the Federal Convention of 1787 (Farrand ed.) 583 (New Haven, 1937); Madison's Notes, Documents Illustrative of the Formation of the Union of the American States 716 (Washington, Government Printing Office, 1927).

text to claim more than were granted. For why declare that things shall not be done which there is no power to do? . . . This may serve as a specimen of the numerous handles which would be given to the doctrine of constructive powers, by the indulgence of an injudicious zeal for bills of rights.[121]

2. *Terms of the Constitution and the Bill of Rights*

The United States Constitution, as adopted originally, expressly prohibits a religious test as a qualification "to any office or public trust under the United States."[122] It is tenable to say that this prevents the use of such a religious test as a restraint upon the exercise of the right to associate for religious purposes. In no other place did the Constitution itself allude, even by implication, to the right of association. Various amendments to the Constitution, however, were formally proposed by six state ratifying conventions.[123] Some are relevant to freedom of association.

It was proposed by five states, Massachusetts,[124] New Hampshire,[125] New York,[126] North Carolina,[127] and Rhode Island[128] that the Constitution prohibit Congress from creating "any Company with exclusive advantages of commerce."[129] The safeguards of religious freedom later embodied in the First Amendment were proposed in various forms by five states, including New Hampshire,[130] Virginia,[131] New York,[132] North Carolina,[133] and Rhode Island.[134] Four states sought protection for freedom of assembly and petition, including Virginia,[135] New York,[136] North Carolina,[137] and Rhode Island.[138] South Carolina proposed the modification of Article VI, clause 3, of the Constitution by inserting the word "other" between

[121] Madison, Hamilton, Jay, The Federalist 559 (Modern Library, New York, 1937); on Jefferson's insistence on a Bill of Rights, see Dumbauld, Thomas Jefferson and American Constitutional Law, 2 J. Pub. L. 381–83 (1953).

[122] Constitution of the United States, Art. VI, cl. 3.

[123] Dumbauld, The Bill of Rights and What It Means Today 11 (Norman, 1957).

[124] Documents Illustrative of the Formation of the Union of the American States 1018–20 (Washington, Government Printing Office).

[125] Id. at 1024–27.

[126] Id. at 1040.

[127] Id. at 1051; the North Carolina Convention refused to ratify until the changes it requested were made, and did not enter the Union until Nov. 21, 1789.

[128] Id. at 1050; Rhode Island did not ratify until May 29, 1790.

[129] Id. at 1040.

[130] Id. at 1024–27.

[131] Id. at 1030–31.

[132] Id. at 1035.

[133] Id. at 1047.

[134] Id. at 1053.

[135] Id. at 1030.

[136] Id. at 1037.

[137] Id. at 1046–47.

[138] Id. at 1054.

"no" and "religious."[139] Thereby, the oath or affirmation required of legislators and officers by the first part of that clause would be recognized to be a "religious test."

Acting upon the various proposals,[140] Congress submitted twelve amendments to the legislatures of the states on September 25, 1789.[141] The first two, relating to apportionment of the House of Representatives and requiring the intervention of an election of Representatives before any variance in the compensation of Senators and Representatives could go into effect, failed of ratification.[142] Interestingly, an amendment had been rejected by the Senate which would have provided that "The equal rights of conscience, the freedom of speech or of the press, and the right of trial by jury in criminal cases, shall not be infringed by any State."[143] That amendment, which would have enforced certain of the basic rights against the states, was described by Madison as "the most valuable of the whole list."[144] Madison also proposed an amendment that "The people shall not be restrained from peaceably assembling and consulting for their common good; nor from applying to the Legislature by petitions, or remonstrances, for redress of their grievances."[145] This was incorporated in the proposed amendments submitted by Congress to the states.[146] The last ten of the twelve amendments submitted to the states were adopted and became effective in December of 1791.[147]

In the Bill of Rights, as adopted, the right of association is nowhere specifically protected. But it impliedly finds its support by derivation from the rights of assembly, petition and religion embodied in the First Amendment to the Constitution,[148] which provides that:

[139] Id. at 1023.

[140] Of course, Congress was not influenced by the proposals of the Rhode Island convention, which was not held until May 29, 1790; Dumbauld, The Bill of Rights and What It Means Today 31–32 (Norman, 1957).

[141] Documents Illustrative of the Formation of the Union of the United States 1063 (Washington, Government Printing Office, 1927); Norton, The Constitution of the United States 194 (New York, 1956).

[142] Documents, id. at 1063–65.

[143] The Constitution of the United States of America (Corwin ed.) 750 (Washington, Government Printing Office, 1953); see Dumbauld, The Bill of Rights and What It Means Today 41, 206–209 (Norman, 1957).

[144] Corwin, id. at 750, quoting 1 Annals of Congress 755.

[145] Dumbauld, The Bill of Rights and What It Means Today 207 (Norman, 1957).

[146] Id. at 220.

[147] 1 Harlow, The Growth of the United States 248 (New York, 1943).

[148] The Constitution of the United States of America (Corwin ed.) 805–810 (Washington, Government Printing Office, 1953).

Congress shall make no law respecting an establishment of religion, or prohibiting the free exercise thereof; or abridging the freedom of speech or of the press; or the right of the people peaceably to assemble, and to petition the government [149] for a redress of grievances.

3. *The Federalist*

In the debate in New York preceding ratification of the Constitution, Alexander Hamilton, James Madison, and John Jay, under the nom-de-plume of Publius,[150] presented a series of closely reasoned expositions favoring ratification to the readers of New York newspapers. To those articles, published in the spring of 1788 under the title *The Federalist,*[151] is given much of the credit for the ratification by the New York Convention on July 26, 1788, by a vote of 30 to 27.[152] From them, certainly, we have gained much information about the meaning of the Constitution, and considerable insight into the deeper legal and political aspects of that instrument.

One of the most-quoted parts of *The Federalist* is essay Number 10, written by Madison. It contains his denunciation of factions, i.e., of unions of citizens "who are united and actuated by some common impulse of passion, or of interest, adverse to the rights of other citizens, or to the permanent and aggregate interests of the community." [153] Recognizing that the spirit of faction cannot be eradicated without the imposition of inadmissible uniformity and control, Madison advocated the control of its evil effects.[154] For this purpose, he favored the representative form of government as the primary means to prevent the despotism of a faction, whether of a minority or of a majority of the citizens.[155] Hamilton, in Number 9 of *The Federalist,* had similarly advised a firm republican union of the states as a necessary barrier against the evils of faction and insurrection.[156]

[149] Compare the language of the Bill of Rights of 1689: "That it is the right of the subjects to petition the King, and all commitments and prosecutions for such petitioning are illegal." Dumbauld, The Declaration of Independence and What It Means Today 165 (Norman, 1950).

[150] Madison, Hamilton, Jay, The Federalist 10 (Modern Library, New York, 1937).

[151] Id. at 10.

[152] See The Constitution of the United States of America (Corwin ed.) 14 (Washington, Government Printing Office, 1953).

[153] Madison, Hamilton, Jay, The Federalist 54 (Modern Library, New York, 1937).

[154] Id. at 54–57.

[155] Id. at 58–59.

[156] Id. at 48–53.

It is important for our present purpose that Hamilton and Madison both recognized the inevitability of factionalism, but strongly advocated its restriction, with proper regard for the basic imperatives of individual freedom. Their analysis is instructive in our own efforts to formulate a proper legal function and status for political associations and, inferentially, for other types of associations as well.

4. Tocqueville

Democracy in America, first published in 1835 as the collected observations of Alexis de Tocqueville upon his journey through America, has remained a classic of political and social criticism.[157] In it, Tocqueville analyzed our burgeoning democracy. In it, fortunately for this present undertaking, he made astute observations on various aspects of the right of association in American society.

Even in his day, Tocqueville found that: "In no country in the world has the principle of association been more successfully used, or more unsparingly applied to a multitude of different objects, than in America." [158] Tocqueville noted the ubiquitous character of American voluntary associations in the following comments:

> Societies are formed to resist enemies which are exclusively of a moral nature, and to diminish the vice of intemperance: in the United States associations are established to promote public order, commerce, industry, morality, and religion, for there is no end which the human will, seconded by the collective exertions of individuals, despairs of attaining.[159]
>
> Americans of all ages, all conditions, and all dispositions, constantly form associations. They have not only commercial and manufacturing companies, in which all take part, but associations of a thousand other kinds—religious, moral, serious, futile, extensive or restricted, enormous or diminutive. . . . Wherever, at the head of some new undertaking, you see the Government in France, or a man of rank in England, in the United States you will be sure to find an association.[160]

Tocqueville proved himself an admirer of the American separation of the functions of Church and State, while appreciating the

[157] See generally, Pierson, Tocqueville and Beaumont in America (New York, 1938).

[158] 1 Tocqueville, Democracy in America 197 (New York, 1904).

[159] Id. 1, at 198.

[160] Id. 2, at 593–94.

important leavening influence of religion in the American system. He observed:

Religion in America takes no direct part in the government of society, but nevertheless it must be regarded as the foremost of the political institutions of that country; for if it does not impart a taste for freedom, it facilitates the use of free institutions. . . . I do not know whether all the Americans have a sincere faith in their religion . . . but I am certain that they hold it to be indispensable to the maintenance of republican institutions.[161]

A general unanimity of American opinion on the relations of Church and State was remarked in this passage:

. . . I questioned the members of all the different sects, and I more especially sought the society of the clergy, who are the depositaries of the different creeds and are especially interested in their duration. . . . I found that they differed upon matters of detail alone; and that they mainly attributed the peaceful dominion of religion in their country to the separation of Church and State. I do not hesitate to affirm that during my stay in America I did not meet a single individual of the clergy or of the laity, who was not of the same opinion upon this point.[162]

The freedom of political association Tocqueville found to be most highly developed, and necessary, in the new nation. "In America," he said, "the liberty of association for political purposes is unbounded."[163] Referring to the perils of democracy, he warned:

There are no countries in which associations are more needed, to prevent the despotism of faction or the arbitrary power of a prince, than those which are democratically constituted.[164]

In his comment upon political associations, Tocqueville enumerated three stages in the development of an American political party:

Thus, in the first instance, a society is formed between individuals professing the same opinion, and the tie which keeps it together is of a purely intellectual nature; in the second case, small assemblies are formed, which only represent a fraction of the party. Lastly, in the third case, they constitute a separate nation in the midst of the nation, a government within the Government.[165]

[161] Id. 1, at 329.
[162] Id. 1, at 332.
[163] Id. 1, at 200.
[164] Id. 1, at 202.
[165] Id. 1, at 199.

The necessity of free political association in a democracy was epitomized in the reflection that: "Political associations may therefore be considered as large free schools, where all the members of the community go to learn the general theory of association." [166]

The necessary relation between freedom of association and a widely extended free press was illuminated by Tocqueville, who noted that "the press is the chiefest democratic instrument of freedom," [167] and offered the following analysis:

> In order that an association among a democratic people should have any power, it must be a numerous body. The persons of whom it is composed are therefore scattered over a wide extent, and each of them is detained in the place of his domicile. . . . Means then must be found to converse every day without seeing each other, and to take steps in common without having met. Thus hardly any democratic association can do without newspapers. There is consequently a necessary connection between public associations and newspapers; newspapers make associations, and associations make newspapers: and if it has been correctly advanced that associations will increase in number as the conditions of men become more equal, it is not less certain that the number of newspapers increases in proportion to that of associations. Thus it is in America that we find at the same time the greatest number of associations and of the greatest number of newspapers.[168]

In short, Tocqueville concluded, "The more we consider the independence of the press in its principal consequences, the more are we convinced that it is the chief and, so to speak, the constitutive element of freedom in the modern world." [169]

Having journeyed from a Europe beset by political upheaval, and having recently witnessed the revolutionary accession to power in his own country of Louis Philippe in 1830,[170] Tocqueville's eye was quick to detect conspiratorial and subversive patterns in the United States. He was not an advocate of an absolute right of association, and thought that ". . . the unrestrained liberty of association for political purposes is the privilege which a people is longest in learning how to exercise." [171] However, he was greatly surprised to find conspiracy and subversion practically nonexistent in the United

[166] Id. 2, at 604.
[167] Id. 2, at 817.
[168] Id. 2, at 599–600.
[169] Id. 1, at 200.
[170] See Hayes, Baldwin & Cole, History of Europe 737–38 (New York, 1949).
[171] 1 Tocqueville, Democracy in America 202–203 (New York, 1904).

States, remarking that ". . . in countries where associations are free, secret societies are unknown. In America there are numerous factions, but no conspiracies."[172]

An opinion by Tocqueville on the proper method of imposing restraint on the right of association is worth an extended quote, especially insofar as it relates to our problem of controlling the pernicious influence of subversive associations:

When some kinds of associations are prohibited and others allowed, it is difficult to distinguish the former from the latter beforehand. In this state of doubt men abstain from them altogether, and a sort of public opinion passes current that tends to cause any association whatsoever to be regarded as a bold and almost an illicit enterprise.[173]

This is more especially true when the executive government has a discretionary power of allowing or prohibiting associations. When certain associations are simply prohibited by law, and the courts of justice have to punish infringements of that law, the evil is far less considerable. Then every citizen knows beforehand pretty nearly what he has to expect. He abstains from prohibited associations and embarks on those which are legally sanctioned. It is by these restrictions that all free nations have always admitted that the right of association might be limited. But if the legislature should invest a man with the power of ascertaining beforehand which associations are dangerous and which are useful, and should authorize him to destroy all associations in the bud or allow them to be formed, as nobody would be able to foresee in what cases associations might be established and in what cases they would be put down, the spirit of association would be entirely paralyzed. The former of these laws would only assail certain associations, the latter would apply to society itself, and inflict an injury upon it. I can conceive that a regular government which respects the rule of law may have recourse to the former, but I do not concede that any government has the right of enacting the latter.[174]

It is with these qualifications that Tocqueville concluded:

Thus I do not think that a nation is always at liberty to invest its citizens with an absolute right of association for political purposes; and I doubt whether, in any country or in any age, it be wise to set no limits to freedom of association.[175]

[172] Id. 1, at 203.
[173] Id. 2, at 604.
[174] Id. 2, at 607n.
[175] Id. 2, at 607.

III. *Freedom of Association and Religion*

A. GENERAL ISSUES

The American constitutional structure is designed to preserve inviolate the freedom of religious belief and the right to join, or not to join, a religious association. This purpose is well realized in fact, and the rights to religious belief and to join or not to join a religious group are well-nigh inviolable. However, there are situations in which the correlative right to practice outwardly the tenets of a religion or of a religious association conflicts with the duty of the State to maintain peace and order. There are other cases in which the right not to practice religion, individually or as a member of an association, may conflict with various sumptuary laws which enact requirements coinciding with the tenets of some religious association; thereby, it may be said, the dissident citizen is compelled to associate with the members of those associations in the practice of their religious beliefs. There are other instances in which the right to refrain from supporting financially a religious association may conflict with the asserted right of the State to promote the public welfare by subvention, with public funds, of some or all religious associations. From the recognition or rejection of these subordinate rights, which ramify from the parent rights of believing, joining, and not joining, may be determined the validity of the overall right of religious association as a fundamental liberty.

B. CONSTITUTIONAL PROVISIONS

As noted already, the Constitution of the United States indirectly protects the right of religious association by the prohibition of religious tests for office.[1] Also, the First Amendment bars Congress from legislating with respect to an establishment of religion, and from prohibiting the free exercise of religion.

The state constitutions presently in force contain many and varied protections of the freedom of religious association.[2]

Free exercise of religion and worship are guaranteed, in varying forms, by the constitutions of all fifty states.[3]

Thirty-seven state constitutions expressly prohibit, with varying formulae, the establishment of any religion to be adhered to, or supported, by the people under compulsion, or to be preferred by the law.[4]

Religious tests as a qualification for public office are barred by the constitutions of twenty-three states.[5] Oklahoma's constitution

[1] Art. VI, cl. 3.

[2] See generally, Legislative Drafting Research Fund, Index Digest of State Constitutions (Columbia University, 1959).

[3] Ala., Art. I, Sec. 3; Alaska, Art. I, Sec. 4; Ariz., Art. XX, Secs. 1, 2; Ark., Art. 2, Sec. 24; Cal., Art. I, Sec. 4; Colo., Art. II, Sec. 4; Conn., Art. I, Sec. 3; Del., Preamble, Art. I, Sec. 1; Fla., Decl. of Rights, Art. 5; Ga., Art. I, Sec. 1, Para. 12, 13; Hawaii, Art. I, Secs. 4, 7; Idaho, Art. I, Sec. 4, Art. XXI, Sec. 19; Ill., Art. II, Sec. 3; Ind., Art. I, Secs. 2, 3, 4; Iowa, Art. I, Secs. 3, 4; Kan., Bill of Rights, Art. 7; Ky., Secs. 1, 5; La., Art. I, Sec. 4; Me., Art. I, Sec. 3; Md., Decl. of Rights, Art. 36; Mass., Decl. of Rights, Art. 2, Amend. XLVI, Sec. 4; Mich., Art. II, Sec. 3; Minn., Art. I, Sec. 16; Miss., Art. III, Sec. 18; Mo., Art. I, Secs. 5, 6; Mont., Art. III, Sec. 4; Neb., Art. I, Sec. 4; Nev., Art. I, Sec. 4, Ordinance 2; N.H., Art. I, Secs. 4, 5; N.J., Art. I, Secs. 3, 5; N.M., Art. II, Sec. 11, Art. XI, Sec. 1; N.Y., Art. I, Sec. 3; N.C., Art. I, Sec. 26; N.D., Art. I, Sec. 4, Art. XVI, Sec. 203; Ohio, Art. I, Sec. 7; Okla., Art. I, Sec. 2; Ore., Art. I, Secs. 2, 3; Pa., Art. I, Sec. 3; R.I., Art. I, Sec. 3; S.C., Art. I, Sec. 4; S.D., Art. VI, Sec. 3, Art. XXVI, Sec. 18; Tenn., Art. I, Sec. 3, Art. XI, Sec. 15; Tex., Art. I, Sec. 6; Utah, Art. I, Secs. 1, 4; Vt., Art. I, Sec. 3; Va., Art. I, Sec. 16; Wash., Art. I, Sec. 11, Art. XXVI; W.Va., Art. III, Sec. 15; Wis., Art. I, Sec. 18; Wyo., Art. I, Sec. 18, Art. XXI, Sec. 2.

[4] Ala., Art. I, Sec. 3; Alaska, Art. I, Sec. 4; Ark., Art. II, Sec. 24; Colo., Art. II, Sec. 4; Conn., Art. I, Sec. 4; Del., Art. I, Sec. 1; Fla., Decl. of Rights, Art. 6; Hawaii, Art. I, Sec. 3; Idaho, Art. I, Sec. 4; Ill., Art. II, Sec. 3; Ind., Art. I, Sec. 4; Iowa, Art. I, Sec. 3; Kan., Bill of Rights, Art. 7; Ky., Sec. 5; La., Art. I, Sec. 4; Me., Art. I, Sec. 3; Md., Decl. of Rights, Art. 36; Mass., Amend. XI; Mich., Art. II, Sec. 3; Minn., Art. I, Sec. 16; Miss., Art. III, Sec. 18; Mo., Art. I, Secs. 6, 7; Mont., Art. III, Sec. 4; Neb., Art. I, Sec. 4; N.H., Art. I, Sec. 6; N.J., Art. I, Secs. 3, 4; N.M., Art. II, Sec. 11; Ohio, Art. I, Sec. 7; Pa., Art. I, Sec. 3; R.I., Art. I, Sec. 3; S.C., Art. I, Sec. 4; S.D., Art. VI, Sec. 3; Tenn., Art. I, Sec. 3; Tex., Art. I, Sec. 6; Utah, Art. I, Sec. 4; Vt., Art. I, Sec. 3; W.Va., Art. III, Sec. 15.

[5] Ala., Art. I, Sec. 3; Alaska, Art. I, Sec. 3; Ariz., Art. II, Sec. 12; Del., Art. I, Sec. 2; Ga., Art. I, Sec. 1, Para. 13; Hawaii, Art. I, Sec. 4; Ind., Art. I, Sec. 5;

prohibits any religious test for the exercise of any civil or political rights.[6] West Virginia has a similarly broad provision.[7] Seven states prohibit religious tests for teachers and students in public schools.[8] Religious tests for jurors are expressly prohibited by the constitutions of eleven states.[9] In nine state constitutions, a religious test is expressly forbidden as a qualification for enfranchisement or the exercise of other political rights.[10]

Eight states constitutionally provide, however, that the protections accorded to religious liberty do not automatically dispense with oaths or affirmations.[11] Eight states require in their constitutions a belief in the existence of God as a test for holding public office.[12] Massachusetts's constitution exhorts the voters to bear in mind, in choosing officers, that constant adherence to principles of piety is advisable in public affairs.[13]

Some states retain in their constitutions admonitions which nominally serve to restrict the generally recognized freedom of worship, but which have virtually no practical effect. For example, Massachusetts [14] suggests that all persons ought to worship the Supreme Being. Delaware's constitution is similar in this respect.[15] Vermont states that religious denominations should keep the Lord's

Iowa, Art. I, Sec. 4; Kan., Bill of Rights, Art. 7; Me., Art. I, Sec. 3; Minn., Art. I, Sec. 17; Mo., Art. I, Sec. 5; Neb., Art. I, Sec. 4; N.J., Art. I, Sec. 4; N.M., Art. VII, Sec. 3; Ohio, Art. I, Sec. 7; Ore., Art. I, Sec. 4; R.I., Art. I, Sec. 3; Va., Art. IV, Sec. 58; Wash., Art. I, Sec. 11; W.Va., Art. III, Sec. 15; Wis., Art. I, Sec. 19; Wyo., Art. I, Sec. 18.

[6] Okla., Const., Art. I, Sec. 2.

[7] W.Va., Const., Art. III, Secs. 11, 15.

[8] Ariz., Art. XI, Sec. 7, Art. XX, Sec. 7; Colo., Art. IX, Sec. 8; Idaho, Art. IX, Sec. 6; Mont., Art. XI, Sec. 9; N.M., Art. XII, Sec. 9; Utah, Art. X, Sec. 12; Wyo., Art. VII, Sec. 12.

[9] Ariz., Art. II, Sec. 12; Cal., Art. I, Sec. 4; Mo., Art. I, Sec. 5; N.M., Art. VII, Sec. 3; N.D., Art. I, Sec. 4; Ore., Art. I, Sec. 6; Tenn., Art. I, Sec. 6; Utah, Art. I, Sec. 4; Wash., Art. I, Sec. 11; W.Va., Art. III, Sec. 11; Wyo., Art. I, Sec. 18.

[10] Alaska, Art. I, Sec. 3; Ark., Art. II, Sec. 26; Ill., Art. II, Sec. 3; Kan., Bill of Rights, Art. 7; Mich., Art. II, Sec. 3; Minn., Art. I, Sec. 17; N.M., Art. VII, Sec. 3; Utah, Art. I, Sec. 4; W.Va., Art. III, Sec. 11.

[11] Ark., Art. II, Sec. 26; Colo., Art. II, Sec. 4; Idaho, Art. I, Sec. 4; Ill., Art. II, Sec. 3; Mont., Art. III, Sec. 4; Neb., Art. I, Sec. 4; Ohio, Art. I, Sec. 7; Tex., Art. I, Sec. 5.

[12] Ark., Art. II, Sec. 26, Art. XIX, Sec. 1; Md., Decl. of Rights, Art. 37; Miss., Art. III, Sec. 18, Art. XIV, Sec. 265; N.C., Art. VI, Sec. 8; Pa., Art. I, Sec. 4; S.C., Art. XVII, Sec. 4; Tenn., Art. I, Sec. 4, Art. IX, Sec. 2; Tex., Art. I, Sec. 4. In Torcaso v. Watkins, 367 U.S. 488, 496 (1961), the Supreme Court invalidated the Maryland requirement as an invasion of "freedom of belief and religion."

[13] Mass., Decl. of Rights, Art. 18.

[14] Mass. Decl. of Rights, Art. 2.

[15] Del. Const., Art. I, Sec. 1.

day and maintain religious worship.[16] Virginia, somewhat hopefully, exhorts that all persons should practice Christian forbearance, love, and charity.[17] The constitutions of nineteen states expressly warn that the religious freedoms recognized in the constitution do not warrant the commission of acts of licentiousness, bigamy, or other practices inconsistent with the peace of the state.[18]

The state constitutional provisions discussed herein, as well as ordinary legislation, must be viewed in the light of the United States Constitution, including the so-called supremacy clause in Article VI,[19] the First Amendment,[20] and the Fourteenth Amendment, which last provides in relevant part that:

> . . . No State shall make or enforce any law which shall abridge the privileges or immunities of citizens of the United States; nor shall any State deprive any person of life, liberty, or property, without due process of law; nor deny to any person within its jurisdiction the equal protection of the laws.

In *Gitlow v. New York* [21] the Supreme Court casually discarded a long-standing position [22] by announcing that: "For present purposes we may and do assume that freedom of speech and of the press—which are protected by the First Amendment from abridgement by Congress—are among the fundamental personal rights and 'liberties' protected by the due-process clause of the Fourteenth Amendment from impairment by the States." [23] This dictum was confirmed as law two years later.[24] Later cases have brought other

[16] Vt. Const., Art. I, Sec. 3.

[17] Va. Const., Art. I, Sec. 16.

[18] Ariz., Art. II, Sec. 12; Cal., Art. I, Sec. 4; Colo., Art. II, Sec. 4; Conn., Art. I, Sec. 3; Fla., Decl. of Rights, Art. V; Ga., Art. I, Sec. 1, Para. 13; Idaho, Art. I, Sec. 4; Ill., Art. II, Sec. 3; Me., Art. I, Sec. 3; Minn., Art. I, Sec. 16; Miss., Art. III, Sec. 18; Mo., Art. I, Sec. 5; Mont., Art. III, Sec. 4; Nev., Art. I, Sec. 4; N.Y., Art. I, Sec. 3; N.D., Art. I, Sec. 4; S.D., Art. VI, Sec. 3; Wash., Art. 1, Sec. 11; Wyo., Art. I, Sec. 18.

[19] "This constitution, and the laws of the United States which shall be made in pursuance thereof; and all treaties made, or which shall be made, under the authority of the United States, shall be the supreme law of the land; and the judges in every state shall be bound thereby, anything in the constitution or laws of any state to the contrary notwithstanding."

[20] The Bill of Rights was originally not intended to operate against the states. Barron v. Baltimore, 32 U.S. (7 Pet.) 243, 247 (1833); see also Permoli v. Municipality of New Orleans, 44 U.S. (3 How.) 589, 609 (1845).

[21] 268 U.S. 652 (1925).

[22] See Warren, The New "Liberty" under the Fourteenth Amendment, 39 Harv. L. Rev. 432, 436 (1926).

[23] 268 U.S. at 666.

[24] Fiske v. Kansas, 274 U.S. 380 (1927).

rights protected by the First Amendment within the compass of the Fourteenth Amendment, thus making them effective against the states.[25] Thereby, for the vindication of the rights of religious freedom against any imposition thereon by a state, recourse may be had to the commands of the First Amendment as well as to those of state constitutions and laws.

However, the nature and extent of the application of the First Amendment freedoms as restrictions upon the states have been matters of recent inquiry.[26] If the Fourteenth Amendment, whether by the privileges and immunities clause [27] or the due-process clause, as is probable, literally incorporates the First Amendment, then the states are barred from intruding upon those rights "equally," and in the same way, as Congress.[28] But if the Fourteenth Amendment does not literally incorporate the First,[29] then the protection of any First Amendment freedom against state action will depend upon a finding that the freedom "is within the liberty safeguarded by the due-process clause of the Fourteenth Amendment from invasion by state action." [30] If the latter hypothesis is correct, then, because the Federal Government exercises only delegated powers, the restraint imposed upon it by the First Amendment is greater than the restraint imposed on the states by the "liberty" guarantee of the Fourteenth. This idea was elaborated by Mr. Justice Jackson in his dissent in *Beauharnais v. Illinois:* [31]

> The history of criminal libel in America convinces me that the Fourteenth Amendment did not "incorporate" the First, that the powers of Congress and of the States over this subject are not of the same dimensions, and that because Congress probably could not enact this law it does not follow that the States may not. . . .
>
> As a limitation upon power to punish written or spoken words, Four-

[25] See DeJonge v. Oregon, 299 U.S. 353 (1937) (freedom of assembly); Cantwell v. Connecticut, 310 U.S. 296 (1940) (freedom of religion).

[26] See Rogge, The First & the Fifth 38–53, 314 (New York, 1960).

[27] It was early settled that the privileges and immunities clause did not literally incorporate the Bill of Rights. Slaughter-House Cases, 83 U.S. (16 Wall.) 36 (1873).

[28] See opinion of Mr. Justice Douglas for the Court in Murdock v. Pennsylvania, 319 U.S. 105, 108 (1943); dissenting opinion of Mr. Justice Black in Adamson v. California, 332 U.S. 46, 71–72, 75 (1947); dissenting opinion of Mr. Justice Black in Beauharnais v. Illinois, 343 U.S. 250 (1952); concurring opinion of Mr. Justice Black in Speiser v. Randall, 357 U.S. 513, 530 (1958) (". . . the First Amendment is applicable in all its particulars to the States.")

[29] See dissent of Mr. Justice Jackson in Beauharnais v. Illinois, ibid.

[30] Near v. Minnesota, 283 U.S. 697, 707 (1931).

[31] 343 U.S. 250, 288 (1952).

teenth Amendment "liberty" in its context of state powers and functions has meant and should mean something quite different from "freedom" in its context of federal powers and functions.[32]

Mr. Justice Harlan, in his opinion in *Roth v. United States*[33] cogently expressed the distinction:

> . . . our function in reviewing state judgments under the Fourteenth Amendment is a narrow one. We do not decide whether it is based on assumptions scientifically substantiated. We can inquire only whether the state action so subverts the fundamental liberties implicit in the Due Process Clause that it cannot be sustained as a rational exercise of power. . . . The States' power to make printed words criminal is, of course, confined by the Fourteenth Amendment, but only insofar as such power is consistent with our concepts of "ordered liberty." Palko v. Connecticut, 302 U.S. 319, 324, 325. . . .
>
> . . . I agree with Mr. Justice Jackson that the historical evidence does not bear out the claim that the Fourteenth Amendment "incorporates" the First in any literal sense.

The proposition that freedom of association is one of the fundamental liberties guaranteed against encroachment by the states was affirmed by a unanimous court in *NAACP v. Alabama,*[34] discussed above in the Introduction, where Mr. Justice Harlan said, "It is beyond debate that freedom to engage in association for the advancement of beliefs and ideas is an inseparable aspect of the 'liberty' assured by the Due Process Clause of the Fourteenth Amendment, which embraces freedom of speech."

It is reasonable to conclude, from the unequivocal character of the Constitutional provisions discussed herein, that the basic rights of personal religious belief, and to join or not join a religious association, enjoy a practical invulnerability to restriction by the Federal

[32] See Rogge, The First & the Fifth 38–53, 314 (New York, 1960); see Patterson, The Forgotten Ninth Amendment 19–26, 36–43 (Indianapolis, 1955), where the author suggests that the Ninth Amendment would be an appropriate vehicle for the protection against both Federal and state governments of fundamental rights not enumerated in the Bill of Rights.

[33] Roth v. United States, 354 U.S. 476, 501–503 (1957). Apparently, the Supreme Court has not accepted the Jackson-Harlan theory of nonincorporation, as far as the First Amendment is concerned; the recent opinions of the Court, however, have left in some doubt the extent to which the Court adopts the literal incorporation idea. See McKay, Book Review, 15 Rutgers L. Rev. 145, 150, 151 (1960). Compare Bartkus v. Illinois, 359 U.S. 121 (1959), holding that the Fourteenth Amendment did not literally incorporate the Fifth Amendment protection against double jeopardy.

[34] 357 U.S. 449, 460 (1958).

Government or the states. We now turn to a consideration of the corollaries of those basic liberties.

C. FREEDOM TO SUPPORT AND PRACTICE TENETS OF RELIGIOUS ASSOCIATIONS

The problems to be discussed here have been resolved in the past usually by application of the establishment and free-exercise clauses of the First Amendment. Without analyzing in detail the merits of particular cases, or of the application of those clauses to the problems involved, the purpose here is to show that the issues could have been resolved by reference to the newly recognized freedom of association, with, in some cases, more satisfactory results.

1. Mormons

In assessing the freedom to associate for religious purposes and to practice religion, it must not be thought that it is an absolute imperative, or that it admits of no infringement for the sake of a higher good. The Church of Jesus Christ of Latter-Day Saints, known as the Mormon Church, has provided several occasions for the recognition by legislatures and courts of the permissibility of reasonable qualification of this freedom. Because the Mormons held to polygamy as a compulsory tenet of their religion, they quickly became the targets of restrictive legislation. In *Reynolds v. United States,*[35] the Supreme Court sustained the convictions of Mormon defendants for practicing polygamy. Rejecting the claim that the prohibiting statute interfered with the legitimate religious beliefs of the members, the court concluded that to excuse the defendants on that ground "would be to make the professed doctrines of religious belief superior to the law of the land, and in effect to permit every citizen to become a law unto himself." [36]

Later, in upholding a territorial law against polygamy, the court said "whilst legislation for the establishment of religion is forbidden, and its free exercise permitted, it does not follow that everything which may be so-called can be tolerated. Crime is not the less odious because sanctioned by what any particular sect may designate as

[35] 98 U.S. 145 (1878).
[36] 98 U.S. at 167.

religion." [37] In other cases, Federal restrictions on both the advocacy and practice of polygamy have been uniformly upheld over protests from the Mormons.[38]

Similarly, state laws against polygamy and related practices have experienced no difficulty in the courts.[39]

Clearly, the experience of the Mormons indicates that the right of religious association is not a license for the commission of acts which in themselves are seriously inimical to the peace and order of the community. The result would seem to be in accord with the prescription of Locke concerning religious freedom, that ". . . no opinions contrary to human society, or to those moral rules which are necessary to the preservation of civil society are to be tolerated by the magistrate." [40] The fact that a religious group commands polygamy as a religious practice does not give immunity against civil prohibition of such an act which would be unlawful if performed by an individual not associated with the religious group. This inability of a religious association to confer upon its members a privilege to ignore the penal law was recognized by the Supreme Court in the *Reynolds* and *Davis* cases.[41]

2. *Jehovah's Witnesses*

Probably no American religious association has generated a stronger adverse reaction than the Jehovah's Witnesses. Because the campaigns of the Witnesses have been markedly aggressive and ubiquitous, and because they apparently welcome prosecution as a means of testing their rights, we can observe in their experience the lengths to which police power may go in controlling the outward acts of religious associations, and we can see whether the efforts of those associations to recruit new members enjoy any distinctive privilege.

[37] Davis v. Beason, 133 U.S. 333, 345 (1890).

[38] See Late Corp. of the Church of Jesus Christ of Latter-Day Saints v. United States, 136 U.S. 1 (1890) (revocation of charter of church); Cleveland v. United States, 329 U.S. 14 (1946) (Mann Act).

[39] See State v. Barlow, 107 Utah 292, 153 P.2d 647 (1944), app. dis. 324 U.S. 829 (1945) (state bigamy law); In re State in interest of Black, 3 Utah 2d 315, 283 P.2d 887 (1955), app. dis., 350 U.S. 923 (1955) (parents teaching legitimacy of polygamy may be deprived of custody).

[40] Locke, Letter on Toleration 208 et seq. (New York, 1957).

[41] Reynolds v. United States, 98 U.S. 145, 165, 166 (1870); Davis v. Beason, 133 U.S. 333, 343, 344 (1890).

Often, local authorities have sought to deny to the Witnesses the use of public places for their assemblies and proselytizing. Licensing restrictions are most frequently used and are upheld if reasonable and nondiscriminatory in their content and application.

The validity of an enactment requiring a license for such activity will turn primarily upon whether sufficient controls are placed upon the discretion of the issuing officer. It is not essential that the statute or ordinance itself contain the governing standards, and it will suffice if they have been inferred in judicial construction by the state courts.[42] However, if nothing in the enactment or its construction prevents an arbitrary denial of the permit by the administrator, it will be invalidated.[43] It goes without saying that the courts will protect the members of a religious association from invidious discrimination in denying permission for public devotional and proselytizing activities.[44] It is difficult to find a meaningful distinction in these cases between the right of the Witnesses as members of an association to use the public places, and their right to do so as individuals without affiliation. It would seem that the individual's right in such a situation neither increases nor decreases when he seeks to exercise it in association with others. It is true that many regulations aimed at the Witnesses seem to be prompted by animus toward the group as a whole based upon the unfavorable reaction of a community to the sect.[45] Occasionally, the aversion of the community may be justified.[46] But regardless of the unpopularity of the association which he joins, the individual's right to practice and proselytize, which is basically an individual right, continues to be protected against unreasonable prior restraint.[47] His act of association, however, does not confer on the member of the sect any license to violate the substantive law preserving the public peace[48] and, if he is wrongfully denied a permit to practice and proselytize,

[42] See Cox v. New Hampshire, 312 U.S. 569 (1941), where the Supreme Court upheld a statute, itself containing no standards, since it was construed by the state court to require uniform and fair treatment of each application for a license.

[43] Saia v. New York, 334 U.S. 558 (1948); Kunz v. New York, 340 U.S. 290 (1951) (involving a Baptist minister); compare, Kovacs v. Cooper, 336 U.S. 77 (1949) (relevant discussion of standards in nonreligious case).

[44] Niemotko v. Maryland, 340 U.S. 268 (1951); Fowler v. Rhode Island, 345 U.S. 67 (1953).

[45] See, e.g., Taylor v. Mississippi, 319 U.S. 583 (1943).

[46] For a discussion of the tactics of the Witnesses, see dissenting opinion of Mr. Justice Jackson in Douglas v. Jeannette, 319 U.S. 157, 166–74 (1943).

[47] See Niemotko v. Maryland, 340 U.S. 268 (1951).

[48] Chaplinsky v. New Hampshire, 315 U.S. 568 (1942).

he must pursue the ordinary civil remedies to correct the wrong decision and may not disregard it with impunity.[49]

One of the main tactics of the Jehovah's Witnesses has been the distribution of handbills in the public streets. In a number of cases, all involving Witnesses, the Supreme Court has invalidated ordinances prohibiting the reasonable distribution of religious handbills in public places.[50] Interestingly, the distribution of commercial handbills enjoys no such protection.[51]

It sometimes happens that the collective activity of members of an association in promoting its cause will conflict with the asserted individual rights of nonmembers. Here again, the proselytization of the Witnesses, and the reaction thereto of nonbelievers, have occasioned much of the law on the point as it affects religious associations. For example, the door-to-door canvassing employed by the Witnesess was attacked by an ordinance in Ohio which flatly forbade summoning the occupant of any residence to the door for the purpose of giving him any sort of handbill. The court, in a five-to-four decision, invalidated the ordinance, although it indicated that it might be valid if it restricted the offense to the summoning of any householder who had appropriately indicated his unwillingness to be disturbed.[52] One type of regulation which might be sanctioned by the dictum in *Martin v. Struthers* was involved in *Breard v. Alexandria*,[53] where a municipal prohibition against door-to-door solicitation without the prior consent of the occupant was upheld as applied to salesmen soliciting orders for nationally known periodicals. Since the *Breard* case did not involve religious solicitation, we cannot be certain that a similar restriction on religious canvassing would be upheld, but the *Breard* decision is persuasive in that direction. In fact, Mr. Justice Black, joined by Mr. Justice Douglas, in dissenting in *Breard*, expressed the opinion[54] that the decision virtually overruled *Martin v. Struthers*.[55] As in the cases involving the

[49] Poulos v. New Hampshire, 345 U.S. 395 (1953); compare United States v. United Mine Workers, 330 U.S. 258 (1947).

[50] See Lovell v. City of Griffin, Georgia, 303 U.S. 444 (1938); Schneider v. Town of Irvington, New Jersey, 309 U.S. 147 (1939); Jamison v. Texas, 318 U.S. 413 (1943).

[51] See Valentine v. Chrestensen, 316 U.S. 52 (1942).

[52] Martin v. Struthers, 319 U.S. 141 (1943); accord: Largent v. Texas, 318 U.S. 418 (1943).

[53] 341 U.S. 622 (1951).

[54] 341 U.S. at 649–50.

[55] See Peterman, Municipal Control of Peddlers, Solicitors and Distributors, 22 Tul. L. Rev. 284 (1947); Comment, 50 Mich. L. Rev. 576 (1952).

use of public places, the courts will invalidate an enactment requiring a permit for canvassing if no standards are imposed to control the discretion of the issuing officer.[56]

A new approach to the problem of the relations between religious associations and nonmembers was taken in *Marsh v. Alabama,*[57] where the court extended the constitutional right to distribute religious literature on the public streets to distribution of it on the sidewalk of a company-owned town, even over the objection of the company. The majority, through Mr. Justice Black, held that the privately owned town would be treated the same as a publicly owned one, and that the public interest in the maintenance of free communication is the same in either case. The Marsh decision raises an interesting point in that the court essayed to compel the company and the townspeople to enter into legal relations with the defendant, i.e., to accord to him the rights of a licensee on real property, to associate with him, and to submit to his importunings to join his association. Thereby, defendant's right of religious association carries with it, in its proselytizing manifestation, a power over nonmembers which could not be claimed by a defendant who was seeking merely to induce a listener to enter into business dealings.[58] On the other hand, the case may be considered as merely an extension of the prior holdings [59] that a municipality may not constitutionally prohibit such proselytizing on city streets. Another distinctive feature of the Marsh decision is its emphasis upon the right of the residents to receive the information as well as the right of the defendant to disseminate it.[60]

Municipalities have attempted to impose upon the Jehovah's Witnesses the usual license taxes or fees imposed upon commercial canvassers. In *Jones v. Opelika,*[61] a bare majority of the court found such a nondiscriminatory tax valid. However this position was later changed, and the court held invalid such a tax, even if nondiscriminatory, as an unlawful tax on the exercise of religious freedom.[62]

[56] Cantwell v. Connecticut, 310 U.S. 296 (1940).

[57] 326 U.S. 501 (1946).

[58] See Valentine v. Chrestensen, 316 U.S. 52 (1942); on the equality of the freedoms protected by the First Amendment, see Prince v. Massachusetts, 321 U.S. 158, 164 (1944).

[59] See Jamison v. Texas, 318 U.S. 413 (1943).

[60] In accord with Marsh on a similar set of facts is Tucker v. Texas, 326 U.S. 517 (1946).

[61] 316 U.S. 584 (1942).

[62] Murdock v. Pennsylvania, 319 U.S. 105 (1943); accord: Follett v. McCormick, 321 U.S. 573 (1944).

The result emphasizes the preferred position of freedom of religion and, impliedly, freedom of religious association. Merely commercial canvassing enjoys no such protection.[63] The fact that the religious tracts are sold, and not given away free of charge, does not transform the enterprise into a taxable commercial one so long as the selling is merely incidental to the main object of religious propagation.[64]

A somewhat different problem is presented where the corporate position of a religious association, and the individual convictions of its members, conflict with the dictates of the government when it seeks to impose, on behalf of society, a civic duty upon the members which, the government asserts, overrides their right to adhere to their religious practice. Here again we are indebted to the Witnesses for our present understanding of the constitutional issue. Their refusal to salute the flag was considered in *Minersville School District v. Gobitis*,[65] where the court upheld the expulsion from public school of Witnesses who refused to salute the flag. The Gobitis decision elicited much unfavorable comment,[66] and was reversed in 1943.[67] Mr. Justice Jackson, for the majority in Barnette, proclaimed: "If there is any fixed star in our constitutional constellation, it is that no official, high or petty, can prescribe what shall be orthodox in politics, nationalism, religion, or other matters of opinion or force citizens to confess by word or act their faith therein. If there are any circumstances which permit an exception, they do not now occur to us." [68] On the same day, the court invalidated a Mississippi flag-salute statute.[69]

The foregoing selection will give a fair idea of the variety and scope of the official and unofficial efforts to impede the proselytizing

[63] See Jamison v. Texas, 318 U.S. 413, 417 (1943); Valentine v. Chrestensen, 316 U.S. 52, 55 (1942).

[64] Murdock v. Pennsylvania, 319 U.S. 105, 112 (1943).

[65] 310 U.S. 586 (1940).

[66] See Fennell, The "Reconstructed Court" and Religious Freedom: The Gobitis Case in Retrospect, 19 N.Y.U.L. Rev. 31 (1941); Heller, A Turning Point for Religious Liberty, 29 Va. L. Rev. 440 (1943); Million, Validity of Compulsory Flag Salutes in Public Schools, 28 Ky. L.J. 306 (1940).

[67] West Virginia State Board of Educ. v. Barnette, 319 U.S. 624 (1943).

[68] 319 U.S. at 642; see dissent by Mr. Justice Frankfurter, 319 U.S. at 652: "The constitutional protection of religious freedom terminated disabilities, it did not create new privileges. It gave religious equality, not civil immunity. Its essence is freedom from conformity to religious dogma, not freedom from conformity to law because of religious dogma."

[69] Taylor v. Mississippi, 319 U.S. 583 (1943).

work of the Witnesses.[70] More importantly, the cases involving the Witnesses are instructive on the general principles of the right of religious association and the right to act in furtherance of the aims of such association.[71] Freedom of religious association, we may conclude, enjoys such a preferred position that it not only guarantees the right to practice religious tenets peaceably, but it also affords exemption, as in the flag-salute case, from the operation of some ordinary secular laws which happen to conflict with the religious belief of the members. It may be argued that the rights claimed under this freedom of religious association are not different from the ordinary individual rights of religious freedom. This contention has plausibility when the matter is viewed in a vacuum. However, in reality, the practices of the Witnesses, e.g., canvassing, ceremonies, distribution of literature, are ones which would rarely, if ever, be undertaken by an individual not affiliated with some organized religious group. Not only does the ritual of the group induce the individual to perform the acts in question, but the stability and genuineness of the group to which he adheres provide a sort of *prima facie* proof of the individual's own sincerity. Since the individual Witnesses were acting to advance the tenets of their group, and not to advance merely individual conceptions, the newly recognized freedom of association [72] may be properly advanced as an additional ground for the vindication of their rights. It may possibly be employed as an alternative ground to the free-exercise and establishment clauses of the First Amendment, thereby avoiding the nearly absolutist interpretations which are so identified with those familiar guarantees. It is true that the application of freedom of association to the foregoing cases would probably not change the result in any of them. In those cases which upheld the religious practice in question, the freedom of religious association would provide a protection sufficient for the occasion. In the cases which have permitted

[70] See Prince v. Massachusetts, 321 U.S. 158 (1944) where a child labor law, reflecting the state's interest in protecting its children, was successful in frustrating the pamphleteering efforts of a nine-year-old Witness; see also, Board of Zoning Appeals v. Decatur, Indiana, Company of Jehovah's Witnesses, 233 Ind. 83, 117 N.E.2d 115 (1954), on the requirement of reasonableness in application of zoning laws to churches; Brundel, Zoning Out Religious Institutions, 32 Notre Dame Law 627 (1957); Note, Churches and Zoning, 70 Harv. L. Rev. 1428 (1957).

[71] See Elias, The Jehovah's Witnesses Cases, 16 U. Kan. City L. Rev. 140 (1948); Howerton, Jehovah's Witnesses and the Federal Constitution, 17 Miss. L.J. 347 (1946); Waite, The Debt of Constitutional Law to Jehovah's Witnesses, 28 Minn. L. Rev. 409 (1944).

[72] NAACP v. Alabama, 357 U.S. 449 (1958).

restrictions upon religious practice, the freedom of religious association could be well employed because it is more readily seen to be subject to qualification than the traditional freedoms of religious exercise and from religious establishment, which are guaranteed in specific terms in the First Amendment. It may be possible, then, to preserve the religious exercise and establishment clauses of the First Amendment from an undue dilution. The former could thereby be saved mainly for those matters of belief or doctrine where its protection is, practically speaking, absolute. The latter could be reserved for those cases in which there is a public compulsion of religious support in a dimension serious enough to bring into play the traditional concept of an establishment of religion.

3. *Other Police-Power Regulations*

In addition to the strictures aimed at Jehovah's Witnesses, there are miscellaneous police-power regulations which otherwise bear upon the right to associate for religious purposes.

Immediately there come to mind the laws compelling Sunday as a day of rest. They have been attacked on the ground that they enact into law the religious practices of sects observing Sunday as a day of religious observance. Thereby, it may be said, they compel dissidents to associate with those sects in their observance of Sunday as a religious day.[73] Today, most states restrict the performance of work on Sunday,[74] but the laws are generally sustained not for religious reasons, but rather on the ground that one day of rest each week is conducive to the good order of society.[75] The contentions that such laws constitute an unlawful establishment of religion and infringe upon the rights of religious exercise and association have been rejected by the Supreme Court.[76] In the McGowan and McGinley cases, the Maryland and Pennsylvania Sunday-closing statutes were sustained against objections raised, by individuals of unspecified religious affiliation in the McGowan case, and by a corpo-

[73] The prototype of the modern statutes was the English statute forbidding any person to exercise "wordly labor or business or work of their ordinary calling on the Lord's Day, works of necessity and charity excepted." Sec. 29 Car. II, c. 7 (1676).

[74] See New York Penal Law, Secs. 2143, 2146, 2147.

[75] See State v. Grabinski, 33 Wash. 2d. 603, 206 P.2d 1022 (1949); People v. Friedman, 302 N.Y. 75, 96 N.E.2d 184 (1950), app. dis. 341 U.S. 907 (1951).

[76] McGowan v. Maryland, 366 U.S. 420 (1961); Gallagher v. Crown Kosher Super Market, 366 U.S. 617 (1961); Two Guys from Harrison-Allentown Inc. v. McGinley, 366 U.S. 582 (1961); Braunfeld v. Brown 366 U.S. 599 (1961).

ration in McGinley. The McGowan majority, through Chief Justice Warren, found the exemptions granted by the law not violative of equal protection, and emphasized "the evolution of Sunday laws as temporal statutes" [77] in disposing of the contention that the law was one respecting an establishment of religion.[78]

The question whether Sunday laws unconstitutionally impede Sabbatarians in the free exercise of their religion was raised by the plaintiffs in *Gallagher* (a corporation operating a kosher market, whose stockholders, officers, and directors were Orthodox Jews) and *Braunfeld* (individual Orthodox Jewish merchants). The opinion of Chief Justice Warren in the *Braunfeld* case, for four members of the court, observed that "freedom to hold religious beliefs and opinions is absolute," [79] but religious practices may be restricted when the practices themselves conflict with the public interest. Noting that the statute in question does not prohibit a religious practice but merely imposes an indirect burden on the exercise of religion [80] by making it "more expensive," [81] the Chief Justice found the non-religious purpose of the statute to be a sufficient justification for that indirect burden.[82] In *Gallagher* and *Braunfeld*, it may be said that plaintiffs were not only compelled to associate in the Sunday observance, but were also prevented, by the economic necessity of working six days a week, from practicing the tenets of their own religious association which observes Saturday as a day of rest.[83] The plaintiffs in *Gallagher* and *Braunfeld* failed to secure exemption, on account of the creed of their religious association, from a general law. The cases may be distinguished from the flag-salute case [84] by the presence in *Gallagher* and *Braunfeld* of an adequate secular reason for the statutes.

Spiritism, fortunetelling, and other cult observances are, of course,

[77] 366 U.S. at 436.

[78] Chief Justice Warren also wrote the majority opinion in the McGinley case, which he described as "essentially the same as" McGowan. Note Mr. Justice Frankfurter's comprehensive tabulation of colonial and present Sunday laws at 366 U.S. 551.

[79] 366 U.S. at 603.

[80] 366 U.S. at 606.

[81] 366 U.S. at 605.

[82] In both cases, Justices Brennan and Stewart dissented vigorously on the free exercise question, with the latter stating that the statute "compels an Orthodox Jew to choose between his religious faith and his economic survival." 366 U.S. at 616. Mr. Justice Douglas also dissented in both cases.

[83] In McGowan and McGinley, the objectors were not themselves members of any religious association.

[84] West Virginia State Bd. of Educ. v. Barnette, 319 U.S. 624 (1943).

subject to reasonable regulation, even where they are conducted by a religious association.[85] A belief in faith healing is no defense to a parent prosecuted for failure to provide required medical care to a child, even where the parent is a member of a bona-fide religious association which believes in healing by faith. The law regulates the action, or inaction, and not the beliefs.[86]

Statutes outlawing snake handling have been upheld, even against practitioners associated as a religious group with that practice as a ritual.[87] It is no objection to a program of public-water fluoridation that it interferes with the beliefs of a religious association which is opposed to medication.[88] Nor is religious belief a valid objection to a public program of compulsory vaccination.[89]

Members of religious associations are not afforded by their membership any immunity against the general criminal laws of the community. But the religious nature of the enterprise may have an important effect on the procedural conduct of a prosecution. In *United States v. Ballard,*[90] a Federal prosecution for fraudulently using the mails to solicit funds for the defendant's "I Am" religious movement, the Supreme Court held that the trial court had properly withdrawn from the jury any consideration of the truth or falsity of the religious representations made. Mr. Justice Douglas, for the majority, said any inquiry into the truth of defendant's religious beliefs, as distinguished from his good faith, would be an inadmissible encroachment on the free exercise of religion. It is important that the court did permit an inquiry into the good faith of defendant's religious beliefs. Arguably, an inquiry into the individual's good faith is in

[85] See State v. Delaney, 122 Atl. 890 (N.J., 1923); People v. Ashley, 184 App. Div. 520, 172 N.Y. Supp. 282 (1918); State v. Neitzel, 69 Wash. 567, 125 Pac. 939 (1912); City of St. Louis v. Hellscher, 295 Mo. 293, 242 S.W. 652 (1922); McMasters v. State, 21 Okla. Cr. 318, 207 Pac. 566 (1922).

[86] People v. Pierson, 176 N.Y. 201, 68 N.E. 243 (1903); Beck v. State, 29 Okla. Cr. 240, 233 Pac. 495 (1925); see Mitchell v. Davis, 205 S.W.2d 812 (Tex. Civ. App., 1947).

[87] Hill v. State, 38 Ala. App. 404, 88 So. 2d 880 (1956); cert. den. 264 Ala. 697, 88 So. 2d 887 (1956); Harden v. State, 188 Tenn. 17, 216 S.W.2d 708 (1948), noted in 2 Vand. L. Rev. 694 (1949); Lawson v. Commonwealth 291 Ky. 437, 164 S.W.2d 972 (1942); see Kirk v. Commonwealth, 186 Va. 839, 44 S.E.2d 409 (1947).

[88] Kraus v. Cleveland, 121 N.E.2d 311 (Ohio Ct. App., 1954) aff'd. 163 Ohio St. 559, 177 N.E.2d 609 (1955), app. dis. 351 U.S. 935 (1956); noted in 3 St. Louis U.L.J. 284 (1955).

[89] Commonwealth v. Green, 268 Mass. 585, 168 N.E. 101 (1929); Viemeister v. White, 179 N.Y. 235, 72 N.E. 97 (1904); Seubold v. Fort Smith Special School Dist., 218 Ark. 560, 237 S.W.2d 884 (1951).

[90] 322 U.S. 78 (1944).

order in any case in which he asserts his belief in the doctrines of a religious association.[91]

The general independence of religious associations from government interference in their internal affairs [92] was illustrated in *Kedroff v. St. Nicholas Cathedral of the Russian Orthodox Church in North America.*[93] There, the Supreme Court held that it was an unconstitutional abridgement of religious freedom for a state to attempt by statute [94] to transfer control of the New York properties of the Russian Orthodox Church from the central authorities of the Church to the American authorities, who were not dominated by the government of Soviet Russia. In a later phase of the case, the Supreme Court held it would be equally objectionable for a state court to attempt the interference as a matter of common law. The exercise of state power is evident, whether the legislature or a court is the implementing agency.[95]

Other incidental regulations of religious associations could be mentioned.[96] The examples cited, however, will demonstrate the general subjection of the right of religious association to the police power of the government, reasonably exercised upon an external matter and not impinging at all upon the sanctuary of internal religious belief or directly and substantially upon the free exercise of that belief.

4. Associations and Persons Objecting to Military Service

The power of Congress to raise an army and a navy includes the power to impose compulsory military service in both war and peacetime.[97] In the exercise of that power, Congress may, but need not, exempt from such service clergymen and those who, individually or as members of a religious group, have religious scruples against bearing arms.[98] The *Arver* decision rejected as manifestly unsound

[91] See Mr. Justice Brennan's opinion in Braunfeld v. Brown, 366 U.S. at 615.

[92] See Watson v. Jones, 80 U.S. (13 Wall.) 679 (1872).

[93] 344 U.S. 94 (1952).

[94] New York Religious Corporations Law, Art. 5-C.

[95] Kreshik v. St. Nicholas Cathedral of the Russian Orthodox Church in North America, 363 U.S. 190 (1960).

[96] For instance, the decision in Pierce et al. v. Society of Sisters, 268 U.S. 510 (1925) seems to have indicated the right of a religious association itself to maintain schools for its adherents as well as the right of the parents to send their children to such schools.

[97] Arver v. United States, 245 U.S. 366 (1918); United States v. Herling, 120 F.2d 236 (2d Cir., 1941); Billings v. Truesdale, 321 U.S. 542 (1944).

[98] Arver v. United States, 245 U.S. 366 (1918).

the contention that the World War I draft law, because it provided for religious exemptions, violated the nonestablishment and free exercise clauses of the First Amendment.

It is important for our purpose to note that Congress lent direct encouragement to religious associations, and to the freedom to practice pacifistic tenets of such groups, by requiring that one who seeks exemption as a minister or ministerial student must be connected with "a church, a religious sect, or organization of which he is a member." [99] The exemption does not apply to everyone whom a particular group may designate as a minister. The statute excludes from the exempt category those who preach only "irregularly or incidentally" [100] and draft boards have been upheld in refusing exemptions to Jehovah's Witnesses who were not ministers in the sense in which Congress used the term, even though the Witnesses consider each of their number to be a minister.[101]

Conscientious objectors, as opposed to clergy and clerical students, must show an objection based on religious belief, either individually or as a member of a bona-fide pacifistic denomination; a nonreligious ethical objection is not sufficient.[102]

A draft board may dictate that a conscientious objector "perform such civilian work contributing to the maintenance of the national health, safety or interest as the local board may deem appropriate," [103] and the objector is not allowed to refuse on religious grounds to perform such work.[104]

When a person who would otherwise be exempt for conscience' sake from military service voluntarily attends a state university at which Reserve Officer Training Corps military training is compulsory, he is obliged to undergo the training as a price of continuing in the school he chose to attend.[105] It has been held that a pacifist applicant may be denied admission to the bar where the state constitution requires military service of all male adults in time of war, and the applicant balked, for religious reasons, at swearing to comply

[99] 50 U.S.C. App. Secs. 456(g), 466(g).

[100] 50 U.S.C. App. Sec. 466(g).

[101] United States v. Mroz, 136 F.2d 221 (7th Cir. 1943); Martin v. United States, 190 F.2d 775 (4th Cir. 1951); United States v. Hoepker, 223 F.2d 921 (7th Cir. 1955), cert. den. 350 U.S. 841 (1955).

[102] 50 U.S.C. App. Sec. 456(j); see United States v. Bendik, 220 F.2d 249 (2d Cir. 1955).

[103] 50 U.S.C. App. Sec. 456(j) (1951).

[104] Johnston v. United States, 351 U.S. 215 (1956).

[105] Hamilton v. Regents of the Univ. of California, 293 U.S. 245 (1934); see Heisler, The Law versus the Conscientious Objector, 20 U. Chi. L. Rev. 441 (1953).

with that obligation.[106] Justices Douglas, Murphy, Rutledge, and Black dissented.[107]

Naturalization will not be denied to an alien who is opposed, "by reason of religious training and belief," to bearing arms on behalf of the United States.[108] Personal religious belief will suffice, and the alien need not show that his belief is prescribed by any sect to which he belongs.[109]

The conclusion to be drawn from the law governing military service exemptions is that one may not, by personal belief or by religious association, entitle himself to constitutional immunity from the requirement to defend the nation. Rather, the immunity which exists is not a constitutional one, but is merely statutory and given at sufferance of Congress. In the same category is the enactment opening the gates to citizenship for such conscientious objectors. While Congress and the courts have recognized the vital function of religion and religious associations, there is accorded to the right of religious belief and association no absolute value that would, as a matter of right, transcend the constitutional obligation of the government to conduct defense and set the requirements for citizenship. Further, the mere fact that an individual is associated with a pacifistic group is not alone sufficient to qualify him for the relevant exemptions or disabilities unless he is himself imbued with the requisite pacifistic belief; his association with the group, however, seems to be evidence of his own adherence to its precepts.

D. FREEDOM NOT TO JOIN OR SUPPORT RELIGIOUS ASSOCIATIONS

1. The Meaning of the Establishment Clause of the First Amendment

We have seen, of course, that there are no established, publicly supported churches in the United States today.[110] The First Amendment prevents Congress from legislating on the subject and this

[106] In re Summers, 325 U.S. 561 (1945).

[107] See Application of Steinbugler, 297 N.Y. 713, 77 N.E.2d 16 (1947) (reaching opposite result from Summers decision). The concept of freedom of religious association should not change the result in the Summers case.

[108] 8 U.S.C. Sec. 1448.

[109] In re Hansen, 148 F. Supp. 187 (D.C. Minn., 1957); see Girouard v. United States, 328 U.S. 61 (1946).

[110] Supra p. 43.

interdiction, by the presently accepted construction,[111] is applicable to the states. Much controversy has occurred over the meaning of this First Amendment prohibition against Congress legislating "respecting an establishment of religion."

On the one hand it has been contended that the evil to be prevented is preferential treatment of any particular religion or religions by the government.[112] This position, recognizing a right in government to act in favor of religions without discrimination, draws further support from the encouragement of religion which was written into the Northwest Ordinance of 1787.[113] It is reflected in the majority opinion of Mr. Justice Douglas in *Zorach v. Clauson* [114] wherein it is stated that:

> We are a religious people whose institutions presuppose a Supreme Being. . . . We sponsor an attitude on the part of government that shows no partiality to any one group and that lets each flourish according to the zeal of its adherents and the appeal of its dogma. When the state encourages religious instruction or cooperates with religious authorities by adjusting the schedule of public events to sectarian needs, it follows the best of our traditions.[115]

The contrasting approach draws upon the statement by Thomas Jefferson in his letter to the Baptists of Danbury, Connecticut, in 1802, in which he declared:

> Believing with you that religion is a matter which lies solely between man and his God, that he owes account to none other for his faith or his worship, that the legislative powers of Government reach actions only, and not opinions, I contemplate with sovereign reverence that act of the whole American people which declared that their legislature should "make no law respecting an establishment of religion, or prohibiting the free exercise thereof," thus building a wall of separation between church and State.[116]

[111] See Murdock v. Pennsylvania, 319 U.S. 105 (1943).

[112] See 2 Story, Commentaries Secs. 1870–79 (Boston, 1833). Story considered preference of the Christian religion over other religions to be constitutional; see Daniel Webster's argument that Christianity is part of the common law of Pennsylvania, in Vidal v. Girard's Ex'rs, 43 U.S. (2 How.) 127, 198 (1844); see the statement by Mr. Justice Brewer that "this is a Christian nation," in Church of the Holy Trinity v. United States, 143 U.S. 457, 471 (1892); Cooley, Principles of Constitutional Law 224–25 (1898).

[113] Supra pp. 30–31.

[114] 343 U.S. 306 (1952).

[115] 343 U.S. at 313–14.

[116] 8 The Writings of Thomas Jefferson 113 (Washington ed., 1861).

In this famous letter, enunciating the "wall-of-separation" metaphor, Jefferson was objecting to the establishment of the Congregational Church as the official Church of the State of Connecticut.[117] In 1879, a unanimous Supreme Court appraised Jefferson's statement as "almost an authoritative declaration of the scope and effect of the amendment.[118]

This second viewpoint of the establishment clause found expression beyond the original meaning of Jefferson's metaphor in the opinion of Mr. Justice Black, for a divided Supreme Court in 1947:

> The "establishment of religion" clause of the First Amendment means at least this: Neither a state nor the Federal Government can set up a church. Neither can pass laws which aid one religion, aid all religions, or prefer one religion over another. Neither can force or influence a person to go to or to remain away from church against his will or force him to profess a belief or disbelief in any religion. No person can be punished for entertaining or professing religious beliefs or disbeliefs, for church attendance or non-attendance. No tax in any amount, large or small, can be levied to support any religious activities or institutions, whatever they may be called, or whatever form they may adopt to teach or practice religion. Neither a state nor the Federal Government can, openly or secretly, participate in the affairs of any religious organizations and vice versa.[119]

It is necessary at this point merely to note the existence of the conflict over the meaning of the establishment clause.[120] There can be no thought of an established Church, in the literal sense of a state-supported compulsory Church, in this nation today. However, the problem of defining the constitutional restriction laid upon government is necessarily a continuing one.[121] In any inquiry into certain detailed aspects of the matter, as it bears upon the right of religious association, it will be helpful to bear in mind these general and conflicting thoughts on the nature and extent of the prohibition.

[117] O'Neill, Religion and Education under the Constitution 25 (New York, 1949).

[118] Reynolds v. United States, 98 U.S. 145, 164 (1879).

[119] Everson v. Board of Education, 330 U.S. 1, 15, 16 (1947), upholding a New Jersey statute allowing the public bus transportation for parochial-school students.

[120] See Corwin, The Constitution and What It Means Today 190 et seq. (Princeton, 1958).

[121] See Kauper, Church, State and Freedom: A Review, 52 Mich. L. Rev. 829 (1954).

2. *Public Subsidies to Religious Associations*

While formal establishment of religion no longer poses a threat to freedom of conscience and of association in our society, there are many instances of governmental subvention of some or all religions, in forms which may vary in kind or only in degree from actual establishment. It may be argued reasonably that the newly articulated freedom of association provides an alternative ground for the decision of cases involving government subsidies to religion. A taxpayer who does not adhere to the aided religion is obviously being compelled to contribute to its support. If the right not to join a religious association includes, as it should, the right not to support it, he may allege that his freedom of association is infringed. In deciding upon his contention, the conflicting interpretations of the establishment clause, as discussed above, would affect the meaning to be given to the right of association in this context. However, the semantic difficulties occasioned by the absolutist language of the First Amendment prohibition [122] and by the restricted historical meaning of an establishment of religion [123] could be mitigated by application of the new freedom of association which is still in a plastic state. There are many such aids to religious associations which have not been seriously questioned. Municipalities obviously "aid" church or synagogue in providing traffic policemen to direct the attending worshippers. The Congress of the United States and the armed forces have their chaplains. Attendance at church services is compulsory at the United States Military and Naval Academies. Veterans receive training for the ministry at government expense under legislation providing general educational benefits for veterans. Thanksgiving Day is a national holiday. Examples of this sort of "aid" could be multiplied.[124]

While such activities of government do aid religion and religious associations, most have been sanctioned by a long-standing historical prescription [125] and many are reinforced by the argument that for the state to withdraw essential services from religious groups

[122] "Congress shall make no law respecting an establishment of religion. . . ."

[123] See generally, O'Neill, Religion and Education under the Constitution (New York, 1949).

[124] See the enumeration by Mr. Justice Douglas in the opinion of the court in Zorach v. Clauson, 343 U.S. 306 (1952).

[125] See Mr. Justice Reed's dissent in Illinois ex rel. McCollum v. Board of Educ., 333 U.S. 203 (1948).

would betoken an attitude on the part of government of active hostility toward religion. Religious groups, for example, could not survive without the police protection to which all are entitled. Or, to deny formal religious ministrations to draftees in the armed services would surely inhibit their free exercise of religion. There are more substantial types of aid, however, which do cause genuine concern.

Public aid to schools conducted by religious groups is a continuing cause of controversy. It would be an undue excursion afield for us to discuss here, for example, the released-time program[126] or its checkered career in the courts.[127] Nor can we discuss the merits of the controversies occasioned by the introduction of prayer and scripture reading into the public schools.[128] But we can and should note the possibility of deciding those cases on the basis of freedom of association, as at least an alternative rationale.[129] Insofar as those cases involve personal participation by the dissenting citizen, e.g., prayers in the public schools, it may be argued that the dissident is being compelled, not only to support, but to practice, the religious beliefs of those with whom he does not choose to associate himself. The associational theory could be applied, as an alternative rationale, to other miscellaneous instances of public support of reli-

[126] See Religion and the State (Symposium), 14 Law & Contemp. Prob. 3 (1949); New York Times, Sept. 21, 1947, p. 22.

[127] See Illinois ex rel. McCollum v. Board of Educ., 333 U.S. 203 (1948); Zorach v. Clauson, 343 U.S. 306 (1952); Sutherland, Due Process and Disestablishment, 62 Harv. L. Rev. 1306 (1949); Reed, Church, State and the Zorach Case, 27 Notre Dame Law. 529 (1952); Pfeffer, Church and State: Something Less Than Separation, 19 U. Chi. L. Rev. 1 (1951).

[128] See Doremus v. Board of Educ., 342 U.S. 429 (1952); Schempp v. School Dis. of Abington Township, 177 F. Supp. 398 (E.D. Pa., 1959); Miami Military Institute v. Leff, 129 Misc. 481, 220 N.Y. Supp. 799 (1926); Engel v. Vitale, 370 U.S. 421 (1962).

[129] In Engel v. Vitale, 370 U.S. 421 (1962), the Court invalidated, as an establishment of religion, the voluntary recitation by public school students of a nondenominational prayer composed by the New York State Board of Regents. It may be argued that the students prevented by the decision from reciting a prayer they wish to recite are thereby compelled to practice the tenets of such nontheistic religions as ethical culture, which does not approve of such prayers. On the other hand, if the Court had upheld the prayer, ethical culture adherents could have argued that they were thereby compelled to associate in the practice of theistic religion. A decision upon either objection would require due consideration of the religious background of many of the institutions and traditions of this nation. In Torcaso v. Watkins, 367 U.S. 488, 495 (1961), Mr. Justice Black, speaking for the Court, said, "Among religions in this country which do not teach what would generally be considered a belief in the existence of God are Buddhism, Taoism, Ethical Culture, Secular Humanism and others." On the question of standing to sue and other procedural difficulties in challenging the expenditure of public funds, see Massachusetts v. Mellon, 262 U.S. 447 (1923); Doremus v. Board of Educ., 342 U.S. 429 (1952); Sutherland, Due Process and Disestablishment, 62 Harv. L. Rev. 1306 (1949).

gious groups including, for example, the use of public-school buildings for Sunday school and similar purposes,[130] the utilization by a religious association of the fruits of an exercise of the power of eminent domain,[131] the integration of religious schools into the public-school system,[132] the provision by the government of secular textbooks to all school children, including those attending nonpublic schools,[133] and public financial assistance to pupils attending religious schools or to such schools themselves.[134]

While educational subventions have bulked largest in our constitutional literature, there are frequent subsidies to sectarian hospitals, orphanages, and the like,[135] in addition to the prevalent exemption of religious associations from taxation.[136] In all such instances, the right not to join a religious association, and the correlative right not to support it, may provide some clarification.[137]

These varied types of public aid to religious associations are men-

[130] See State ex rel. Gilbert v. Dilley, 95 Nebr. 527, 145 N.W. 999 (1914).

[131] See 64th St. Residences v. City of New York, 4 N.Y.2d 268, 150 N.E.2d 396 (1958), cert. den. sub. nom. Harris v. City of New York, 357 U.S. 907 (1958).

[132] Compare Zellers v. Huff, 55 N.M. 501, 236 P.2d 949 (1951) with New Haven v. Torrington, 132 Conn. 194, 43 Atl.2d 455 (1945); see Blum, Religious Liberty and Religious Garb, 22 U. Chi. L. Rev. 875 (1955).

[133] See Cochran v. Louisiana Board of Education, 281 U.S. 370 (1930).

[134] This is, of course, a large subject, with current significance. See Almond v. Day, 197 Va. 419, 89 S.E.2d 851 (1955), noted in 42 Va. L. Rev. 437 (1956); Quick Bear v. Leupp, 210 U.S. 50 (1908); Manning, Aid to Education—Federal Fashion, Aid to Education—State Style, 29 Fordham L. Rev. 495, 525 (1961); note, Federal Aid to Education—for Some or for All? 23 Temp. L.Q. 227 (1950).

It could be argued that governmental aid limited to public schools would force the limitation or closing of many sectarian schools because of inability to compete with the publicly financed institutions. Thereby, it could be said, the member of the religious group would suffer an impairment of his right to associate, and to have his children associate, with members of his own religious group. If so, it would then appear to be incumbent upon the proponents of aid limited to public institutions to show that a sufficient public interest required the limitation and the consequent restriction upon the right of association. On the criteria employed in judging the sufficiency of an asserted public interest as a justification of an infringement upon freedom of association, see the NAACP cases discussed herein pp. 112 et seq.

[135] Bradfield v. Roberts, 175 U.S. 291 (1899); Craig v. Mercy Hospital-St. Memorial, 209 Miss. 427, 47 So. 2d 867 (1950); Bennett v. City of La Grange, 153 Ga. 428, 112 S.E. 482 (1922); Schade v. Alleghany County, 386 Pa. 507, 126 A.2d 911 (1956).

[136] United States Internal Revenue Code (1954), Secs. 170, 501, 2055, 2522; see Pfeffer, Church, State and Freedom 183–90 (Boston, 1953); Lundberg v. County of Alameda, 46 Cal. 2d 644, 298 P.2d 1 (1956), app. dis. sub. nom. Heisey v. County of Alameda, 352 U.S. 921 (1956).

[137] Of interest is the Blaine Amendment to the United States Constitution, proposed in 1876 but never ratified, which would have expressly prohibited all public support, federal and state, of sectarian schools; it exempted Bible reading in the schools from its interdiction, H.R. 1, 44th Cong., 1st Sess. (1876); Ames, The Proposed Amendments to the Constitution of the United States during the First Century of Its History, 777–78. H.R. Doc. No. 353, Pt. 2, 54th Cong., 2d Sess.

tioned here only insofar as they shed light upon the viability of freedom of association as a practical constitutional concept. The unsatisfactory and contradictory analyses in this area, in terms of the establishment and free-exercise clauses of the First Amendment, could be improved, in some cases, by employment of the freedom not to associate. For example, the free exercise and establishment arguments against most indirect public subventions of religion are weakened by the facts that there usually is no substantial impairment of the dissenting taxpayer's right to exercise his own religion and that the treatment of indirect aid as an "establishment of religion" involves a considerable stretching of that concept. When the taxpayer objects, however, that he is being compelled to associate with others in their religious endeavors, his objection may carry a greater plausibility even though he still must surmount the hurdles created by the nonabsolute character of freedom of association and the *de minimis* nature of his interest in most such public subsidies.

E. FREEDOM NOT TO PRACTICE RELIGION

Sumptuary Laws and Other Aspects

As we have seen, our fundamental laws adequately prevent a state dictation of formal religious belief or affiliation. Similarly, our laws and traditions endeavor to insure that no person shall be compelled to participate in a religious practice or observance against his will. However, in the area of practice, as distinguished from belief and affiliation, there are laws which do prevent certain actions which are licit in the eyes of many, but illicit in the eyes of some of our religious denominations. They have usually been analyzed in the past in terms of establishment and free exercise of religion. In some cases, the associational approach may lend clarification through a conception of the sumptuary law as a compulsion of association in the practice of a religious belief, especially where such a law is not based upon adequate nonreligious grounds.

About these sumptuary laws, their wisdom and effect, there are sharply divided opinions. Included among such enactments are those attempting to censor obscenity from literature and the arts.[138]

[138] See Roth v. United States, 354 U.S. 476 (1957); Kingsley Int'l Pictures Corp. v. Regents, 360 U.S. 684 (1959); Annotation, Constitutionality of federal and state regulation of obscene literature—federal cases, 4 L. Ed. 2d 1821 (1959); Times Film Corp. v. Chicago, 365 U.S. 43 (1961).

The prohibition of published obscenity directly involves the right of free speech and, analytically, it depends little upon the latent religious issues.[139] There are other sumptuary laws, however, which are more obviously based upon particular religious beliefs. Arguably, the State, in enacting them, is compelling dissident citizens to observe the favored religious practice. The crime of blasphemy, for example, which is the showing of disrespect to God or to persons or things considered sacred, has been considered a serious offense by Jewish, Christian ecclesiastical, and English common law.[140] It was widely proscribed by the states in the early years of our history, and the ban was actively enforced through the first third of the nineteenth century.[141] It is still a crime in fourteen states.[142] Only a few cases have arisen in this century[143] and the crime has lapsed into almost utter desuetude. It is interesting to speculate about the possible fate of a blasphemy prosecution in the Supreme Court of the United States, which has rejected[144] as too indefinite for censorship the standard of "sacrilegious," defined by a highest state court[145] as meaning that "no religion, as that word is understood by the ordinary, reasonable person, shall be treated with contempt, mockery, scorn and ridicule . . ."[146]

Although the prospect of a serious enforcement of the blasphemy laws today is so remote as to be fanciful, they do constitute an example of the endowment of a religious practice with an official and compulsory character. Apart from the question of vagueness raised

139 For a detailed treatment, see Chafee, Free Speech in the United States 529–48 (Cambridge, 1941); Schroeder, Constitutional Free Speech (New York, 1919); Lockhart & McClure, Literature, the Law of Obscenity and the Constitution, 38 Minn. L. Rev. 295 (1954); Note, Constitutional Law—Freedom of Press—Validity of Motion Picture Licensing Statute, 58 Mich. L. Rev. 134 (1959). Lockhart & McClure, Censorship of Obscenity: The Developing Constitutional Standard, 45 Minn. L. Rev. 5 (1960); Lockhart & McClure, Obscenity Censorship: The Constitutional Issue—What Is Obscene?, 7 Utah L. Rev. 289 (1961).

140 3 Stokes, Church and State in the United States, 149 (New York, 1950).

141 People v. Ruggles, 8 Johns. (N.Y.) 290 (1811); see The Blasphemy of Abner Kneeland, 8 New England Q. 29 (1935).

142 Conn., Dela., Me., Md., Mass., Mich., N.H., N.J., N.D., Okla., Pa., R.I., S.D., Vt.; 3 Stokes, Church and State in the United States, 149 et seq. (New York, 1950).

143 See Schroeder, Constitutional Free Speech 14, 34 (New York, 1919).

144 Burstyn v. Wilson, 343 U.S. 495 (1952).

145 Burstyn v. Wilson, 303 N.Y. 242, 258, 101 N.E.2d 665, 672.

146 See the charge by Lord Coleridge in a blasphemy prosecution that "if the decencies of controversy are observed, even the fundamentals of religion may be attacked," Regina v. Ramsey, 15 Cox C.C. 231, 238 (1893). See Torcaso v. Watkins, 367 U.S. 488 (1961) (invalidating Maryland requirement of belief in God as condition of holding public office, as infringing freedom of religion).

in *Burstyn v. Wilson* above, such a prosecution may well be vulnerable to the defense that the statutes exalt the precepts of the favored religious groups to a position where all other citizens are compelled to practice them, in violation of the freedom not to associate in the practice of religion. On the other hand, it may be said that the only thing forbidden is interference with the religious beliefs and activities of others by deprecation of their religions.

A similar problem is presented by the statutes which prohibit the dissemination of information or equipment in furtherance of contraception.[147] The conflicting religious positions on this matter are well known.[148] It is possible to argue that such laws compel adherence by dissidents to the precepts of the Roman Catholic Church, and thereby compel them to associate with Catholics in the practice of their religion.

Legislation restricting birth control is defended on constitutional grounds as a proper exercise of the police power to protect public health, welfare, and morals. Most state courts have held the statutes reasonable and constitutional[149] but some have disagreed.[150] The Connecticut and Massachusetts statutes have been especially fruitful as a source of constitutional litigation. Citizens opposing the statutes in those states have found it difficult, however, to frame the issues in a form suitable for constitutional adjudication by the Supreme Court of the United States.[151] The most recent attempt failed to penetrate the jurisdictional barrier in a carefully constructed trio of Connecticut cases.[152] All were suits for declaratory judgments

[147] For compilations of the state statutes now in force, see note, Connecticut's Birth Control Law: Reviewing a state statute under the Fourteenth Amendment, 70 Yale L.J. 322 (1960); note, Birth Control Legislation, 9 Clev.-Mar. L. Rev. 245 (1960); Sulloway, The Legal and Political Aspects of Population Control in the United States, 25 Law & Contemp. Prob. 593, 600–601 (1960). The Federal statutes are 18 U.S.C. Secs. 1461, 1462; 19 U.S.C. Sec. 1305(a); see Stone and Pilpel, The Social and Legal Status of Contraception, 22 N.C.L. Rev. 212 (1944).

[148] For the Roman Catholic position, see Pope Pius XI, Encyclical on Christian Marriage; Five Great Encyclicals 93 (New York, 1939). For the views of other denominations, see Fagley, The Population Explosion and Christian Responsibility (New York, 1960); 3 Stokes, Church and State in the United States, 72 (New York, 1950).

[149] See, e.g., Commonwealth v. Allison, 227 Mass. 57, 116 N.E. 265 (1917); People v. Sanger, 222 N.Y. 192, 118 N.E. 637 (1918).

[150] See, e.g., State v. Kinney Bldg. Drug Stores, Inc., 56 N.J. Super, 37, 151 A.2d 430 (Essex County Ct., 1959).

[151] See Commonwealth v. Gardner, 305 U.S. 559 (1938), and Tileston v. Ullman, 318 U.S. 44 (1943), both dismissed on jurisdictional grounds.

[152] Poe v. Ullman, 367 U.S. 497 (1961).

that the statute [153] prohibiting the use of contraceptives is contrary to the due-process clause of the Fourteenth Amendment. The Supreme Court rejected all three appeals for lack of a genuine case or controversy, with Mr. Justice Frankfurter, for four members of the court, noting that only one prosecution [154] had been brought under the statute since its enactment in 1879, and that the State's Attorney had not actually threatened to prosecute in the cases before the court.

It should be noted that the latent religious issue was not alluded to in *Poe v. Ullman*. Nevertheless, it is there, and birth-control legislation will continue to be regarded by many as an attempt to impose a sectarian practice upon a dissident segment of the population, and consequently an impingement upon the right not to practice religion.[155] The religious issue has come to the surface on a number of occasions, notably in the 1958 controversy over the dissemination of contraceptive advice in the New York City public hospitals,[156] and the 1959 recommendation by the President's Committee to Study the United States Military Assistance Program (the Draper Committee) that the United States "assist those countries with which it is cooperating in economic aid programs, on request, in the formulation of their plans designed to deal with the problem of rapid population growth." [157] It still has not received, and is not likely to receive, a final constitutional determination. At least academically, however, it offers a clear illustration of an issue involving the right not to associate in the practice of religious beliefs.

In this discussion of freedom not to practice religion, a brief mention should be made of the customs, in some places, of declaring religious feasts to be public holidays, and of issuing governmental

[153] Conn. Gen. Stat. Rev., 1958, Sec. 53–32.

[154] State v. Nelson, 126 Conn. 412, 11 A.2d 856 (1940) (later dismissed on motion of prosecution after constitutionality of statute was upheld in this decision).

[155] The state's attorney in Poe v. Ullman justified the statute as protective of public morals, in that the practice of contraception is immoral in itself and the ready availability of contraceptive devices would promote fornication and adultery. See dissenting opinion of Mr. Justice Harlan, 367 U.S. at 545.

[156] See Sulloway, The Legal and Political Aspects of Population Control in the United States, 25 Law & Contemp. Prob. 593 (1960); Planned Parenthood Federation of America, The Anatomy of a Victory (New York, 1959).

[157] President's Committee to Study the United States Military Assistance Program, Third Interim Report, Economic Assistance Programs and Administration, 42–45 (1959); New York Times, Nov. 26, 1959, p. 43; The Brooklyn Tablet, Nov. 21, 1959, p. 8.

proclamations seeking divine aid or benediction. The problem of so-called Sunday laws has been elaborated above.[158] Thanksgiving, Christmas, and Good Friday proclamations and holidays are obviously of a different order and represent a minimal, although genuine, compulsion of religious observance on the part of dissident citizens. Most of such practices, however, are reinforced by usage, and the absence of constitutional adjudication apparently reflects a tacit public consensus of their desirability or at least harmlessness.[159]

Another incidental but interesting aspect of the freedom not to practice religion is found in the frequent statutes [160] requiring that a child being adopted must be assigned to an adopting parent of the same faith as the child's putative faith at birth, wherever such is possible or practicable. Such a statute does affect adversely those would-be adopting parents who find themselves deprived of custody because of their presumed inability to rear the child in the religion of his birth, and arguably exert compulsion upon such parents to qualify by affiliating with the religion of the child. However, the statutes have been sustained as reasonable and not an undue infringement of religious freedom.[161]

Other cases arguably involve the freedom of religious association of children of divorced parents or of mixed marriages. A requirement in a divorce decree that the "child shall be reared in the Roman Catholic Religion" was successfully attacked in an Iowa case,[162] where the majority opinion, in addition to finding the provision too vague, intimated that judicial enforcement of the decree would constitute state action [163] and raise a serious question of constitutionality. Problems have also arisen concerning antenuptial agreements between parents to raise the children of the marriage in a particular faith. Although there are authorities to the contrary,[164] the weight of modern authority does not accord-

[158] Supra p. 55.

[159] For a discussion of a few of the instances in which such practices have been challenged outside of the courts, see 3 Stokes, Church and State in the United States, 177–78 (New York, 1950); for descriptions of, and quotations from, various prayer, fast and thanksgiving proclamations which are issued with continuing frequency by the Federal Government and the states, see Stokes, id. at 179–200.

[160] See New York Domestic Relations Court Act, Secs. 86(3), 88(1), (5).

[161] See Petition of Goldman, 331 Mass. 647, 121 N.E.2d 843 (1954), cert. den. 348 U.S. 942 (1955); Re Adoption of Anonymous, 207 Misc. 240, 137 N.Y.S. 2d 720 (1955).

[162] Lynch v. Uhlenhopp, 248 Iowa 68, 78 N.W. 2d 491 (1956).

[163] See Shelley v. Kramer, 334 U.S. 1 (1948).

[164] See Weinberger v. Van Hessen, 260 N.Y. 294, 183 N.E. 429 (1932); Denton v. James, 107 Kan. 729, 193 Pac. 307 (1920); Williston, Contracts (1938), Sec. 1744.

binding legal effect to such agreements.[165] Rather, the courts will follow the general principle that the controlling factor in any case involving the upbringing of children is the moral and physical welfare of the children concerned.[166] This approach would seem to be in accord with the inherent parental right, secure from judicial invasion, to control the religion of an infant child.[167] The choice of the child himself, as to the religious group with which he chooses to associate, is not controlling as long as the child is in parental custody, even though the child may be old enough to make an intelligent choice.[168] The court, however, may consider the child's wishes in deciding which course of action will best promote the child's welfare.[169]

F. GENERAL CONCLUSIONS CONCERNING FREEDOM OF RELIGIOUS ASSOCIATION

The problems discussed here in terms of freedom of religious association have been treated in the past under the traditional First Amendment classifications. This analysis, however, supports the conclusion that the newly recognized freedom of association provides a workable, and in some cases superior, rationale. In addition, certain general outlines of the freedom of religious association can be deduced:

1. The right to join, and the right not to join, a religious association are constitutionally inviolate. Similarly to the right of internal belief, the right to effect a mere affiliation with a religious association, as well as the right not to do so, cannot be restricted or even regulated by the government. This absolutist principle does not apply to any act beyond the bare affiliation.

[165] See Martin v. Martin, 308 N.Y. 136, 123 N.E.2d 813 (1954) (per curiam opinion; Weinberger v. Van Hessen not mentioned by court but cited by counsel and dissenting opinion); In re Walsh's Estate, 100 Cal. App. 2d 194, 223 P.2d 322 (1950); note, Enforceability of Anti-Nuptial Contracts in Mixed Marriages, 50 Yale L.J. 1286 (1941); Pfeffer, Religion in the Upbringing of Children, 35 B.U.L. Rev. 333, 360–64 (1955).

[166] See State ex rel. Baker v. Bird, 253 Mo. 569, 162 S.W. 119 (1913); People ex rel. Sisson v. Sisson, 271 N.Y. 285, 2 N.E.2d 660 (1936).

[167] Meyer v. Nebraska, 262 U.S. 390 (1923); Pierce v. Society of Sisters, 268 U.S. 510 (1925).

[168] See Prieto v. St. Alphonsus Convent of Mercy, 52 La. Ann. 631, 27 So. 153 (1900).

[169] Matter of Vardinakis, 160 Misc. 13, 289 N.Y. Supp. 355 (Dom. Rel. Ct., N.Y. Co., 1936); Boerger v. Boerger, 26 N.J. Super. 90, 97 A.2d 419 (1953); see generally, Friedman, The Parents' Right to Control the Religious Education of a Child, 29 Harv. L. Rev. 485 (1916).

2. The rights to practice the tenets of a religious association, and to support it, are subject to reasonable regulation in the interest of public peace and order. The individual, by associating with a religious group, does not thereby gain immunity for the performance of acts which otherwise would menace the public peace and order, but he may thereby gain a limited immunity from some secular laws.

3. The negative right not to practice the tenets of a religious association is subject to limitation of an uncertain degree, through sumptuary laws enacting the precepts of some religious groups, where such laws are justified also on a secular ground.

4. The negative right not to support a religious association is subject to limitation of an uncertain degree, through public subvention of the activities of some religious associations.

IV. Freedom of Association and Livelihood

A. GENERAL ISSUES

In our highly organized society, the individual's access to employment, or to the practice of his profession, involves in some cases the intervention of a group between him and his job. The authority of such an intermediate group is founded sometimes on consent and sometimes on compulsion of the person to join or to accede to its representation of him. The purpose here is to trace the recognition of the individual's right to join such a group; the contemporaneous rise to power of the groups themselves; the attribution to some groups of powers to represent even nonmembers; the duty of the individual, in some situations, to join such a group; and his immunity against infringement of his freedom of political association by the group to which he is compelled to belong. Labor unions offer the prime example of such intermediate groups and their history illustrates each of the problems involved. Professional associations, while differing materially from labor unions, have also occasioned controversy in some of the areas to be considered. Both types are particularly instructive in our examination of freedom of association, because in them the issues of compulsory association and support have been distinctly raised and exhaustively analyzed.

B. HISTORICAL DEVELOPMENT OF LABOR ASSOCIATIONS IN THE UNITED STATES

Soon after the adoption of the Constitution, economic causes occasioned the first permanent American trade unions. The introduction of machinery and the accumulation of capital are among the reasons for the appearance of a definable employer-employee division.[1] Naturally enough, the journeymen employees were soon inclined to organize to obtain better wages and conditions, and to counter the growing power of the masters.[2] At this period, the first permanent American unions appeared.[3] These craft unions were local in nature, with no connecting organization, although there was occasional correspondence on matters of common interest.[4] Only a few instances of collective bargaining are recorded, although the strike was frequently used.[5]

In the second quarter of the nineteenth century, the local unions began the process of amalgamation and cooperation for economic and political ends.[6] The Philadelphia Mechanics' Union of Trade Associations, for example was formed in 1827 and shortly developed into the Workingmen's Party.[7] Increasing inter-city contacts led to the formation, in the 1830's, of what amounted to national federations of local unions.[8] Interrupted by the panic of 1837, the growth of unions, and their consolidation, resumed in the 1840's [9] and continued at a moderate pace until the Civil War, which lent considerable impetus to the growth of local unions and to regional amalgamation.[10] The National Labor Union, which was open to all trades, ran its course between 1866 and 1872 and provided the earliest example, though unsuccessful, of a functioning national union.[11] Upon its demise, the leadership was assumed by the Knights of Labor, founded in 1869, which dominated the labor scene until its decline shortly after the Haymarket Riot in Chicago in 1886.[12] The aim of

[1] See Hoxie, Trade Unionism in the United States 81 et seq. (New York, 1936); Gregory, Labor and the Law 14 (New York, 1958).

[2] See Newman, The Law of Labor Relations 2–4 (Buffalo, 1953).

[3] The Philadelphia cordwainers, after a short-lived attempt in 1792, succeeded in launching the first permanent union in 1794. In the next two decades, shoemakers, typesetters, printers, and carpenters established fairly permanent unions in various eastern cities. Rayback, A History of American Labor 54 et seq. (New York, 1959).

[4] Hoxie, Trade Unionism in the United States 81 et seq. (New York, 1936).

[5] Rayback, A History of American Labor 55 (New York, 1959).

[6] United States Department of Labor, Brief History of the American Labor Movement 4–5 (Washington, 1957).

[7] Rothenberg, Labor Relations 11 (Buffalo, 1949); Hoxie, Trade Unionism in the United States 81 et seq. (New York, 1936).

[8] Newman, The Law of Labor Relations 4 (Buffalo, 1953).

[9] See Commerce Clearing House, Labor Law Course 1053 (Chicago, 1957).

[10] Hoxie, Trade Unionism in the United States 81–87 (New York, 1936).

[11] Commerce Clearing House, Labor Law Course 1053 (Chicago, 1957); United States Department of Labor, Brief History of the American Labor Movement 7–8 (Washington, 1957).

[12] Commerce Clearing House, id. at 1053; Hicks & Mowry, A Short History of American Democracy 460–61 (Boston, 1956).

the Knights was the organization of the workers of all trades into one brotherhood.[13] Its membership was consequently heterogeneous and often divided.[14] The Knights of Labor gave place to the American Federation of Labor, founded in 1886 and organized on a homogeneous basis whereby its membership was composed almost entirely of the members of craft unions.[15] It constituted the main body of organized unionism until the depression of the 1930's.[16] Throughout its history, the American Federation of Labor had faced competition from unions organized on industrial, rather than craft, lines.[17] This cleavage in the union movement was accentuated by the combination of the depression and the permissive legislation of the 1920's and 1930's.[18] Finally, the leading industrial unionists formed the Committee for Industrial Organization, subsequently renamed the Congress of Industrial Organizations.[19] After years of competition, the A.F. of L. and the C.I.O. merged in 1955 as the American Federation of Labor and Congress of Industrial Organizations.[20] In addition to the combined A.F.L.-C.I.O., there are various independent unions, such as the railroad brotherhoods and others.[21]

The total membership of all unions in the United States in 1958, excluding 1,052,000 Canadian members of the United States unions, was 17,029,000 comprising 33.7 percent of the nonagricultural work force. The percentage has almost trebled since 1930, and the pattern of its growth is instructive in assessing the effects of the various regulatory statutes and of economic conditions.[22]

[13] Newman, The Law of Labor Relations 4 (Buffalo, 1953).

[14] Rothenberg, Labor Relations 12 (Buffalo, 1949).

[15] Id. at 13.

[16] Newman, The Law of Labor Relations 5 (Buffalo, 1953); on the general organization and operations of the AFL see Rothenberg, id. at 13–24.

[17] Rothenberg, id. at 27–28.

[18] Newman, The Law of Labor Relations 5 (Buffalo, 1953).

[19] Rothenberg, Labor Relations 28–30 (Buffalo, 1949); on the general organization and operation of the CIO see Rothenberg, id. at 29–37.

[20] Commerce Clearing House, Labor Law Course 1056 (Chicago, 1957).

[21] Id. at 1155; Rothenberg, Labor Relations 39 (Buffalo, 1949).

[22]

1930: 11.7%	1938: 27.8%	1945: 35.8%	1952: 32.9%
1931: 12.5	1939: 28.9	1946: 34.9	1953: 34.1
1932: 13.0	1940: 27.2	1947: 34.0	1954: 35.1
1933: 11.5	1941: 28.2	1948: 32.2	1955: 33.6
1934: 12.0	1942: 26.1	1949: 33.0	1956: 33.8
1935: 13.4	1943: 31.4	1950: 31.9	1957: 33.3
1936: 13.8	1944: 34.1	1951: 33.7	1958: 33.7
1937: 22.8			

Sources: United States Department of Commerce, Historical Statistics of the United States 98 (Washington, 1960); United States Department of Commerce, Statistical Abstract of the United States 229 (Washington, 1961).

C. THE RIGHT TO JOIN LABOR ASSOCIATIONS

English common law in the eighteenth century developed the theory that combined action by workers to raise their wages was criminal conspiracy.[23] The gist of the offense was the combination, since concededly the workers could individually refuse to work for less than a certain wage.[24] It should be noted that combinations of workers were not declared per se unlawful, but only those combinations aimed at improving wages and conditions; since there are few other meaningful purposes of workers' combinations, the distinction is of little significance.[25]

It has been said that the American courts in the post-Revolutionary period adopted this common-law approach and branded all combinations of workers to improve wages and conditions as criminal conspiracies.[26] On the other hand, it has been urged more precisely that what was forbidden by the American courts was not the mere combination to improve wages and conditions, and not even the use of the strike for that limited purpose, but rather the employment of unlawful means, e.g., picketing, violence, or closed-shop practices, to attain that end.[27]

In the earliest recorded American case on the point, the trial judge charged the jury that a combination of workmen to raise their wages is unlawful, whether its purpose be to benefit themselves or to injure nonmembers.[28] In the next three decades, there were at

[23] Rex v. Journeymen Tailors of Cambridge, 8 Mod. 10 (1721); Rex v. Eccles, 1 Leach C.C. 274 (1783).

[24] See Gregory, Labor and the Law 19 (New York, 1958).

[25] In Rex v. Journeymen Tailors of Cambridge, the unlawful object of the combination was the raising of wages above the rate fixed by a statute; it was thus a conspiracy to violate a general statute law, and therefore unlawful; see Commonwealth v. Hunt, 4 Metcalf 111, 122 (Massachusetts, 1842); in Rex v. Eccles, the object does not appear to have been violative of such an express statute, and Lord Mansfield remarked that "every man may work at what price he pleases, but a combination not to work under certain prices is an indictable offence."

[26] See Horn, Groups and the Constitution 69 et seq. (Stanford, 1956); Dulles, Foster R., Labor in America 30 (New York, 1949); Morris, Government and Labor in Early America 206–207 (New York, 1946); Gregory, Labor and the Law 20–25 (New York, 1958).

[27] Witte, Early American Labor Cases 41 Yale L.J. 825, 825–27 (1926); Petro, The Labor Policy of a Free Society 191–92 (New York, 1957).

[28] Commonwealth v. Pullis (Philadelphia Mayor's Court; The Philadelphia Cordwainers' Case) (1806); 3 A Documentary History of American Industrial Society (Commons et al. eds.) 60 (Cleveland, 1910–1911); see Nelles, The First American Labor Case, 41 Yale L.J. 165 (1931).

least eighteen prosecutions of workmen for conspiracy.[29] In only two did the court follow the dictum of Recorder Levy in the Philadelphia case, that a combination to raise wages is itself unlawful.[30] In all the others, there was present some distinctly unlawful element in addition to the mere act of combination.[31]

Any remaining doubts as to the common-law attitude toward the right to join labor associations were dissipated by *Commonwealth v. Hunt*.[32] The defendants had agreed not to work for any person who should employ anyone not a member of defendants' association. This was held not to be an unlawful purpose or means. Chief Justice Shaw defined the distinction between the lawfulness of the combination as such and the lawfulness of its object:

> The manifest intent of the association is, to induce all those engaged in the same occupation to become members of it. Such a purpose is not unlawful. . . . But in order to charge all those, who become members of an association, with the guilt of a criminal conspiracy, it must be averred and proved that the actual, if not the avowed, object of the association, was criminal.[33]

After *Commonwealth v. Hunt*, the criminal conspiracy theory was infrequently used in labor cases [34] but this result may well be ascribed to the inappropriateness of the theory and the fact that the decision was really a restatement of the general common law rather

[29] Witte, Early American Labor Cases, 41 Yale, L.J. 825, 826 (1926).

[30] People v. Melvin (The New York Cordwainers' Case), 2 Wheeler Cr. Cas. 262 (Ct. Gen. Sess., New York City, 1810); see Morris, Government and Labor in Early America 206–207 (New York, 1946); Gregory, Labor and the Law 26–27 (New York, 1958); People v. Fisher, 14 Wend. 9 (Sup. Ct., New York, 1835). (Intrepretation of statutory prohibition of conspiracy to commit any act injurious to trade or commerce.)

[31] Commonwealth v. Moore (Philadelphia Mayor's Court, 1827); 4 A Documentary History of American Industrial Society (Commons et al. eds.) 99 (Cleveland, 1910–1911); Witte, Early American Labor Cases, 41 Yale L.J. 825, 827–28 (1926); but see Commonwealth ex rel. Chew v. Carlisle, Brightly 36 (Pennsylvania, 1821), in which the court expressed the view that a combination of employers to depress wages is as criminal as a combination by employees to raise them, but that it is a good defense for the employers that their combination was required to resist the unlawful combination of the employees. Gregory, id. at 25–26. See also the Pittsburgh Cordwainers' Case in Commons et al. eds., id. at 15.

[32] 4 Metcalf 111 (Massachusetts, 1842).

[33] 4 Metcalf at 129.

[34] Between 1842 and the Civil War, it was used three times, and was used on eighteen recorded occasions, between 1863 and 1880. In the 1880's it was used more often, though most of the cases are unreported. Witte, Early American Labor Cases, 41 Yale L.J. 825, 829 (1926).

than to any revolutionary influence of the decision.[35] The criminal conspiracy approach does not appear to have been used to prevent the mere joining of a union, but rather the seeking of further illegal purposes, within the common law illegal-purpose idea described in the Hunt case.[36] In the post-Civil War period, some success was attained in repealing or amending favorably the statutes in some industrial states which, embodying the illegal-purpose doctrine, punished labor activity as a criminal conspiracy.[37] After the 1880's the criminal-conspiracy weapon was wholly supplanted by the injunction as a means of controlling the activity of labor associations.[38] The right merely to join a labor association, however, was not subject to injunction [39] and was recognized without dispute, in criminal and civil cases, throughout at least the last two-thirds of the nineteenth century.[40]

While the common law recognized the right of an employee to join a labor association, it also recognized his right under freedom of contract to execute a so-called yellow-dog contract with his employer whereby he pledged not to join a union, and the corresponding right of the employer to insist upon such a contract as a condition of employment.[41] The yellow-dog contract is an obvious interference with the employee's freedom of association, i.e., with his right to decide whether to join or not to join a labor union. As such, because of the inequality of bargaining power between an individual employee and an employer, it has been justly stigmatized.[42] It also may

[35] Petro, The Labor Policy of a Free Society 192 (New York, 1957); and see the discussion in Gregory, Labor and the Law 27–29 (New York, 1958).

[36] See Witte, Early American Labor Cases, 41 Yale L.J. 825, 828–32; Landis & Manoff, Cases on Labor Law 35 (Chicago, 1942); for a later explicit enunciation of the illegal-purpose rule, see Carew v. Rutherford, 106 Mass. 1 (1870).

[37] Witte, id. at 828–31.

[38] See Gregory, Labor and the Law 29–30 (New York, 1958); 2 Labor Relations and the Law (Mathews ed.) 635 (Boston, advance printing, 1953).

[39] Horn, Groups and the Constitution 69 et seq. (Stanford, 1956).

[40] "And it is no crime for any number of persons, without an unlawful object in view, to associate themselves together and agree that they will not work for or deal with certain men or classes of men, or work under a certain price, or without certain conditions." Carew v. Rutherford, 106 Mass. 1, 14 (1870); Vegelahn v. Guntner, 167 Mass. 92 (1896); see National Protective Ass'n v. Cumming, 170 N.Y. 315, 63 N.E. 369 (1902).

[41] Hitchman Coal & Coke Co. v. Mitchell, 245 U.S. 229 (1917); see also, Adair v. United States, 208 U.S. 161 (1908) (federal anti-yellow-dog statute declared unconstitutional); Coppage v. Kansas, 236 U.S. 1 (1915) (state anti-yellow-dog statute declared unconstitutional).

[42] See Gregory, Labor and the Law 174 et seq. (New York, 1958); Abernathy, The Right of Association, 6 S.C.L.Q. 32, 53 (1953); see also dissent of Mr. Justice

be criticized as an undue subordination of the right of association to the freedom to contract. In this context, the abolition of yellow-dog contracts may be considered as a step forward in the development of the freedom of labor association. Conversely, the later institution of compulsory unionism may be considered an arrest of that development.

The yellow-dog contract was relegated to the discard by the Norris-La Guardia Act of 1932,[43] which declared it to be the public policy of the United States that the employee, as well as the employer, should "have full freedom of association, self-organization, and designation of representatives of his own choosing, to negotiate the terms and conditions of his employment. . . ."[44] The act went on to render unenforceable, rather than void, any contract whereby either an employer or employee agreed not to join an employers' or employees' association.[45] Earlier, the Railway Labor Act had flatly prohibited yellow-dog contracts in the railroad industry.[46] The right to join labor associations was reaffirmed in the National Industrial Recovery Act,[47] the Wagner Act,[48] and the amendatory Taft-Hartley Act.[49]

Labor unions, although endowed with some public responsibilities, are still essentially private groups,[50] and thereby, in large part, unencumbered by the restrictions of due process. The question arises, therefore, of their capacity to deny admittance to their ranks

Day in Coppage v. Kansas, 236 U.S. at 40, wherein he stated that an object of the anti-yellow-dog statute was "to protect the liberty of the citizen to make such lawful affiliation as he may desire with organizations of his choice." But see Petro, The Labor Policy of a Free Society 49–50 (New York, 1957), pointing out that the yellow-dog contract, although violative of "the principle of free employee choice," may have been justified, in fact, in the early years of this century when, because of the disruptive tactics of unions, "the 'yellow-dog' contract might well have seemed more like a promise by employees not to sabotage than one forfeiting a basic property right."

[43] Act of March 23, 1932; 47 Stat. 70–73; 29 U.S.C. Secs. 101–15.

[44] Sec. 2.

[45] Sec. 3.

[46] Act of May 20, 1926; 44 Stat. 577–87; 45 U.S.C. Secs. 151–63; on the affirmation by the War Labor Conference Board, in World War I, of the right to join a union, see Metz, Labor Policy of the Federal Government 27 (Washington, 1947).

[47] Act of June 16, 1933; 48 Stat. 195; 15 U.S.C. Secs. 701–12; declared unconstitutional on other grounds in Schechter v. United States, 295 U.S. 495 (1935).

[48] National Labor Relations Act. Act of July 5, 1935; 49 Stat. 449–57.

[49] Labor Management Relations Act of 1947. Act of June 23, 1947; 61 Stat. 136; 29 U.S.C. Secs. 151 et seq.; see Millis & Brown, From the Wagner Act to Taft-Hartley 174–89 (Chicago, 1960).

[50] See dissent of Mr. Justice Minton in Brotherhood of Railroad Trainmen v. Howard, 343 U.S. 768, 778 (1952).

for racial reasons. A union certified as a bargaining agent under either the Railway Labor Act or the National Labor Relations Act, as amended, is under a statutory duty to represent fairly all employees whom it is authorized to represent, whether or not they are members of the union.[51] This duty of fair representation extends beyond the negotiation of the collective contract and includes the necessary day-to-day adjustments.[52] However, it has not yet been held that unions may not exclude applicants from membership on the basis of race.[53] The National Labor Relations Board will not recognize as an appropriate bargaining unit any unit based solely and completely on race.[54] However, the mere fact that a union excludes Negroes from its membership will not cause the Board to deny it certification.[55] Nor is segregation of Negroes in a separate local a bar to certification.[56]

An implement for attacking union racial discrimination may be found in the various Fair Employment Practices Commission laws.[57] FEPC laws, with compulsory enforcement powers, are found in twelve states.[58] The Supreme Court has held that a state has power to prohibit, by such laws, racial discrimination by labor unions in admission to membership,[59] and the laws have been held to be so operative against union discrimination.[60]

Although reliance has been placed by the courts on the private

[51] Steele v. Louisville & N.R. Co., 323 U.S. 192 (1944); Tunstall v. Brotherhood of Locomotive F. & E., 323 U.S. 210 (1944); Brotherhood of Railroad Trainmen v. Howard, 343 U.S. 768 (1952); Syres v. Oil Workers Int'l Union, Local 23, 350 U.S. 892 (1955).

[52] Conley v. Gibson, 355 U.S. 41 (1957).

[53] See Davis v. Railway Carmen, 272 S.W.2d 147 (Tex. Civ. App., 1954); Oliphant v. Brotherhood of Locomotive F. & E. 156 F. Supp. 89 (N.D., Ohio, 1957), 262 F2d 359 (6th Cir., 1958); but see concurring opinion of Mr. Justice Murphy in the Steele case, 323 U.S. at 208, arguing that such discriminatory exclusion by a certified union would violate the Fifth Amendment.

[54] See American Tobacco Co., 9 NLRB 579 (1938); Taxicabs of Cincinnati, 83 NLRB 1150 (1949).

[55] Sloss Sheffield Steel & Iron Co., 14 NLRB 186 (1939); Veneer Prod. Inc., 81 NLRB 492 (1949); Pacific Maritime Ass'n, 110 NLRB 1647 (1954).

[56] See Atlanta Oak Flooring Co., 62 NLRB 973 (1945).

[57] See Berger, The New York State Law Against Discrimination: Operation and Administration, 35 Cornell L.Q. 747 (1950).

[58] Colo., Conn., Mass., Mich., Minn., N.J., N.M., N.Y., Ore., Pa., R.I., Wash. Kovarsky, A Review of State FEPC Laws, 9 Lab. L.J. 478, 483 (1958).

[59] Railway Mail Ass'n v. Corsi, 326 U.S. 88 (1945) (New York statute).

[60] International Bhd. of Elec. Workers, Local 35 v. Commission on Civil Rights, 140 Conn. 537, 102 Atl.2d 366 (1953); contra, in Wis., where the FEPC law lacks enforcement provisions, Ross v. Ebert, 82 N.W.2d 315 (Wis., 1957).

character of unions, with the result that the edicts of the Fourteenth Amendment do not inhibit them, it would seem plausible to argue that the recognition of unions as collective-bargaining agents involves a delegation to them of state power. Just as political parties lose their character as strictly private groups and may not discriminate in the admission of members,[61] it could be said that labor unions ought to be subject to the same treatment.[62] There is a relevant distinction, however. By the very nature of the primary election process, the denial of membership by a political party results in foreclosure of the applicant from the exercise of his franchise. Especially is this so in the predominantly one-party South, where exclusion from the primary election constitutes a total obliteration of any meaningful right to vote. The labor union, unlike the political party, does not, by its denial of membership, automatically deprive the employee of any of his statutory rights. Those rights are protected by the existing prohibition against actual discrimination by the union in the exercise of its bargaining function. It may be that some discriminations are so subtle that, though they work a substantial hardship, they cannot be detected. For such clandestine and unprovable practices, admission of the injured minority to membership, and voting rights, in the union may provide the only remedy. However, such is not the law, and it is doubtful whether the courts will presume, on the strength of mere allegations, the existence of discrimination so evanescent that it cannot be construed as a discriminatory exercise of bargaining authority and can be remedied only by compelling an open membership. Nor does it seem desirable for the courts so to endow the labor association with an indelible public character where a substantial need for such a course is not demonstrated. The reprehensible character of discrimination does not make it unconstitutional in every case. The state of the law in this area of racial discrimination warrants the conclusion that freedom of association, insofar as it relates to labor associations, is the freedom to enter into a consensual arrangement, and that it does not include a right on the part of an individual to compel the mem-

[61] Rice v. Elmore, 165 F.2d 387 (4th Cir., 1947), cert. den. 333 U.S. 875 (1948); see United States v. Thomas, 362 U.S. 58 (1960).

[62] See Lawrence v. Hancock, 76 F. Supp. 1004 (DCSD, W.Va., 1948); Department of Conservation v. Tate, 231 F.2d 615 (4th Cir., 1956), cert. den. 352 U.S. 838 (1956) (private lessees who operate publicly owned facilities may not discriminate racially). Burton v. Wilmington Parking Authority, 365 U.S. 715 (1961).

bers of a group to enter into association with him. As we shall see in the next section, however, there are situations where there is a duty to join a labor association—that is, where the members of a group can compel the individual to associate with them.

D. THE DUTY TO JOIN LABOR ASSOCIATIONS

The progression from the right to join a labor union to the imposition of a duty to join one was accomplished through the medium of the collective contract. The attribution to the union of representative power was a natural extension of the right of the employees to join such an association for the very purpose of having it represent them. The addition of the element of compulsion, either to join or to accede to representation by the union, is a development rooted in public policy. It is our aim here to inquire whether that policy is consistent with freedom of association and whether, if it infringes upon that freedom, the infringement is justified.

At common law, voluntary unincorporated associations have never been regarded as legal entities.[63] Since labor unions, with few exceptions, have been unincorporated,[64] they were prevented by this common-law rule from suing or being sued in their own names.[65] Collective-bargaining contracts, with the union acting on behalf of the employees, were thus unenforceable by either party and were therefore not recognized as contracts by the common law.[66]

It remained for positive law to whittle away this nonentity status of labor unions and to institutionalize collective bargaining. The Sherman Anti-Trust Act[67] was construed to include unions within the category of "persons" liable to damage suits under the act.[68] The Clayton Act[69] was similarly applied.[70] The Norris-La Guardia

[63] Teller, Labor Disputes and Collective Bargaining, Sec. 462 (New York, 1940).

[64] Gregory, Labor and the Law 380 (New York, 1958).

[65] Donovan v. Danielson, 244 Mass. 432, 138 N.E. 811 (1923); Oster v. Brotherhood of Locomotive F. & E., 271 Pa. 419, 114 Atl. 377 (1921).

[66] See Rice, Collective Labor Agreements in the American Law, 44 Harv. L. Rev. 572 (1931).

[67] Act of July 2, 1890; 26 Stat. 209, 15 U.S.C. Secs. 1–7 (1934).

[68] United Mine Workers of America v. Coronado Coal Co., 259 U.S. 344 (1922).

[69] Act of October 15, 1914; 38 Stat. 730, 731, 736–40; 15 U.S.C. Secs. 12, 15, 15A, 15B, 16, 17, 25–27; 28 U.S.C. Secs. 381–83, 386–90; 29 U.S.C. Sec. 52.

[70] See Bedford Cut Stone Co. v. Journeymen Stone Cutters' Ass'n, 274 U.S. 37 (1927).

Act [71] declared the national policy in favor of the right of employees to bargain collectively and forbade injunctive interference with it. It was the Wagner Act,[72] however, which signaled the real development of collective bargaining. The act did not convert unincorporated unions into legal entities, a step which would have given the collective agreement the status of an ordinary enforceable contract. Rather, it decreed that a union representing a majority of the employees in a bargaining unit was the exclusive agent of all employees in that unit, whether members of the union or not, for purposes of negotiating terms of employment.[73] The Wagner Act [74] prohibited coercion or interference by the employer with the employees in the exercise of their right to affiliate with unions and bargain collectively. It contained no protection against such interference or coercion by the union. Moreover, the act authorized the employer and union to include a closed-shop or union-shop provision in the collective agreement, thereby requiring compulsory membership of all employees in the union certified as bargaining agent.[75] The Wagner Act was closely emulated by several state labor relations acts,[76] which have application to intrastate commerce.[77]

The Taft-Hartley Act [78] reaffirmed the existing policy in favor of collective bargaining.[79] Although it did not declare unions to be full legal entities, the Taft-Hartley Act did provide that they may sue or be sued in their association names,[80] and that they may be compelled to respond in damages for the commission of certain boycotts and other unlawful acts.[81] It affirmed the enforceability of collective contracts.[82] But it substituted for the Wagner Act allowance of both closed-shop and union-shop agreements a provision [83] permitting the

[71] Act of March 23, 1932; 47 Stat. 70–73; U.S.C. Secs. 101–15.
[72] Act of July 5, 1935; 49 Stat. 449–57; 29 U.S.C. Secs. 151–66.
[73] See Petro, The Labor Policy of a Free Society 184–85 (New York, 1957). The Railway Labor Act contained a similar recognition of the right of collective bargaining. Act of May 20, 1926; 44 Stat. 577–87; 45 U.S.C. Secs. 151–63.
[74] Sec. 8(a).
[75] See Rosedale Knitting Co., 20 NLRB 326 (1940).
[76] See, e.g., New York Labor Law, Art. 20.
[77] See Consolidated Edison Co. v. NLRB, 305 U.S. 197 (1938); Wisconsin Labor Relations Bd. v. Rueping Leather Co., 228 Wisc. 473, 279 N.W. 673, 117 A.L.R. 398 (1938).
[78] Act of June 23, 1947; 61 Stat. 140; 29 U.S.C. 141, 168.
[79] Sec. 7.
[80] Sec. 301(b).
[81] Sec. 303(b).
[82] Sec. 301(a); see Association of Westinghouse Employees v. Westinghouse Elec. Corp. 348 U.S. 437 (1955).
[83] Sec. 8(a)(3).

union shop but not the closed shop. Taft-Hartley prohibited union coercion of employees in the exercise of their rights as well as coercion by employers.[84] Moreover, it declared that union-shop agreements are not valid in states or territories which prohibit them by state or territorial law.[85]

It is central to our inquiry that these statutes have made the collective contract a permanent feature of the employer-employee relation [86] and that they settled beyond doubt that an employee must accede to representation by a duly certified union and, in some instances, must join that union. But, of course, the union security devices do not enjoy unvarying favor. It is a reflection of the opposition to them in some quarters that the Taft-Hartley Act explicitly affirmed the right of the states and territories to prohibit them. The controversy over the various state laws which so prohibit compulsory union membership reaches to the very heart of the concept of freedom of association.

1. The Right-to-Work Question

There are five basic types of collective agreements which, either expressly or in practical effect, require membership by the employees in the contracting union. The closed shop requires that an individual be a member of the union at the time he begins employment, and remain so during his employment. Abandonment of membership by an employee will justify his discharge.[87] The union shop does not require that the employee be a member of the union at the time he is hired, but it does require him to join within a specified time thereafter. Maintenance of membership requires all existing members to continue as such, after a grace period within which they can drop their membership, and requires nonmembers who choose to join the union after that period to remain members during the term of the contract; the nonmembers, however, are not compelled to join the union. The agency shop requires all employees, whether members of the union or not, to pay dues to the union.

[84] Sec. 8(b)(1).
[85] Sec. 14(b).
[86] See Torff, Collective Bargaining 16 et seq. (New York, 1953). Naturally, the activities of unions in recruiting members and gaining or enforcing collective contracts raise issues of free speech which it is not our purpose to analyze. See, for example, Thomas v. Collins, 323 U.S. 516 (1945).
[87] See United Fruit Co., 12 NLRB 404 (1939).

Preferential hiring, the fifth type, requires the employer to hire union members insofar as they are available and qualified. Only in the first three types is there a direct compulsion of employees to join, or remain in, the union. Preferential hiring may in fact compel membership as strongly as any, but the compulsion of the individual is not a mandatory matter of contract. Similarly, the agency shop exerts an economic, rather than a legal, leverage in favor of membership.[88]

Historically, the closed shop has been a prime objective of labor unions. In fact, there are records of closed shops even in the seventeenth century in New York City.[89] From the early years of the nineteenth century, the pressure for the closed shop became increasingly strong.[90] Toward the end of that century and the beginning of the twentieth, the closed-shop movement collided with a contrary movement grounded on then-prevailing ideas of public policy in favor of freedom of contract and against monopoly.[91] There ensued the controversy over the yellow-dog contracts, which we have discussed above. The open-shop drive was particularly strong after World War I.[92]

It was, therefore, a triumph for the American labor movement when the Wagner Act[93] permitted all the forms of compulsory unionism discussed above. The Wagner Act, however, did not legalize those agreements in states in which they were illegal by state law.[94] The Senate Report on the bill which was to become the Wagner Act explains the function of Section 8(3):

> . . . the proviso in question states that nothing in this bill, or in any other law of the United States, or in any code or agreement approved or prescribed hereunder, shall be held to prevent the making of closed-shop agreements between employers and employees. In other words, the bill does nothing to facilitate closed-shop agreements or to make them legal in any State where they may be illegal; it does not interfere with the

[88] See generally, Commerce Clearing House, 2 Lab. L. Rep. (Labor Relations) 4510 (New York, 1960).

[89] See Sultan, Historical Antecedents to the Right-to-Work Controversy, 31 So. Cal. L. Rev. 221, 224–25 (1958).

[90] See United States Department of Labor, Brief History of the American Labor Movement 65 (Washington, 1957).

[91] See Teller, Labor Disputes and Collective Bargaining Sec. 98 (New York, 1940).

[92] See generally, 5 Toner, The Closed Shop in the American Labor Movement (Catholic University of America 1941); Wolman, Ebb & Flow in Trade Unionism 230–31 (New York, 1936).

[93] Sec. 8(3).

[94] Algoma Plywood & Veneer Co. v. Wisconsin E.R.B. 336 U.S. 301 (1949).

status quo on this debatable subject but leaves the way open to such agreements as might now be legally consummated.[95]

It was, therefore, only in the absence of contrary state law that a closed-shop contract made pursuant to the Wagner Act justified discharges of employees who relinquished their membership in the union.[96] Congress had left the way open for state restrictions of compulsory unionism which were not inconsistent with the national legislation,[97] and those state restrictions would apply even though interstate commerce were involved.[98]

The Taft-Hartley Act reaffirmed this policy.[99] Under the Taft-Hartley Act, however, the closed-shop[100] and preferential-hiring systems[101] are unlawful. The union-shop, maintenance-of-membership, and agency-shop arrangements are lawful when made pursuant to the statutory procedures and when not contrary to state law.[102] The issue of restrictive state laws, therefore, involves the power of the states to prohibit those types of compulsory-membership agreements which are otherwise legitimated by the national enactment.[103]

The Railway Labor Act was amended in 1951 to permit the making of union-shop agreements with a sixty-day period of grace rather

[95] S. Rep. No. 573, 74th Cong., 1st Sess. at 11–12.

[96] Colgate-Palmolive-Peet Co. v. NLRB 338 U.S. 355 (1949).

[97] For state statutes and decisions on the relation between the closed shop and the closed union, see Teller, Labor Disputes and Collective Bargaining Sec. 99 (New York, 1940).

[98] See Algoma Plywood & Veneer Co. v. Wisconsin E.R.B. 336 U.S. 301 (1949).

[99] "Nothing in this Act shall be construed as authorizing the execution or application of agreements requiring membership in a labor organization as a condition of employment in any state or territory in which such execution or application is prohibited by state or territorial law." Sec. 14(b).

[100] Carpenter & Skaer, 93 NLRB 188 (1951); Local 466, Elec. Workers, 126 NLRB 110 (1960).

[101] NLRB v. Shuck Constr. Co., 243 F.2d 519 (9th Cir., 1957).

[102] Sec. 8(a)(3); see Public Serv. Co. of Colorado, 89 NLRB 418 (1950). But see contra General Motors Corp. v. NLRB 303 F.2d 428 (6th Cir., 1962).

[103] The employee is protected against the closed union under Taft-Hartley by the provision that an employee may not be discharged for lack of union membership, under a union shop or agency shop agreement, where the employer has reasonable grounds for believing that membership was not available to the employee on the same terms and conditions generally applicable to other members, or that membership was denied or terminated for reasons other than failure of the employer to tender the periodic dues and fees uniformly required as a condition of membership: Secs. 8(a)(3), 8(b)(2); Radio Officers' Union v. NLRB, 347 U.S. 17 (1954). Sec. 2, Eleventh of the Railway Labor Act was so construed in Railway Employees' Dep't v. Hanson, 351 U.S. 225 (1956); see note, Labor Law-Agency Shop Lawful Form of Union Security Under Labor Management Relations Act, 30 Fordham L. Rev. 530 (1962), arguing that the union shop is in effect unenforceable under these provisions of Secs. 8(a)(3) and 8(b)(2) of the Taft-Hartley Act.

than the thirty-day period stipulated by Taft-Hartley.[104] Moreover, the act specifically authorized such agreements notwithstanding "any other provisions of this Act, or of any other statute or law of the United States, or Territory, thereof, or of any State. . . ."[105] Having thus preempted its field, the act prevails over contrary state enactments which purport to prohibit such agreements.[106]

Even before the adoption of the Taft-Hartley Act in 1947, some states had enacted strictures against union security agreements.[107] After Taft-Hartley, with its express sanction of such laws, they increased rapidly. To date, twenty states have such laws.[108] Seventeen of the right-to-work laws have been construed to forbid the agency shop as well as the other forms of compulsory unionism.[109]

The right-to-work laws have been sustained by the Supreme Court against constitutional attack on grounds of free speech, peaceable assembly, and petition, equal protection, due process, and impairment of contract.[110] The cases involved the North Carolina statute and the Nebraska constitutional amendment in the first decision, and the Arizona constitutional amendment in the second. The North Carolina and Nebraska provisions also forbade discrimination by employers on account of union membership. The Arizona amendment did not so provide, but since "yellow-dog" contracts were forbidden by another Arizona law, the Supreme Court held that there was no denial of equal protection of the laws. Mr. Jus-

[104] Railway Labor Act, Sec. 2, Eleventh; 44 Stat. 577; 45 U.S.C. Sec. 152.

[105] Sec. 2, Eleventh.

[106] Railway Employees' Dep't v. Hanson, 351 U.S. 225 (1956).

[107] See Constitution of Arizona, Art. XXV, effective November 28, 1946; Constitution of Nebraska, Art. 15, effective December 11, 1946; Constitution of Florida, Declaration of Rights, Sec. 12 (1944).

[108] Ala. (1953); Ariz. (Constitutional amendment, 1946); Ark. (Constitutional amendment, 1947); Fla. (Constitutional amendment, 1944); Ga. (1947); Ind. (1957); Iowa (1947); Kan. (Constitutional amendment, 1958); La. (1956). (The original Louisiana right-to-work law, passed in 1954, was repealed in 1956 and replaced by the present statute, which applies only to agricultural workers.) Miss. (1954); Neb. (Constitutional amendment, 1946); Nev. (1952); N.C. (1947); N.D. (1947); S.C. (1954); S.D. (Constitutional amendment, 1954); Tenn. (1947); Tex. (1947); Utah (1955); Va. (1947). For details, see CCH Lab. L. Rep., II 41025 (1 & 2 State Laws) (1961).

[109] Note, Labor Law-Agency Shop Lawful Form of Union Security Under Labor Management Relations Act, 30 Fordham L. Rev. 530, 536 (1962). In Indiana (Meade Elec. Co., Inc. v. Hagberg, 129 Ind. App. 631, 159 N.E.2d 408 [1959] and North Dakota (Op. Atty. Gen., August 24, 1959) the agency shop is legal, and in Florida (see Op. Atty. Gen., August 25, 1952), there appears to be some doubt.

[110] Lincoln Fed. Labor Union v. Northwestern Iron & Metal Co. and Whittaker v. North Carolina, 335 U.S. 525 (1949); AFL v. American Sash & Door Co., 335 U.S. 538 (1949) (Mr. Justice Murphy dissenting).

tice Black epitomized the associational issue in his opinion for six members of the court in the Lincoln case:

> There cannot be wrung from a constitutional right of workers to assemble to discuss improvement of their own working standards, a further constitutional right to drive from remunerative employment all other persons who will not or cannot participate in union assemblies. The constitutional right of workers to assemble, to discuss and formulate plans for furthering their own self-interest in jobs cannot be construed as a constitutional guarantee that none shall get and hold jobs except those who will join in the assembly or will agree to abide by the assembly's plans. For where conduct affects the interests of other individuals and the general public, the legality of that conduct must be measured by whether the conduct conforms to valid law, even though the conduct is engaged in pursuant to plans of an assembly.[111]

Mr. Justice Frankfurter, in his concurrence, warned of the dangers involved in hypostatizing a group, citing an analysis by Harold Laski [112] and observing that at "the point where the mutual advantage of association demands too much individual disadvantage, a compromise must be struck." [113]

What the court did in these two decisions was to find the right-to-work legislation to be a reasonable adjustment of the competing individual and group interests. The decisions were in fact an implicit affirmation of the freedom of association. The court inferentially placed the freedom not to associate on a plane of equality with the positive freedom to associate. Except for Mr. Justice Frankfurter's remarks on the right of association, the opinions were couched in orthodox First Amendment language, without explicit reliance upon the concept of freedom of association which was to find expression by a later Supreme Court. A treatment of this basic right-to-work issue in frank terms of freedom of association would have made possible a simpler and clearer analysis.[114] Moreover, the associational concept would seem to support the conclusion reached

[111] 335 U.S. at 531.

[112] "As soon as we personify the idea, whether it is a country or a church, a trade union or an employer's association, we obscure individual responsibility by transferring emotional loyalties to a fictitious creation which then acts upon us psychologically as an obstruction, especially in times of crisis, to the critical exercise of a reasoned judgment." Laski, Morris Cohen's Approach to Legal Philosophy, 15 U. Chi. L. Rev. 575, 581 (1948).

[113] Citing Dicey, Law and Public Opinion in England 465, 466 (London, 1926); 335 U.S. at 544–46.

[114] See International Ass'n of Machinists v. Street, 367 U.S. 740 (1961).

by the court. Since it has been held not to violate the employee's freedom of association for Congress to authorize the union shop, as a step toward the achievement of industrial stability,[115] it is difficult indeed to argue that it is a violation of that freedom for a state to outlaw the union shop. While the union shop compels an employee to become a member of a private association, the right-to-work laws exert compulsion only insofar as they compel the union members to refrain from seeking to force their fellow employees to join their association. Clearly, the compulsion of the right-to-work laws is less than that of the union shop. If the standard, then, is the free exercise of the associational right, and if the greater compulsion is held to be consistent with that standard, the lesser compulsion of the right-to-work laws ought to be even more secure from constitutional attack.[116]

The contention has been made, in favor of right-to-work laws, that union security agreements are substantially indistinguishable from yellow-dog contracts and that both are incompatible with freedom of employee choice.[117] Judicial construction of various state anti-yellow-dog statutes, relying on legislative history, has rejected the parallel, and generally union security agreements are held not to be interdicted by those statutes.[118] The analogy does draw some support, though, from the fact that some of the state right-to-work laws characterize compulsory unionism and yellow-dog contracts together as seemingly equally undesirable practices.[119] Historically, of course, their origins are different [120] but analytically the right-to-work laws and the anti-yellow-dog laws seek the same end result, of protecting the free choice of employees to associate or not as they see fit.

115 Railway Employees' Dep't AFL v. Hanson, 351 U.S. 225 (1956).

116 But see Mr. Justice Rutledge's reservations in the American Sash and Door Co. case about the constitutionality under the Thirteenth Amendment of a statute which would allow the enjoining of a strike for a union shop; the issue was not before the court. 335 U.S. at 559. See Giboney et al. v. Empire Storage and Ice Co., 336 U.S. 490 (1949).

117 See Petro, The Labor Policy of a Free Society 50–51 (New York, 1957).

118 See Denver Local Union v. Perry Truck Lines, Inc. 101 P.2d 436 (Colorado, 1940); American Furniture Co. v. Teamsters' Union, Local 200, 222 Wis. 338, 268 N.W. 250 (1936); McKay v. Retail Auto. Salesmen, 16 Cal. 2d 311, 106 P.2d 373 (1940), cert. den. 313 U.S. 566 (1941); Shafer v. Registered Pharmacists Union, 16 Cal. 2d 370, 106 P.2d 403 (1940).

119 See, e.g., Amendment 34, Constitution of Arkansas: "No person shall be denied employment because of membership in or affiliation with or resignation from a labor union, or because of refusal to join or affiliate with a labor union. . . ."

120 See Shafer v. Registered Pharmacists Union, 16 Cal. 2d 379, 106 P.2d 403 (1940).

It has been argued that right-to-work laws are unfair in that the nonunion employee gains the benefits of the union's bargaining activities without sharing the cost of the union operation.[121] It is considered immoral, and violative of the democratic concept of majority rule, to permit the "free rider" to reap directly the benefits he has not earned, and to compel the union, a voluntary association, to confer its benefits upon him.[122] On the other side, it is said that it is the unions themselves which contend for the right to represent exclusively all employees, whether members or not; therefore, the nonunion employee in an open shop with an exclusive union bargaining agent is not a "free rider" but a "forced rider" since he is deprived of his right to bargain individually by the union's own insistence on exclusive representation.[123] Further, it is said, the "benefits" of unionization are more apparent than real, and the activities of unions ought not to be regarded as an effective cause of the rising standard of living.[124]

It is not within our purview to assess the economic and statistical arguments for and against right-to-work laws. For example, it has been shown that right-to-work states have below-par per-capita personal incomes,[125] but that the rate of economic growth in those states is above the national average.[126] Neither conclusion is persuasive without an assessment of the total economic picture. We are concerned here rather with the associational element. The "free rider" and majority-rule arguments are pertinent.[127] So also is the contention that right-to-work laws so weaken unions as to make the right of association ineffective and disrupt the processes of collective bargaining.[128] It can hardly be contended, however, that

[121] See pamphlet American Federation of Labor, The Right to Wreck! (Washington, 1954).

[122] See Toner, Right-to-Work Laws: Public Frauds 8 Lab. L.J. 193 (1957).

[123] Keller, The Case of Right-to-Work Laws 42 (Chicago, 1956). See also Chamber of Commerce of the United States, The Right of the Right to Work (Washington, 1962).

[124] See Bradley, Involuntary Participation in Unionism (Washington, D.C., American Enterprise Association, Inc., 1956).

[125] CIO, Economic Outlook, January, 1955.

[126] National Right to Work Committee, Do Right-to-Work Laws Help or Hurt the Economy? (Washington, D. C., 1955).

[127] See Toner, Right-to-Work Laws: Public Frauds, 8 Lab. L.J. 193, 198 (1957), for distinction between direct benefits received by employees from union activity and incidental benefits received by the general public from the activity of religious associations; the latter indirect benefit obviously cannot be used to label nonmembers of religious associations as "free-riders."

[128] See Torff, Collective Bargaining 77–79 (New York, 1953).

unions today are in the same struggling position that they were in during the first third of this century.[129] There may be situations in which a particular union has insufficient strength in a bargaining unit to survive without some form of union security; but in such cases, its very weakness is likely to prevent it from obtaining a union security agreement even if it were lawful to do so.[130] But on the whole, the unions do not appear to be faced with a stark alternative of union security or atrophy. Indeed, there is evidence that right-to-work laws exercise no impeding influence on the growth of unions, either numerically or percentage-wise.[131]

Ultimately, the arguments for union security, whether the "free-rider" objection, the advocacy of democratic-majority rule, or the assertion that a strong union is essential to the right of association, can be reduced to an advocacy that the union should be given some governmental powers over the society of employees among whom it operates.[132] The granting to unions, which are certified as bargaining agents, of power to represent and bind nonmembers, involves some attribution, or delegation, of government power to the union.[133] The union security concept, though, goes beyond the collective-bargaining device. In the compulsion of membership, or of payments to the union, we find unmistakable analogies to the functions and perquisites of government. It was apparently this point which induced Mr. Justice Frankfurter, in upholding the state right-to-work laws, to caution against the tendency to hypostatize the labor association.[134] Compulsory unionism is pluralistic in some aspects.[135] As in the case of collective bargaining, it confers upon the union an exemption from the laws otherwise applicable to persons and associations.[136] It is only by carving an exception to the

[129] Id. at 75.

[130] See Shister, Economics of the Labor Market 187 (1956).

[131] See Niebank, In Defense of Right-to-Work Laws, 8 Lab. L.J. 459, 460–62 (1953).

[132] Id. at 512.

[133] See J. I. Case Co. v. NLRB, 31 U.S. 332 (1944); in Railway Employees' Dep't v. Hanson, 351 U.S. 225, 231–32 (1956), the Supreme Court recognized that the private collective-bargaining agreement, implemented by Federal enforcement machinery, is subject to the First and Fifth Amendments which bind the Federal Government.

[134] AFL v. American Sash & Door Co., 335 U.S. 538, 544–46 (1949).

[135] See 1 Teller, Labor Disputes and Collective Bargaining, Sec. 77 (New York, 1940); Jaffe, Law Making by Private Groups, 51 Harv. L. Rev. 201 (1938).

[136] See Teller, id. at 231, to the effect that collective bargaining realistically requires that unions be exempted from some traditional legal doctrines, such as the law governing injunctions, conspiracy, and the liability or inability of unincorporated associations to sue.

general rule that an individual is free not to associate with a group, that we can legitimize compulsory unionism within the framework of the newly recognized freedom of association. In effect, the resultant privileged status will make the labor association a quasi-governmental body, to an even greater degree than was done by the institution of compulsory collective bargaining. Exceptional treatment of that sort, entailing an abridgement of the general right not to associate, is tenable only for constitutionally sufficient reasons of policy. But the matter may be sufficiently debatable, at this time, to allow that the judgment of the legislature be respected. If Congress chooses, for pragmatic reasons of labor peace in interstate commerce, to permit, but not compel, union security agreements even where state law prohibits them, that judgment will not be disturbed by the courts today.[137] Nor can it be disturbed, if the constitutional justification of union security is really debatable, without transforming freedom of association into an absolute imperative. Similarly, a legislative judgment that union security is undesirable and ought to be prohibited should not, and will not, be disturbed by the courts.[138] The basic issues of union security and "right-to-work," therefore, have been removed by the courts from the arena of constitutional decision at this time. Whether there shall be compulsory or voluntary unionism is a matter for the appropriate legislature to decide. It would be desirable for the legislature to consider the right of association as an advisory, nonconstitutional standard on this point, and to refrain from infringing upon it without a genuinely compelling reason. Moreover, the courts ought not to shrink from the realization and declaration that the legislature, in permitting compulsory unionism, is endowing the labor union with a governmental character, and that means ought to be provided, at least, for the protection of the individual member of the bargaining unit and for the enforcement of the fiduciary responsibilities attendant upon that semipublic status of the erstwhile private group.

[137] Railway Employees' Dep't, AFL v. Hanson, 351 U.S. 225 (1956); the court rejected a contention that union security agreements violate the employees' freedom of association.

[138] Lincoln Fed. Labor Union v. Northwestern Iron & Metal Co. and Whittaker v. North Carolina, 335 U.S. 525 (1949); AFL v. American Sash & Door Co., 335 U.S. 538 (1959).

E. COMPULSORY MEMBERSHIP AND FREEDOM OF POLITICAL ASSOCIATION

There may be situations in which the courts need not defer to the legislative authorization of union security, and in which the implementation of union security agreements would involve a patent and unsupportable infringement of freedom of association. The political activities of unions threaten to present this constitutional issue in an inescapable form.

The Taft-Hartley Act forbade, with criminal penalties, any corporation or labor organization "to make a contribution or expenditure in connection with any election" at which federal officials are chosen, including primary elections.[139] This prohibition of expenditures is very broad in its language, but it has been restrictively construed by the courts. The Supreme Court has held that it does not penalize the expenditure of union funds for the publication of a union newspaper containing advocacy of a candidate's cause and the distribution of such newspaper to its usual readers.[140] But where a union used its general funds to pay for a television broadcast advocating candidates, there was a violation of the act, the unrestricted character of the publication distinguishing the case from the advocacy in the union newspaper.[141] The act has been held not to prohibit the payment of compensation by the union to employees of the union who were assigned political duties.[142] The act has resulted in changes in the forms of corporate and union political activities, but has not greatly diminished those activities.[143]

The relation between union security and union political activity was before the Supreme Court in *International Association of Machinists v. Street.*[144] Defendant unions, having union-shop agree-

[139] Sec. 304; 2 U.S.C. Sec. 251; 18 U.S.C. Sec. 610.

[140] United States v. CIO, 335 U.S. 106 (1948).

[141] United States v. United Auto. Workers, 352 U.S. 567 (1957); compare, United States v. Painters' Local 481, 172 F.2d 854 (2d Cir., 1949).

[142] United States v. Construction & Gen. Laborers' Local 264, 101 F. Supp. 869 (D.C., Mo., 1951).

[143] See Bicks & Friedman, Regulation of Federal Election Finance: A Case of Misguided Morality, 28 N.Y.U.L. Rev. 975, 992–96 (1953), for discussion of Sec. 304 and its predecessors; see also Brown, State Regulation of Union Political Action, 6 Lab. L.J. 769 (1955).

[144] 367 U.S. 740 (1961); in the later proceeding on remand, the Supreme Court of Georgia held that, if the trial court should prove unable to devise a practical method for protecting the protesting members "from any harm caused by withdrawal from the general fund of any monies for political purposes," then the court should enjoin the unions "from spending any monies for political purposes." International Association of Machinists v. Street, 217 Ga. 351, 122 S.E.2d 220, 222 (1961).

ments made pursuant to the Railway Labor Act (Section 2, Eleventh), had expended, over the objection of plaintiff members, union funds in support of political causes to which plaintiffs were opposed.[145] Plaintiffs sued to enjoin the enforcement of the union-shop agreement, on freedom of association and other constitutional grounds. Mr. Justice Brennan, for four members of the court, sidestepped the constitutional issue and held that the Railway Labor Act was not intended to authorize such political expenditures of an employee's dues money over his objection. The remedies suggested on remand by the opinion included an injunction against a political expenditure by the union of so much of his dues money as is the proportion of the union's total expenditures made for such political activities to the union's total budget, or alternatively, restitution to the employee of that part of his money which the union spent despite his notification not to do so. As Justices Douglas, Whittaker, and Black indicated, these remedies may well be so cumbersome as to effect a practical denial of relief on the one hand, and an entanglement of the union in accounting procedures on the other.

The associational issue was presented directly in the dissenting opinion of Mr. Justice Black, stating that the act does authorize such political expenditures, but that it is thereby unconstitutional. He found the act violative of freedom of speech, insofar as it authorizes the expenditures in question, regardless of whether the political activities are helpful to the union in its collective-bargaining role.[146] He urged the refund of all dues paid by the protesting employees. The governmental character of unions enjoying union security agreements was also intimated by Mr. Justice Black:

> There is, of course, no constitutional reason why a union or other private group may not spend its funds for political or ideological causes if its members voluntarily join it and can voluntarily get out of it. . . . How to spend its money is a question for each voluntary group to decide for itself in the absence of some valid law forbidding activities for which the money is spent. But a different situation arises when a federal law steps in and authorizes such a group to carry on activities at the expense of persons who do not choose to be members of the group as well as

[145] No contention was made that the expenditures violated Federal or state criminal prohibitions of union political activity. 367 U.S. at 773.

[146] See 367 U.S. at 790, for Mr. Justice Black's analogy of the use of compulsory dues for political purposes to the religious assessment so vigorously opposed by Jefferson and Madison.

those who do. Such a law, even though validly passed by Congress, cannot be used in a way that abridges the specifically defined freedoms of the First Amendment. . . .[147]

Unions composed of a voluntary membership, like all other voluntary groups, should be free in this country to fight in the public forum to advance their own causes, to promote their choice of candidates and parties and to work for the doctrines or the laws they favor. But to the extent that Government steps in to force people to help espouse the particular causes of a group, that group—whether composed of railroad workers or lawyers—loses its status as a voluntary group. . . .[148]

Mr. Justice Frankfurter (dissenting, joined by Mr. Justice Harlan, and stating that the act authorizes the political expenditures and that it is constitutional) considered the political use of dues to be constitutional in the light of the historical prevalence of union political activity and the practical necessity of that activity to efficient collective bargaining. His opinion analogized between the dues paid to the union and taxes paid to the Federal Government; the citizen, of course, cannot dispute the mode of Federal expenditure.[149] It is sufficient, he thought, that plaintiffs' rights to participate in the shaping of union policy, and to speak individually, are preserved. Plaintiffs' constitutional claim was described by him as "miniscule."[150]

The tenor of the Frankfurter opinion appears to reinforce the conclusion, offered above, that the basic justification for a system of union security must be an attribution to the union of governmental characteristics. The political use of compulsory dues has drawn the issue beyond any real evasion. Nevertheless, the question of the union's governmental role persists, whether the dues are used for political purposes or not. Furthermore, it would seem—once the issue is so clearly drawn—that the analysis of Mr. Justice Black[151] offers the solution which will most effectively safeguard the right of free political association. Nor should it be said that the Black approach is that of a doctrinaire ideologue, nor that the plaintiffs' complaint in *Street* is *de minimis*. On the contrary, the analogy to the issues framed by Madison's *Remonstrance*[152] is clear enough,

[147] 367 U.S. at 788–89.
[148] 367 U.S. at 796.
[149] 367 U.S. at 808–10.
[150] 367 U.S. at 818.
[151] See also concurring opinion of Mr. Justice Douglas, 367 U.S. at 775.
[152] See 367 U.S. at 790; it was stipulated in the court below in Street that the union-shop agreement was negotiated by the union without any notice of such negotia-

and the infringement of plaintiffs' rights is substantial enough[153] to justify the conclusion that a denial that their claim has substantive merit is a denial that there is such a thing as the freedom not to associate for political purposes. For that freedom to be meaningful, as it ought, it must be insulated at some point from the inroads of pragmatic devices based upon current legislative concepts of public policy. Arguably, that point is reached even in the simple compulsion of union membership under union security agreements. But if it is not attained in the Street situation, it is difficult to conceive of any case in which it would be reached. While the institution of collective bargaining and compulsory membership may be argued, with deference to the legislative judgment, to be consonant with freedom of association, that freedom is clearly and unduly impinged upon when there is added the element of associational political activity contrary to the expressed desire of the protesting member.

F. THE INTEGRATED BAR

Lest it be thought that labor associations have been the only source of controversy over the duty to associate, attention should be called to the question of the integrated bar. The so-called "integrated bar"—as distinguished from voluntary bar associations organized by the attorneys themselves—is a state-organized bar, to which all attorneys must belong in order to practice their profession.[154] At the present time, there are integrated bars in twenty-six states.[155] The state court decisions have uniformly upheld the integrated bar against constitutional attack.[156]

tion given to the employees, without any opportunity for them to "express their wishes pro or con with respect to such negotiation and execution of the union shop agreement, or any opportunity to ratify or reject" the agreement, and without any authorization from the employees "other than such authority as might be implied" from the union's status as collective bargaining representative. 215 Ga. 27, 108 S.E.2d 796, 798 (1959).

[153] See stipulations by the parties in the Street case that the amounts and proportion of plaintiffs' dues money, employed for political purposes of which plaintiffs disapprove, are "substantial." 215 Ga. 27, 108 S.E.2d 796, 798–800 (1959).

[154] See Re Nebraska State Bar Ass'n, 133 Neb. 283, 275 N.W. 265 (1937).

[155] Ala., Alaska, Ariz., Calif., Fla., Idaho, Ky., La., Mich., Miss., Mo., Nebr., Nev., N.M., N.C., N.D., Okla., Ore., S.D., Texas, Utah, Va., Wash., W.Va., Wis., Wyo. See enumeration of statutes and rules in dissenting opinion of Mr. Justice Frankfurter in International Ass'n of Machinists v. Street, 6 L.Ed. 2d at 1183–84.

[156] See enumeration in dissenting opinion of Mr. Justice Frankfurter in International Ass'n of Machinists v. Street, 367 U.S. at 808.

On the same day it decided the Street case, the Supreme Court passed on the constitutionality of the integrated bar of Wisconsin.[157] Six members of the court upheld the integrated bar, Mr. Justice Whittaker concurred in the result, and Justices Black and Douglas dissented. Mr. Justice Brennan, joined by the Chief Justice and Justices Clark and Stewart, found no violation of freedom of association in the plan, since the only compulsion on the individual attorney is the payment of reasonable dues.[158] He stated that the associational issue was "no different" from the issue in *Railway Employees' Department v. Hanson,*[159] where the court upheld the Railway Labor Act allowance of the union shop with the words: "on the present record, there is no more an infringement or impairment of First Amendment rights than there would be in the case of a lawyer who by state law is required to be a member of an integrated bar." [160] In analogizing the case to the "right-to-work" issue, the opinion of Mr. Justice Brennan appears well founded. The troublesome question in the Street case, the political use of dues, was held not to be involved in *Lathrop* since there was no showing by plaintiff of actual use of his money for specific purposes to which he had objected.[161] Mr. Justice Harlan, joined by Mr. Justice Frankfurter, concurred on the ground that the integrated bar was constitutional, that there was a sufficient showing by plaintiff that his dues were used for legislative activities which he opposed, and that such a use is constitutional. Rejecting the distinction between free association and free speech which was implicit in the opinions of a majority of the court, Mr. Justice Harlan said:

> I am wholly unable to follow the force of reasoning which, on the one hand, denies that compulsory dues-paying membership in an Integrated Bar infringes "freedom of association," and, on the other, in effect affirms that such membership, to the extent it entails the use of a dissident member's dues for legitimate Bar purposes, infringes "freedom of speech." [162]

Mr. Justice Harlan seems justified in his criticism of the intermixture of the concepts of free association and free speech. It would be clearer to decide both issues, the duty to join and the power of the association to propagate political views over the objections of

[157] Lathrop v. Donohue, 367 U.S. 820 (1961).
[158] 367 U.S. at 843.
[159] 351 U.S. 225 (1956).
[160] 351 U.S. at 238.
[161] 367 U.S. at 845–47.
[162] 367 U.S. at 850.

members, with reference to the unifying concept of freedom of association. This was done by Mr. Justice Douglas who, in dissenting, found the integrated bar an unconstitutional violation of freedom of association, inasmuch as it attempted to compel membership in a "guild," and found that the political use of dues also infringed upon the freedom not to associate, since it compelled plaintiff to associate with others in a common political cause. One may justly quarrel with Mr. Justice Douglas' annulment of the integrated bar itself. His simplistic, perhaps absolutist, denial of power in the state to compel membership in an association affecting livelihood is difficult to reconcile with his opinion for the court in the Hanson case, upholding the Congressional authorization of the union shop.[163] In the Railway Labor Act, it is true, Congress did not compel the union shop; but the Congressional authorization and Federal enforcement, when combined with the union security contract made in reliance upon them, worked a compulsion on the individual as real and immediate as that worked upon the integrated lawyer.[164] The theory that a broader latitude is to be accorded to state enactments under the Fourteenth Amendment than to Congress under the unfiltered First[165] may be argued as an additional makeweight in favor of abstention by the courts from interference with the legislative judgment establishing the integrated bar. An additional factor indicating constitutionality is the fact that the states, and particularly state courts, have traditionally exercised a supervisory power over admission to the bar,[166] and over the subsequent conduct of the members of the bar.[167] The exercise of this supervisory interest via the integrated bar does not, of course, convert the practice of law into a privilege which may be withheld at the pleasure of the state.[168]

Mr. Justice Douglas did present the associational issue with clar-

[163] Railway Employees' Dep't v. Hanson, 351 U.S. 225 (1956).

[164] Mr. Justice Douglas distinguishes the two situations on the basis of the historical background of collective bargaining. 367 U.S. at 880–81.

[165] See opinion of Mr. Justice Harlan in Roth v. United States 354 U.S. 476, 500–501 (1957); see also, Rogge, The First & the Fifth 10–11, 35–53 (New York, 1960); but see the review of the Rogge book by Professor McKay in 15 Rutgers L. Rev. 148 (1960), pointing out that the Supreme Court seems to regard the First Amendment as literally incorporated by the Fourteenth.

[166] See Konigsberg v. State Bar of California, 366 U.S. 36 (1961); Re Anastaplo, 366 U.S. 82 (1961).

[167] See Cohen v. Hurley, 366 U.S. 117 (1961).

[168] Concurring opinion of Mr. Justice Harlan in Lathrop v. Donohue, 367 U.S. at 853–55; contra, dissent of Mr. Justice Black, 367 U.S. at 875–77.

ity in the dual aspects of the duty to join an association regulating livelihood and the right not to join, or support, a political association. If an issue is clearly presented, involving the use of compulsory dues for partisan political purposes, it would seem that the right not to join, or support, a political association is impermissibly infringed, whether the issue arises in terms of union security or the integrated bar.[169]

G. GENERAL CONCLUSIONS CONCERNING FREEDOM OF ASSOCIATION AND LIVELIHOOD

1. There is a constitutional right to join an association which exists to facilitate access of its members to a livelihood.

2. His mere presence in the same economic unit may subject an individual to representation by such an association even though he does not choose to join it.

3. There may be imposed, in some situations, a duty to join an association which exists to facilitate access of its members to a livelihood, and a correlative duty not to join a competing association; such an association, in which membership is compelled, performs quasi-governmental functions.

4. An association to which an individual is compelled to belong as a condition of earning a livelihood may not infringe upon his right of free political association by using his dues for political purposes of which he asserts his disapproval.

[169] See dissent of Mr. Justice Black in Lathrop v. Donohue, 367 U.S. at 865.

V. Freedom of Association and Political Parties and Pressure Groups

A. GENERAL QUESTIONS

In our representative and Federal system, encompassing a large geographic area, the election of officials and the administrative conduct of government would be impossible without political parties. Because they are essential, the right to associate in political parties is constitutionally protected, as is the related right to associate in pressure groups which exercise the right to petition the government. The purpose here is to describe those rights, the permissible limitations upon them, their relation to the traditional freedoms of assembly and petition, and their place within the broader framework of the general freedom of association.

B. THE RIGHT TO FORM POLITICAL PARTIES

It is an interesting reflection of the development of freedom of association that the right to form political parties, a right not even mentioned and certainly not favored in the Constitution, is now considered fundamental.[1] It is worth noting how this transformation occurred. As we have seen already, the political parties in the early years of the nation were merely agglomerations of like-minded

[1] See State ex rel. Shepard v. Superior Court, 60 Wash. 370, 382, 111 Pac. 233, 238 (1910).

men, with none of the organizational trappings so familiar to us today.[2] With the age of Jackson, and the supplanting of the caucus by the convention, the party became an institution in its own right as an indispensable implement in the operations of the increasingly democratic electoral system and the administrative structure of divided and separated powers.[3] In the period that followed, the political party, despite its public indispensability, was still regarded by the common law as a purely voluntary association of a private nature.[4] The public interest in the political party, however, was upheld by the legislation in many states in the closing years of the nineteenth century, establishing the primary election and the secret ballot as devices to insure free and fair public participation in the electoral process.[5] The legislative and judicial recognition of the essential public character of the party involved a vindication of the right to form a party.[6] This right to form a political party is a fundamental one and has been postulated usually as a corollary of the constitutional right of suffrage.[7] Other interpretations have related it to the rights of assembly and petition[8] or have described it as simply a right inherent in a free people.[9] It would appear equally tenable to ascribe the right to form political parties to the basic and general right of association. Whatever its basis, the cases agree that no legislature can deny the right to form political parties.[10]

Without an opportunity for access to the ballot, and a chance to put its preachments into practice, the mere right to form a political party would be chimerical. For that reason, the issue of the right to form a party is practically always translated into the issue of the right to place that party on the ballot. In examining the right of access to the ballot, therefore, we will see the practical extent to

[2] Supra p. 32.

[3] See Friedman, Reflections Upon the Law of Political Parties, 44 Calif. L. Rev. 65, 65–67 (1956).

[4] McKane v. Adams, 123 N.Y. 609, 25 N.E. 1057, 20 Am. St. Rep. 785 (1890).

[5] See Eaton v. Brown, 96 Cal. 371, 31 Pac. 250 (1892); People ex rel. Coffey v. Democratic Gen. Comm., 164 N.Y. 335, 58 N.E. 124 (1900); see Friedman, Reflections Upon the Law of Political Parties, 44 Calif. L. Rev. 65, 66–67 (1956).

[6] See generally, Starr, The Legal Status of American Political Parties, 34 Am. Pol. Sci. Rev. 439, 685 (1940); Abernathy, The Right of Association, 6 S.C.L.Q. 32, 43–45 (1953).

[7] Ex parte Wilson, 7 Okla. Crim. Rep. 610, 125 Pac. 739 (1912); Sarlls v. State ex rel. Trimble, 210 Ind. 88, 166 N.E. 270 (1929).

[8] Britton v. Board of Election Comm'rs, 129 Cal. 337, 61 Pac. 1115 (1900).

[9] Davidson v. Hanson, 87 Minn. 211, 92 N.W. 93 (1902).

[10] See generally, Bone, American Politics and the Party System Ch. 11 (New York, 1955); note, The Right to Form a Political Party, 43 Ill. L. Rev. 832 (1949).

which the right to form a political party is subject to qualification and limitation.

In most states the general election is preceded, with respect to some or all elective offices, by direct primary elections or party conventions at which the various parties nominate candidates.[11] Established parties, of course, experience little difficulty in obtaining government recognition of their candidates and in placing their names on the general-election ballot. Incipient parties, however, usually find it impossible to conduct primaries, because the statutes in almost all states define a political party as a political organization which obtained at least a certain percentage or number of the total vote in the last election for a designated state official, usually for governor.[12] A group which did not poll the necessary number of votes in that election is barred from conducting a primary or convention and usually must nominate its candidates for the general election by filing a petition with a stated number of signatures of registered voters.[13] Organizations which fail to meet the petition requirement cannot appear on the general-election ballot and their candidates can receive only write-in votes.[14]

These numerical-strength requirements do render it difficult for third or minor parties to prosper,[15] especially in our plurality electoral system with its lack of proportional representation.[16] But the generally sterile record of minor or third parties in the United States [17] seems to be attributable far more to their lack of organization or of broad popular appeal than to the technical barriers erected by qualification requirements.[18] The election laws of many states do, however, make it difficult for a nascent or embryonic party to present itself to the electorate and thereby they do im-

[11] See, e.g., New York Election Law, Sec. 131 (providing primaries for nomination of candidates for local office); see generally, Starr, The Legal Status of American Political Parties, 34 Am. Pol. Sci. Rev., 439, 685 (1940).

[12] Abernathy, The Right of Association, 6 S.C.L.Q. 32, 43–45 (1953); see New York Election Law, Sec. 2(4).

[13] See New York Election Law, Sec. 138.

[14] See California Elections Code, Sec. 2540.

[15] See note, Legal Obstacles to Minority Party Success, 57 Yale L.J. 1276 (1948); note, Limitations on Access to the General Election Ballot, 37 Colum. L. Rev. 86 (1937).

[16] See Odegard & Helms, American Politics 799–803 (New York, 1947).

[17] See Penniman, Sait's American Parties and Elections Ch. 13 (New York, 1952).

[18] See note, Legal Obstacles to Minority Party Success, 57 Yale L.J. 1276, 1291 (1948); note, Legal Barriers Confronting Third Parties: The Progressive Party in Illinois, 16 U. Chi. L. Rev. 499 (1949).

pede the efforts of such a struggling party to build the support and organization necessary for substantial success.[19]

The statutes excluding from the ballot, and from the conduct of primaries and conventions, parties which polled less than a required vote in a previous election have generally been upheld, usually against claims that they violate the equal-protection clauses of the state or Federal constitutions.[20] The validity of the requirement depends upon the reasonableness of the classification and numerical test employed.[21] The same rationale governs the decisions on the petition requirements imposed upon parties not polling the required vote in the specified previous election. In *MacDougall v. Green*,[22] the Supreme Court upheld an Illinois requirement that, of the 25,000 signatures on the nominating petition, there must be at least 200 from each of 50 of the state's 102 counties. The complaining Progressive Party alleged that this requirement deprived it of equal protection of the laws, since its strength was concentrated in Cook County, wherein 52 percent of the state's registered voters resided. The court, *per curiam*, ruled that it was "allowable State policy to require that candidates for state-wide office should have support not limited to a concentrated locality" and that there was no denial of equal protection.[23]

In addition to the voting strength and petition requirements, there are miscellaneous impediments to the appearance of a minority party on the ballot. Limitations on the use of party levers and of voting machines by small parties have been upheld,[24] even where ample places on the machine were available.[25] If the denial of a place on the machine is arbitrary and unreasonable, it will not be sustained.[26] The relation between the right of political association

[19] Note, Limitations on Access to the General Election Ballot, 37 Colum. L. Rev. 86 (1937); note, Legal Obstacles to Minority Party Success, 57 Yale L.J. 1276, 1292–97 (1948), thoroughly lists and analyzes the state statutes governing the procedures by which a new party can qualify for the general election ballot.

[20] See cases collected in note, Denial of Equal Voting Facilities to Minor Parties, 50 Colum. L. Rev. 712 (1950).

[21] See Snowden v. Hughes, 321 U.S. 1 (1944).

[22] 335 U.S. 281 (1948).

[23] 335 U.S. at 283–84; for other developments in the efforts of the Progressive Party to get on the ballot in Illinois, see note, Legal Barriers Confronting Third Parties: The Progressive Party in Illinois, 16 U. Chi. L. Rev. 499 (1949); see also Christian Nationalist Party v. Jordan, 49 Cal. 2d 448, 318 P.2d 473 (1957); Socialist Party v. Jordan, 49 Cal. 2d 864, 318 P.2d 479 (1957), cert. den. 356 U.S. 952 (1958).

[24] Davidowitz v. Philadelphia County, 324 Pa. 17, 187 Atl. 585 (1936). (There were insufficient levers to accommodate all parties.)

[25] Morrison v. Lamarre, 75 R.I. 176, 65 A.2d 217 (1949).

[26] See La Guardia v. Cohen, 149 Misc. 110, 266 N.Y.S. 739 (1933).

and the right, if such there be, of subversive association, came to the fore in cases involving statutes barring from the ballot parties advocating the unlawful overthrow of the government. The general right of the legislature to exclude such parties was sustained in the leading case of *Communist Party v. Peek,*[27] where the Supreme Court of California held also that an exclusion based simply on whether the party's name contained the word "Communist," or a derivative thereof, was special legislation without reasonable relation to the legitimate legislative purpose.[28] The court also invalidated a section of the statute which conferred upon the secretary of state, with the advice and consent of the attorney general, the power to determine administratively, without notice and hearing, which parties came within the proscription; [29] the statutory provision for judicial review was held insufficient in view of the pressure of time in an election campaign.[30] The test for such legislative strictures on subversive associations is whether the means chosen, and the administration of the statute, bear a reasonable and nondiscriminatory relation to the object.[31] Other incidental restrictions, such as requirements that members of a new party shall not have participated in an existing party's primary,[32] or legislative failure to reapportion representative districts,[33] work some impediment upon the right of political parties to present themselves to the electorate. But the recognition of them, and of the more direct restrictions discussed in detail, does not change the fact that there is a fundamental right to form political parties. It is a right subject to reasonable and nondiscriminatory regulation in its initial exercise and in its access to the ballot. It is, moreover, a right which is not only compatible with the general freedom of association, but is more

[27] 20 Cal. 2d 536, 127 P.2d 889 (1942).

[28] See 20 Cal. 2d at 550, 127 P.2d at 897–98.

[29] But see Cooper v. Cartwright, 200 Okla. 456, 195 P.2d 290 (1948).

[30] The offending statute was reenacted in 1953 in apparent conformity to the Peek decision. California Elections Code, Secs. 2540.4, 2540.9.

[31] In Gerende v. Baltimore Bd. of Supervisors of Elections, 341 U.S. 56 (1951), the Court upheld per curiam a statute denying a place on the ballot to a candidate who refused to execute the required anti-Communist affidavit; see also Beck v. Hummel, 150 Ohio 127, 80 N.E.2d 899 (1948).

[32] See States' Rights Democratic Party v. State Bd. of Elections, 229 N.C. 179, 49 S.E.2d 379 (1948).

[33] See Colegrove v. Green, 328 U.S. 549 (1946); Abe v. Dyer, 256 Fed. 728 (9th Cir., 1958); Radford v. Gary, 352 U.S. 991 (1957). In Baker v. Carr, 369 U.S. 186 (1962), the Supreme Court invalidated the Tennessee Apportionment Act as a denial of equal protection.

readily explained in associational terms than in terms merely of the rights to vote, assemble, and petition.

C. THE RIGHT TO JOIN AND SUPPORT POLITICAL PARTIES

The personal right of an individual to join and support a political party is at the heart of the freedom of political association. The individual in effect elects himself to membership in a political party by registering as a member of it.[34] But the party does not thereby lose all its characteristics as a voluntary association. It may legitimately condition membership upon the sympathy of the individual with its principles and program.[35]

Membership in a party is a necessary condition to the right to vote in the party's primary election.[36] It is not unconstitutional for a state to impose reasonable restrictions, in addition to the limited right of the party to select its own members, on the right to vote at primaries and hence on the right to join political parties.[37] It is obviously invalid for a state to exclude voters from a primary on the open basis of race.[38] Nor can the state do so by conferring authority on the party to determine eligibility to vote, where the party then acts discriminatorily.[39] Nor, in the absence of an enabling statute, can the party itself bar Negro voters from its primary where the primary is recognized by the state as a step in the general-election process.[40] Not even the repeal of all the statutes providing for pri-

[34] See Horn, Groups and the Constitution 101 (Stanford, 1956); New York Election Law, Sec. 186.

[35] New York Election Law, Sec. 332; Matter of Newkirk, 144 Misc. 765, 259 N.Y. Supp. 434 (1931).

[36] California, prior to 1957, provided the leading example of cross-filing, whereby a registered voter could vote in any primary. California Elections Code, Sec. 5800, repealed by Stats. 1957, C. 585, P. 1682, Sec. 1.

[37] Breedlove v. Suttles, 302 U.S. 277 (1937) (nondiscriminatory Georgia poll tax); see Boudin, State Poll Taxes and the Federal Constitution, 28 Va. L. Rev. 1 (1941). Disqualification of those convicted of crime is common; see, e.g., Alabama Code (1940), Tit. 17, Sec. 15.

[38] Nixon v. Herndon, 273 U.S. 536 (1927).

[39] Nixon v. Condon, 286 U.S. 73 (1932). Compare Ray v. Blair, 343 U.S. 214 (1952), where the court upheld the right of a state to authorize a political party to exact a pledge of support for the party's national candidates as a condition of a member's candidacy for presidential elector.

[40] Smith v. Allwright, 321 U.S. 649 (1944), overruling Grovey v. Townsend, 295 U.S. 45 (1935); see United States v. Classic, 313 U.S. 299 (1941) (ruling that party primary which is an integral part of state election is governed by equal protection clause of 14th Amendment).

mary elections will change those primaries from public to private affairs; when the party discriminates racially in such a "private" primary, the state discriminates, and the Fourteenth Amendment applies, since the nominations made in the primary are still accorded effect in the state's general election.[41] In the Circuit Court of Appeals in the Rice case, the defendants vainly argued the private nature of a political party.[42] Chief Judge Parker disposed of that contention and capsulized the transition of the party from a private voluntary association to a public body:

> The party may, indeed, have been a mere private aggregation of individuals in the early days of the Republic, but with the passage of the years, political parties have become in effect state institutions, governmental agencies through which sovereign power is exercised by the people.[43]

In a gambit of desperation, the Democratic Party of Fort Bend County, Texas, formed the "private" Jaybird Democratic Association, which regarded all white voters in the county as members and excluded Negroes from its "primary" election, which it held prior to the official primary to select candidates it would endorse in that official primary and in the general election. The Supreme Court struck down this device as a subterfuge.[44]

The interest of the state in securing a competent electorate justifies the imposition of literacy tests for the exercise of the franchise. Twenty-one states now have such laws, of which seven[45] are in the South.[46] Despite its effect upon the right of the individual to join a political party and vote, the literacy test is constitutionally valid,[47] if nondiscriminatory on its face, but only if its administra-

[41] Rice v. Elmore, 333 U.S. 875 (1948).

[42] "Plaintiff has no more right to vote in the Democratic primary in the State of South Carolina than to vote in the election of officers of the Forest Lake Country Club or for the officers of the Colonial Dames of America. . . ." 165 F.2d at 389.

[43] Ibid.

[44] Terry v. Adams, 345 U.S. 461 (1953) (Mr. Justice Minton dissented on the ground that the Association was a mere private pressure group and that therefore no state action was involved). In accord with Terry v. Adams is Baskin v. Brown, 174 F.2d 391 (4th Cir., 1949). See Malick, Terry v. Adams: Governmental Responsibility for the Protection of Civil Rights, 7 West. Pol. Q. 51 (1954).

[45] Georgia, Alabama, Louisiana, Mississippi, North Carolina, South Carolina, Virginia.

[46] See statutes collected in note, Use of Literacy Tests to Restrict the Right to Vote, 31 Notre Dame Law, 251, 255 (1956); see also Council of State Governments, The Book of States, 1958–1959 20 (Chicago, 1958).

[47] Lassiter v. Northampton County Bd. of Elections, 360 U.S. 45 (1959).

tion is also reasonable and nondiscriminatory.[48] The Civil Rights Act of 1960 authorizes a suit by the Attorney General of the United States, against the State itself, for injunctive relief against a discriminatory denial of voting rights by a state official, even though the official resigned his position prior to the litigation.[49]

No one can doubt that a deprivation of voting rights on the basis of racial discrimination is flagrantly unconstitutional. Analysis of the problem in the past has centered upon the Fourteenth and Fifteenth Amendments, in dealing both with stark refusals to register a voter and the more subtle, but equally invidious, devices designed to inhibit a racial minority in its effort to cast an effective ballot.[50] A deprivation of the right to vote in a primary election (which is the only meaningful election in the Southern states) necessarily deprives a citizen of his right to join a political association. From this and from the essentially public character of such associations, it can be concluded that the deprivation of the right to vote in a primary election is an unlawful abridgement of the freedom of political association. At least in regard to primary elections, therefore, the newly conceived freedom of association ought to provide an alternative vehicle for decision. Its utility in regard to general election discrimination is not so apparent, since the exercise of the franchise in a general election does not depend upon, or result in, affiliation with any particular political party. Nevertheless, the limited applicability of freedom of association in this area ought not to detract from its utility within its range, especially in view of the critical nature of the primary election in some sectors of the nation.

A more obvious limitation of the right of political association can be seen in the Hatch Act which made it unlawful for employees (with some exceptions) of the executive branch of the Federal Government to take "any active part in political management or in political campaigns." [51] This is a direct restraint on the right of political association. Its validation, against objections laid under the First, Fifth, Ninth, and Tenth Amendments, was rested by the Su-

[48] Davis v. Schnell, 81 F. Supp. 872 (S.D. Ala., 1949), aff'd, 336 U.S. 933 (1949).

[49] 42 U.S.C. Sec. 1971; United States v. Alabama, 362 U.S. 602 (1960). On the Federal Commission on Civil Rights, see Hannah v. Larche, 363 U.S. 420 (1960). A civil right of action for deprivation of civil rights is given by 42 U.S.C. Sec. 1983; a municipality is not liable under this last provision; Egan v. City of Aurora, 365 U.S. 514 (1961); Monroe v. Pape, 365 U.S. 167 (1961). Criminal penalties for violation of civil rights are also provided; see 18 U.S.C. Secs. 241, 242.

[50] See Gomillion v. Lightfoot, 364 U.S. 339 (1960).

[51] 18 U.S.C. Secs. 118(j), 118(l).

preme Court on the public interest in the efficiency of the public service. The enactment was held to be a reasonable device to prevent the evils that flow from political activity on the part of government employees.[52] At the same time, the court upheld the act as applied to state employees who are engaged in any activity financed by Federal funds.[53] A similar rationale, emphasizing the public interest in electoral integrity, may be applied to the so-called Corrupt Practices Acts, insofar as they restrict contributions to political campaigns, even by persons not employed by the government, and require reports of contributions and campaign expenditures.[54] As pointed out by Mr. Justice Reed for the court in the *Mitchell* case, "the right of a citizen to act as a party official or worker to further his own political views" is not absolute; it is qualified by the necessity for integrity in the political process.[55] From our analysis, it is plain that what Mr. Justice Reed was referring to was freedom of political association. Today, the Mitchell case could be better resolved in associational terms; more importantly, the decision in *Mitchell* illustrates well the finite character of that freedom.

D. THE RIGHT TO FORM AND JOIN PRESSURE GROUPS: DEVELOPMENT OF THE RIGHT

Political parties are not the only associations exerting an influence on governmental processes. The private pressure group is familiar, not only as a lever for influencing legislators and officials, but also as a source of information for their guidance in formulating public policy.[56] Because the functions of the pressure groups have become so essential in the political process, the right to form and join such groups, although not absolute, is fundamental and constitutionally protected.[57]

The right to associate in pressure groups may be traced to the right of petition.[58] The right to petition the Crown for a redress of

[52] United Public Workers v. Mitchell, 330 U.S. 75 (1947); see Nelson, Public Employees and the Right to Engage in Political Activity, 9 Vand. L. Rev. 27 (1955).

[53] Oklahoma v. United States Civil Service Comm'n, 330 U.S. 127 (1947).

[54] See 18 U.S.C. Secs. 591 et seq.; 2 U.S.C. Secs. 241 et seq.; see Burroughs v. United States, 290 U.S. 534 (1934); see the discussion, supra p. 93, concerning Sec. 304 of the Taft-Hartley Act.

[55] 330 U.S. at 94–95.

[56] Abernathy, The Right of Association, 6 S.C.L.Q. 32, 42 (1953).

[57] See NAACP v. Alabama, 357 U.S. 449 (1958).

[58] Blaisdell, American Democracy under Pressure 93 (New York, 1957).

grievances was enunciated in Magna Carta in 1215.[59] It exerted influence on the legislative, judicial and executive processes of the government, and came to be recognized as a fundamental right of the subject.[60] The Bill of Rights of 1689, therefore, did not create the right of petition, but merely ratified it[61] by providing:

> That it is the right of the subjects to petition the King, and all commitments and prosecutions for such petitioning are illegal.[62]

This right to petition for a redress of grievances was employed by the American colonists in complaining to King George III.[63] The First Continental Congress, in its Declaration and Resolves, showed the connection between the right of assembly and the right of petition.[64] The First Amendment to the Constitution of the United States reaffirmed the right of petition, but in language which left some doubt about its purpose and relation to the right of assembly.[65] That this language constituted the right of petition as the primary right, and the right of assembly as the ancillary right, thereby guaranteeing a right to assemble in order to petition, was indicated by the Supreme Court in 1876.[66] This restricted right of assembly, though seemingly accurate in a historical sense,[67] has yielded today to a recognition that the right of assembly, for any lawful purpose, ". . . is a right cognate to those of free speech and free press and is equally fundamental."[68] The right of petition, too, underwent an expansion, so that it is no longer confined to rather negative demands "for a redress of grievances," but includes as well the right to ask for active and positive government intervention in aid of the

[59] ". . . that if we . . . shall in any circumstances have failed in the performance of them toward any person, or shall have broken through any of these articles of peace and security, and the offense be notified to four barons chosen out of the five-and-twenty before mentioned, the said four barons shall repair to us, or our justiciary, if we are out of the realm, and laying open the grievance, shall petition to have it redressed without delay." Magna Carta, Ch. 61; quoted in Perry, Sources of Our Liberties 21 (Chicago, 1959).

[60] See Adams, Constitutional History of England 245 (New York, 1921); The Constitution of the United States of America (Corwin ed.) 805 (Washington, Government Printing Office, 1953).

[61] Perry, Sources of Our Liberties 228 (Chicago, 1959).

[62] Id. at 246.

[63] For resolutions of the Stamp Act Congress, see id. at 271.

[64] "That they have a right peaceably to assemble, consider of their grievances, and petition the king. . . ." Perry, Sources of Our Liberties 288 (Chicago, 1959).

[65] "Congress shall make no law . . . abridging . . . the right of the people peaceably to assemble, and to petition the government for a redress of grievances."

[66] United States v. Cruikshank, 92 U.S. 542, 552 (1876).

[67] See Blaisdell, American Democracy under Pressure 94 (New York, 1957).

[68] DeJonge v. Oregon, 299 U.S. 353, 364 (1937).

interest or objective promoted by the petitioners.[69] These developments have resulted in part from the rapid growth of the press and communications media, coupled with the increasingly active role of government, and in part from the growth of the private pressure groups which offer obvious advantages in efficiency, variety of technique, and sustained impact in contrast to the simple petition.[70]

Today there are many thousands of voluntary associations, of all sorts and purposes.[71] In one way or another, each of these is actually or potentially a pressure group.[72] That there is a fundamental right to form them cannot be questioned.[73] One may legitimately wonder what is the function of these myriad groups in the operation of government. The answer is that they not only advance their particular, and perhaps selfish, interests by importuning their legislators and administrators, but they provide, in our system founded upon geographical representation, a substitute for the functional representation one finds in some other countries.[74] When the views of the interested occupational and other groups are available to the legislators in a coherent and responsible form, the process of legislation is simplified and the end product is more likely to elicit the support of a majority of those affected; a similar result obtains in the administrative process.[75] Further, the menace of retributive action by a coherent and purposive group can act as a salutary deterrent to the arbitrary exercise of government power.[76]

E. LEGAL RESTRICTIONS ON THE RIGHT TO FORM AND JOIN PRESSURE GROUPS

The recognition of the desirable role and activities of pressure groups does not preclude an acknowledgement that some of them

69 The Constitution of the United States of America (Corwin ed.), 806 (Washington, Government Printing Office, 1953).

70 See Blaisdell, American Democracy under Pressure 92, 215 (New York, 1957); 2 Chafee, Government and Mass Communications 783 (Chicago, 1947).

71 For a full listing, see Gale Research Co., Encyclopedia of American Associations (Detroit, 1959).

72 See Abernathy, The Right of Association, 6 S.C.L.Q. 32, 41–42 (1953); Bone, American Politics and the Party System 71–72 (New York, 1955); McKean, Party and Pressure Politics 430 (Boston, 1949).

73 See Association for the Preservation of Freedom of Choice v. Shapiro, 9 N.Y.2d 376, 174 N.E.2d 487 (1961).

74 See Key, Politics, Parties and Pressure Groups 178 (New York, 1948).

75 See Blaisdell, American Democracy under Pressure 70 (New York, 1957); Abernathy, The Right of Association, 6 S.C.L.Q. 32, 43 (1953).

76 See the editorial, Golden Jubilee of the NAACP, America, August 1, 1959.

do exert a baneful influence and, indeed, that this negative aspect often outweighs the positive good which they do.[77] It was in response to the evident danger inherent in the unmonitored exertion of pressure on legislators that Congress passed the Federal Regulation of Lobbying Act in 1946,[78] the first meaningful regulation of legislative pressure groups in the history of the nation.[79] At that, the act was hardly more than an intelligence device to keep Congress informed of the activities to influence it.[80] It required registration with the House and Senate by every person who is paid to influence legislation before Congress.[81] Each registrant must file quarterly reports listing his affiliation, his salary and expenses, the legislation in which he has an interest, and the names of newspapers and periodicals in which he has published articles.[82] Persons receiving contributions with the "principal purpose" of achieving "directly or indirectly" the passage or defeat of legislation by the Congress must file a quarterly report of contributions and expenditures, identifying all contributors of $500 or more.[83] Persons merely appearing before Congressional committees, the press, and public officials acting in their official capacities, are exempt.[84]

In *United States v. Harriss*,[85] the act was upheld as sufficiently definite and not violative of the rights of speech, press and petition.[86] However, the court was forced to construe the act narrowly in order to sustain it. To warrant a conviction, "one of the main purposes" of the contribution to the lobbyist, or of the lobbyist himself, must have been to influence the passage or defeat of legislation by Congress, but only if "the intended method of accomplishing this purpose must have been through direct communication with members of Congress." [87] In thus excluding from the obligations imposed by

[77] See Turner, Party and Constituency: Pressures on Congress 178 (Baltimore, 1951).

[78] 60 Stat. 839, 2 U.S.C. Secs. 261 et seq.

[79] Bone, American Politics and the Party System 206–208 (New York, 1955).

[80] See Zeller, The Federal Regulation of Lobbying Act, 42 Am. Pol. Sci. Rev. 239 (1948).

[81] 2 U.S.C. Sec. 267.

[82] Ibid.

[83] 2 U.S.C. Secs. 262–66.

[84] 2 U.S.C. Sec. 267.

[85] 347 U.S. 612 (1954).

[86] See note, Federal Regulation of Lobbying Act—Constitutionality and Future Application, 49 Nw. U.L. Rev. 807 (1955); note, The Lobbying Act: An Effective Guardian of the Representative System, 28 Ind. L.J. 78 (1952); note, Regulation of Lobbying, 30 N.Y.U.L. Rev. 1249 (1955).

[87] 347 U.S. at 623.

the act those persons and groups engaged in public-opinion saturation, the court relied upon its construction of a similarly worded House Resolution [88] in *United States v. Rumely.*[89]

Most states have direct regulations of lobbying activities.[90] The others rely upon general corrupt-practices legislation.[91] The state laws are aimed at lobbying in state governments [92] and have no application to activities intended to affect Federal legislation. In fact, it has been held that the Federal Regulation of Lobbying Act has occupied the field with respect to such Federal lobbying.[93]

In evaluating the regulations imposed upon lobbying groups, we should note their marked, though perhaps indirect, effect upon freedom of association. Registration and disclosure can operate as substantial restraints upon the right of association. Moreover, the lobbyist is not exercising a privilege graciously conferred by Congress, but rather is acting under fundamental Constitutional protections of speech, press, petition, and association. The basic character of the rights to be circumscribed would seem to dictate that the regulatory legislation be founded upon a serious and genuine social interest. Accordingly, the Supreme Court in *United States v. Harriss* [94] relied upon the power of Congress to protect itself, in that a revelation of the financing and activities of the various lobbying groups would enable the legislators to evaluate their pleas objectively and distinguish between their importunings and the real "voice of the people." [95]

In no other instance have the substantial effects of disclosure and the indispensability of legislative justification been shown more clearly than in the attempts to control the activities of the National Association for the Advancement of Colored People. The NAACP was founded in 1909 in New York City as a body to aid Negroes in overcoming the prevailing patterns of discrimination in the North

[88] H. R. 298, 81st Cong., 1st Sess. (1949).

[89] 345 U.S. 41 (1953); see also NAM v. McGrath, 103 F. Supp. 510 (Dist. Col., 1952), complaint dismissed as moot, 344 U.S. 804 (1952) (District Court had held Lobbying Act unconstitutional for indefiniteness).

[90] See Council of State Governments, The Book of the States, 1948–1949, 124–30 (Chicago, 1948), placing the number of such states at 35.

[91] Bone, American Politics and the Party System 206–208 (New York, 1955).

[92] See, e.g., New York Legislative Law, Sec. 66.

[93] Smith v. Faubus, 230 Ark. 831, 327 S.W.2d 562 (1959).

[94] 347 U.S. 612 (1954).

[95] 347 U.S. at 625–26.

and the South.[96] It now reports a membership of 350,000 in 44 states and the District of Columbia.[97] Its stated purpose is "to end racial discrimination and segregation in all public aspects of American life."[98] To attain this goal, it employs litigation, legislative action and public education.[99] Operating through local branches and state conferences,[100] the association centers responsibility for its litigation activities in its Legal Defense and Education Fund, which was incorporated under New York law in 1940 and engages in no legislative activities.[101] The association informs the public that it will assist indigent Negroes in litigation directed against unlawful discrimination.[102] Its membership is open to all races and creeds.[103]

That the efforts of the NAACP have been successful in breaking down existing patterns of segregation[104] is verified by the bitterness of the attacks upon it and the despairing ingenuity of the legal weapons employed against it by the hostile states.[105] One restrictive device which bears heavily upon the right to join and support associations such as the NAACP, and which is evocative of the general lobbying cases discussed above, is the membership disclosure requirement.[106]

In the leading case, Alabama sued to oust the NAACP (which is a New York nonprofit membership corporation) from the state because it failed to comply with a statute[107] requiring foreign corporations to qualify before doing intrastate business. The state obtained a court order requiring that the NAACP produce certain records, including a list of all its Alabama members, on the grounds that such information was required in order to answer the associa-

[96] It was proximately motivated by the race riots in Springfield, Ill., in 1908. Ovington, How the National Association for the Advancement of Colored People Began (NAACP, New York, 1914).

[97] Pamphlet, NAACP, Its Program & Objectives (NAACP, New York), undated.

[98] Pamphlet, This Is the NAACP (New York, 1960).

[99] Ibid. On the similar work of the National Urban League, see Bone, American Politics and the Party System 187–88 (New York, 1955).

[100] Comment, Group Action in the Fight for Civil Liberties, 58 Yale L.J. 574, 582 (1949).

[101] See Greenberg, Race Relations and American Law 37 (New York, 1959).

[102] See Symposium, Equality Before the Law: A Symposium on Civil Rights, 54 Nw. U.L. Rev. 330, 390 (1959).

[103] Pamphlet, NAACP, An American Organization (New York, 1960).

[104] See McKay, The Repression of Civil Rights as an Aftermath of the School Segregation Decisions, 4 How. L.J. 9, 11 (1958).

[105] See Greenberg, Race Relations and American Law, Appendix A (New York, 1959).

[106] See, e.g., Ark. Stat. Ann., Secs. 6–817–6–824 (Supp., 1957).

[107] Ala. Code, 10, Secs. 192–98 (1940).

tion's denial that it was conducting intrastate business. On *certiorari* from a judgment of contempt for failure to reveal the names, the Supreme Court reversed, holding that the secrecy of the membership list was essential to the freedom of association of the members and that the order constituted an unwarranted invasion of that freedom.[108] For obvious reasons, the individual members of the NAACP were not parties to the action. The association, therefore, asserted both its own alleged constitutional rights and the constitutional rights of its members. Apparently reluctant to rely upon the idea of group personality and uphold an assertion of the association's own rights, the court said: "We think that petitioner argues more appropriately the rights of its members. . . ."[109] The court went on to find the association and its members "in every practical sense identical"[110] for the purpose of asserting the members' right to silence, a right which would be nullified in the very act of its assertion by the members. Citing *United States v. Rumely,*[111] the court recognized that ". . . inviolability of privacy in group association may in many circumstances be indispensable to preservation of freedom of association, particularly where a group espouses dissident beliefs."[112] Most importantly for our purpose, the court affirmed, for the first time in unmistakable terms, the fundamental character of freedom of association as a basic constitutional liberty.[113] In view of the essential character of this freedom, and the catastrophic effect of disclosure upon the NAACP, the court found that the rather tenuous connection between the disclosure of members' names and the state's capacity to determine whether the association was doing intrastate business was insufficient justification for the resultant restriction upon freedom of association. Significantly, the NAACP had cooperated with the court by producing all information required, apart from the rank-and-file membership list.[114]

That *NAACP v. Alabama* is good law, and that the fundamental

[108] NAACP v. Alabama, 357 U.S. 449 (1958).

[109] 357 U.S. at 458; but later in the opinion the court remarked, "The reasonable likelihood that the Association itself through diminished financial support and membership may be adversely affected if production is compelled is a further factor pointing toward our holding that petitioner has standing to complain of the production order on behalf of its members. . . ." See Pierce v. Society of Sisters, 268 U.S. 510, 534–36.

[110] 357 U.S. at 459.

[111] 345 U.S. 41, 56–58 (1953).

[112] 357 U.S. at 462.

[113] 357 U.S. at 460–61. See Introduction above.

[114] Compare New York ex rel. Bryant v. Zimmerman, 278 U.S. 63 (1928).

position of freedom of association is secure, were affirmed in *Bates v. Little Rock*,[115] where the local NAACP refused to reveal its membership list as required by a municipal license tax ordinance. Finding no sufficient relation between the list and the determination of whether the association was subject to the tax, the court reversed the convictions, relying squarely upon freedom of association and *NAACP v. Alabama*. But while the decisions in *NAACP v. Alabama* and *Bates v. Little Rock* both rested upon the absence of a sufficient connection between membership disclosure and an asserted legitimate legislative purpose, the case of *Shelton v. Tucker*[116] appears to broaden the right of secrecy even beyond those decisions. There the court struck down an Arkansas statute[117] requiring every teacher in a state-supported school to file an annual affidavit listing every organization, without limitation, to which he had belonged or regularly contributed during the preceding five years. Unlike the *Alabama* and *Bates* cases, the court found a relevant connection between disclosure of associational ties and a legitimate legislative objective. However, the court found the means chosen by the legislature, i.e., the disclosure by *all* teachers of *all* associational ties, to be so "unlimited and indiscriminate" as to constitute an impermissible infringement of freedom of association.[118] The court found such infringement in ". . . the pressure upon a teacher to avoid any ties which might displease those who control his professional destiny. . . ."[119] The dissenters (Frankfurter, Harlan, Clark, and Whittaker) considered the statute, at least on its face, to be within the reasonable bounds of legislative authority. Some clarification of the questions raised by these decisions, especially the problems of the sufficiency of the public interest necessary to support the intrusion into associational privacy[120] and the necessity of actual injury to the members of the association, may soon be resolved. The court has granted *certiorari* in a case in which the Supreme Court of Florida sustained the right of a legislative committee investigating subversion to require the disclosure of NAACP membership lists.[121]

[115] 361 U.S. 516 (1960).
[116] 364 U.S. 479 (1960).
[117] Ark. Stat. Ann., Sec. 80–1229 (1960).
[118] Compare Talley v. California, 362 U.S. 60 (1960).
[119] 364 U.S. at 486.
[120] See note, Anonymity: An Emerging Fundamental Right, 36 Ind. L.J. 306 (1961).
[121] Gibson v. Florida Legislative Investigation Comm., 126 So.2d 129 (Florida, 1960), cert. granted, 366 U.S. 917 (1961), case restored to calendar for rearrangement, 369 U.S. 834 (1962).

In any event, it seems clear that the right to associate includes the right to do so in privacy and that this right, albeit not absolute, can be curbed only upon a showing that a clear and serious public purpose will be served by requiring the disclosure of membership, and that no more disclosure is required than is reasonably essential to the achievement of that purpose.[122]

The strictures imposed upon the NAACP by the states have been varied in form and effect. The *NAACP v. Alabama* case arose out of a commonplace statute imposing registration requirements on foreign corporations. Other harassments have been based upon the NAACP's claim to tax-exempt status as a nonprofit corporation. The Supreme Court has denied *certiorari* to review a Georgia decision upholding the right of the state to force disclosure of membership lists to aid the Revenue Commission in determining the tax-exempt status of the NAACP.[123] *Certiorari* was denied because the judgment was not final. The disposition of such an attempt to compel disclosure under the tax laws would depend upon the same considerations—of sufficiency of the legislative purpose, relevance of the means chosen, and genuineness of the impediment to freedom of association—that determined the *Alabama, Bates,* and *Shelton* cases.[124] It is difficult to see what relevance the identities of an association's dues payers have to a tax-exempt status which depends primarily upon the use made of the revenues rather than upon their source.[125] Similarly, the efforts to stigmatize the NAACP as a subversive association, thereby compelling the disclosure of membership lists and a virtual cessation of its activities, would seem to depend upon a factual justification for the conclusion that the association is or may be subversive.[126] That such a factual nexus can be proven is doubtful.[127] Even if there were sufficient grounds for suspicion that the NAACP is subversive, the *Uphaus* decision intimated a distinction between a public sort of association (in that case, a summer camp open to all applicants) and one in which there are genuine rights of associational privacy. For this proposition, the

[122] See note, The Constitutional Right to Anonymity, 70 Yale L.J. 1084 (1961).

[123] NAACP v. Williams, 98 Ga. App. 74, 104 S.E.2d 923 (1958), cert. den. 359 U.S. 550 (1959).

[124] Bates v. Little Rock, in fact, involved a license tax ordinance.

[125] See, e.g., Scofield v. Corpus Christi Golf & Country Club, 127 F.2d 452 (5th Cir., 1942); Miss. Code Ann., Sec. 9220–15 (recompiled 1952).

[126] Uphaus v. Wyman, 360 U.S. 72, 79 (1959).

[127] See pamphlet, NAACP, An American Organization (New York, 1960); Gibson v. Florida Legislative Investigation Comm., 108 So.2d 729 (Florida, 1959).

court cited *NAACP v. Alabama.*[128] It may be, therefore, that, regardless of the reasonableness of a suspicion that the NAACP is subversive, the association cannot be compelled to disclose its membership lists. It will probably never be determined, in a concrete case involving the NAACP, whether the implications of *Uphaus* will be pushed to such an extent.

A different problem is presented by those statutes which seek to curb the NAACP as an association engaged in barratry. Generally, the statutes in question prohibit the solicitation of plaintiffs for the purpose of instituting lawsuits, exempting recognized legal-aid societies, but not exempting all charitable associations.[129] While it has long been considered unlawful for a disinterested person to stir up litigation, the statutes aimed at the NAACP seem to ignore the facts that those policies against barratry are directed against the promotion of litigation for monetary gain,[130] and that persons or associations which assist or encourage litigants for desirable social purposes are generally not considered to have violated the barratry laws.[131] Moreover, the novel Southern barratry legislation is so plainly designed to thwart the constitutional policy in favor of equal rights, and is so lacking in a nondiscriminatory justification, that it may be considered unreasonable and arbitrary on that account.[132] The Supreme Court has granted *certiorari* to review a judgment of the Virginia Supreme Court of Appeals invalidating the barratry provisions of the Virginia statute but upholding other provisions achieving practically the same end through a broadening of the definition of malpractice as grounds for disbarment.[133] We may hope that a definitive resolution of the matter is imminent.[134]

[128] 360 U.S. at 80.

[129] See, e.g., Miss. Code Ann., Sec. 2049–01 (recompiled 1956); Va. Code Sec. 18–349.31 (Supp. 1958); Tenn. Code Ann., Sec. 39–3405 (Supp. 1958).

[130] See Symposium, Equality before the Law: A Symposium on Civil Rights, 54 Nw. U.L. Rev. 330, 397–99 (1959).

[131] Gunnels v. Atlanta Bar Ass'n, 191 Ga. 366, 12 S.E.2d 602 (1940).

[132] See NAACP v. Patty, 159 F. Supp. 503 (E.D., Va., 1958), judgment vacated and remanded sub nom. Harrison v. NAACP, 360 U.S. 167 (1959).

[133] NAACP v. Harrison, 202 Va. 142, 116 S.E.2d 55 (1960) cert. granted, 365 U.S. 842 (1961).

[134] The Virginia antilobbying statute (Ch. 32 of Acts of Assembly of 1956, Code of Va., Sec. 18.1–381) is not in issue in NAACP v. Harrison as it is now presented to the Supreme Court. It was in issue in NAACP v. Patty, 159 F. Supp. 503 (E.D., Va., 1958), and was there held unconstitutional in reliance upon United States v. Harriss, 347 U.S. 612 (1954). The Supreme Court remanded for interpretation by the state courts, and did not reach the constitutional issue. Harrison v. NAACP, 360 U.S. 167 (1959). When the other issues in the Patty case were presented to the

As the Jehovah's Witnesses have done in the realm of religious associations, so the NAACP has literally made much of the constitutional law governing the pressure group. In striving to overcome the hostility of some to their program, they have presented the associational issues involved in such a clear-cut and imperative manner that the courts have been compelled to spell out the fundamental nature, and limitations, of the right of association in this area with an increasing clarity and with a predictable solicitude for the associational rights of the individuals involved.

F. GENERAL CONCLUSIONS CONCERNING FREEDOM OF ASSOCIATION AND POLITICAL PARTIES AND PRESSURE GROUPS

From the foregoing discussion of political parties and pressure groups in their associational context, it is possible to deduce a few constituent principles of freedom of association in relation to them.

1. There is a constitutional right to form a political party, which right is subject to reasonable regulation to insure that only responsible parties with a certain minimal support shall compete for the favor of the electorate.

2. There is a constitutional right to join and support a political party, which right is subject only to such regulation as is reasonably designed to insure the applicant's capacity to exercise rationally his right to vote, or to preserve, as in the case of government personnel, the integrity of governmental processes.

3. There is a constitutional right not to join a political party, which right is legally inviolable. There is a cognate right not to support a party, which has been discussed in connection with the political activities of labor and professional associations.[135]

4. There is a constitutional right to form, join, or support pressure groups, which right is subject to regulations reasonably designed to insure the integrity of governmental processes.

5. There is a constitutional right not to join or support pressure

Virginia courts in the Harrison case now before the Supreme Court, the antilobbying issue was not included. The Virginia statute would seem fatally defective, under the criterion of United States v. Harriss, since it requires registration of those who attempt to influence legislation "in any manner" and is not limited to direct lobbying activities. Other Southern statutes are similarly broad, e.g., N.C. Gen. Stat. Ann., Sec. 120–48 (1943).

[135] See above pp. 93 et seq.

groups, which is governed by the principles discussed in connection with the political activities of labor and professional associations.

6. The foregoing rights are traditionally based upon the freedoms of speech, press, assembly, and petition, but there are facets of them which may be more properly ascribed to freedom of association.

VI. *Freedom of Association and Subversive Associations*

A. GENERAL QUESTIONS

The associations discussed hereinbefore are generally characterized by the integrity and desirability of their aims. However, unlike religious, labor or professional, and political associations, those groups which we describe herein as subversive have carried a reputation for hostility to the basic values of our society. It is in examining the individual's right to associate for subversive purposes, a right most susceptible to regulation, that we can verify whether freedom of association really ranks as a fundamental constitutional right. Obviously, the right to subvert, if such there be, is subject to some regulation or perhaps prohibition in the interest of society in its own preservation. The limits of that regulation or prohibition have not yet been defined, and it is the purpose here, building upon those principles hereinbefore discussed in relation to other associations, to determine whether there is a right to associate for subversive ends and to note the disabilities which the individual may incur by so associating. A further question is whether the right of subversive association is, like the associational rights hereinbefore discussed, an independent constitutional right or whether it really is only a less than fundamental product of the restraints imposed upon government by due process and other constitutional guarantees.

Webster defines the verb "subvert" as meaning, in its primary sense: "To overturn from the foundation; to overthrow; to ruin utterly; to destroy; also, to upset, uproot, or the like." [1] We are here

[1] Webster's New International Dictionary, Second Edition, unabridged (Springfield, 1949).

concerned mainly with subversion of the Constitution, government and society. Plainly, all will not agree as to what constitutes subversion in this respect. An activity which some regard as tending to "overturn" or "ruin utterly" the structure of our society may be regarded by others of equal good will as eminently salutary and proper. Such differences of opinion increase when we ascribe a less radical meaning to the word "subvert," when we include within its compass activities which merely weaken the established fundamental order as well as those which tend to "overthrow" it "from the foundation." If we were to adopt, for purposes of our analysis, a definition of subversion which made the subversive character of an association depend upon the meaning of some pliable word, e.g., "overturn," "destroy," "weaken," we would never arrive at a satisfactory classification. Instead of clarifying the content of the right to associate for subversive ends, we would render it more inexact by introducing an inevitably subjective element into the selection of associations for analysis as subversive.

It is for this reason, to foster clarity of analysis, that this discussion will avoid a vague and shifting definition. We will treat as subversive only those associations which have been the targets of major legislative or administrative restriction. This will insure that only those associations are selected here, to explain the freedom of subversive association, which have been regarded as subversive by a number of contemporaries numerous enough to cause the engines of government repression to be brought directly to bear upon those groups. There are sufficient major historical examples of such associations to permit the drawing therefrom of reasonable conclusions about the freedom of subversive association. In this pragmatic approach, we shall not endeavor to formulate an independent substantive definition of a subversive association. Indeed, the selection for analysis of only those associations which have been stigmatized by the contemporary governments as subversive precludes such a definition, for the prevailing opinion as to what constitutes a subversive association is not constant from era to era. There are essential differences, for example, between the Ku Klux Klan and the Communist Party, despite their common invidious reputations. Yet, for our analysis, they will both be treated as subversive because their contemporaries, acting through their governments, have considered them to be such insofar as they have been targets of hostile and repressive government action.

By skirting the problem of definition, we may deduce principles which will apply to all proscribed and repressed types of associations, rather than only to those which fit a limited substantive definition. We will, however, where appropriate, attempt to generalize as to some substantive characteristics of subversive associations and of the forbidden individual participation therein. We will weigh the necessity of the individual member personally having the intent which is officially branded as subversive, and the necessity of overt activity on his part. We will seek distinctions between the groups we treat as subversive and those which are merely unpopular, or are genuine, though minority, political groups. But primarily, we will deal with the right, if any, of an individual to join any group officially characterized as subversive, the ramifications of that right, its limitations and its status as a fundamental constitutional freedom.

B. ALIEN AND SEDITION LAWS

The newly born United States did not have to wait long for a serious challenge to political freedom. During President Washington's second term in office, opposition to Federal taxation had crystallized in Democratic-Republican Societies, which were largely Jeffersonian in their orientation.[2] When war with France appeared imminent in 1798, these groups and their supporters increased their attacks upon the controlling Federalists and espoused principles which, to the Federalists, savored of revolutionary republicanism.[3] To suppress these hostile utterances, and to minimize foreign influence in American politics, the Federalist majority in Congress enacted in 1798 the Alien and Sedition Laws.[4] The Naturalization Act extended the period of residence required for naturalization from five to fourteen years.[5] The Enemy Alien Act gave the President power in time of war, or the threat thereof, to expel or confine all enemy aliens.[6] The Alien Act authorized the President to deport all aliens whom he might consider "dangerous to the peace and safety of the United States." [7] The Enemy Alien Act and the Alien Act were never formally invoked, although the threat of their operation caused a few aliens to

[2] Horn, Groups and the Constitution 17 (Stanford, 1956).

[3] See 1 Harlow, The Growth of the United States 265 (New York, 1943); Link, Democratic-Republican Societies, 1790–1800 (New York, 1942).

[4] 1 Chitwood & Owsley, A Short History of the American People 306–307 (New York, 1951).

[5] 1 Stat. 566.

[6] 1 Stat. 577.

[7] 1 Stat. 570.

flee the country.[8] The fourth of the Alien and Sedition Laws, however, was enforced before it expired in 1801.[9] This was the Sedition Act.[10] Under this act the Federalists effected about twenty-five arrests, and at least fifteen indictments, with ten convictions.[11] Its administration was blatantly partisan.[12] The issue of the constitutionality of the Sedition Act never reached the Supreme Court, but it was sustained in the lower Federal courts.[13] The Sedition Act was supported as a statutory restatement of the common law of seditious libel, justified under the "necessary and proper" clause [14] of the Constitution and not violative of the First Amendment, which was asserted to prohibit only prior censorship.[15] Against the act it was argued that the

[8] 1 Harlow, The Growth of the United States 266 (New York, 1943).

[9] Smith, Freedom's Fetters 442 (Ithaca, 1956).

[10] "Section 1 . . . If any persons shall unlawfully combine or conspire together, with intent to oppose any measure or measures of the government of the United States . . . or to impede the operation of any law of the United States . . . ; and if any person or persons, with intent as aforesaid, shall counsel, advise or attempt to procure any insurrection, riot, unlawful assembly or combination, . . . he or they . . . shall be punished. . . ." (1 Stat. 596). "Section 2 . . . if any person shall write, print, utter or publish . . . or shall knowingly assist or aid in writing, printing, uttering or publishing any false, scandalous and malicious writing . . . against the government of the United States, or either house of the Congress of the United States, or the President of the United States, with intent to defame . . . or to bring them, or either of them, into contempt or disrepute; or to excite against them, or either or any of them, the hatred of the good people of the United States, or to stir up sedition within the United States, or to excite any unlawful combinations therein, for opposing or resisting any law of the United States, or any act of the President of the United States, done in pursuance of any such law, or of the powers in him vested by the Constitution of the United States . . . or to aid, encourage or abet any hostile designs of any foreign nation against the United States, their people or government, then such person . . . shall be punished. . . ." (1 Stat. 597).

[11] Emerson and Haber, Political and Civil Rights in the United States 277–78 (Buffalo, 1958).

[12] See Hicks & Mowry, A Short History of American Democracy 131–32 (Boston, 1956).

[13] See Emerson and Haber, Political and Civil Rights in the United States 278 (Buffalo, 1958); United States v. Lyon, Wharton's St. Tr. 333 (1798); United States v. Haswell, Wharton's St. Tr. 684 (1800); United States v. Cooper, Wharton's St. Tr. 659 (1800); United States v. Callender, Wharton's St. Tr. 688 (1800). Callender's offense, for which he was convicted, was that he had described Federal judges and ambassadors as "paper jobbers" and "poltroons" and said that President Adams "contrived pretenses to double the annual expense of government, by useless fleets, armies, sinecures and jobs of every possible description." See Robertson, The Trial of James Thompson Callender (Petersburg, Virginia, 1804). See Kilpatrick, The Sovereign States 69 (Chicago, 1957).

[14] Art. I, Sec. 8, cl. 18.

[15] See Emerson and Haber, Political and Civil Rights in the United States 278 (Buffalo, 1958). John Marshall, although he opposed the act, considered it constitutional; Smith, Freedom's Fetters 151 (Ithaca, 1956).

creation of such a crime was outside the delegated powers of the Federal Government,[16] and that the provisions of the act abridged the freedoms of speech, press and petition.[17] The opposition to the act was proclaimed most cogently in the Virginia and Kentucky Resolutions, written by Madison and Jefferson respectively.[18] Despite the strictures imposed upon combinations by the act, the debate concerning its wisdom and constitutionality ignored the associational problems involved.[19] Indeed, the Republican minority in Congress did not even seriously oppose section one of the act. They conceded that it was directed against "seditious practices" and not against words, beliefs, and opinions; they thought, however, that it was useless, since adequate laws existed to punish individual or combined forceful opposition to the law.[20] Their opposition was concentrated upon section two, which punished mere utterances, and they emphasized freedom of speech.[21]

The drama of the Sedition Act is important for us because its points up the fact that what we now regard as a fundamental right was almost wholly unrecognized at the start of our history. If a statute such as the Sedition Act were enacted today, freedom of association almost certainly would be advanced as a basis for a constitutional challenge of both section one and section two.[22] The episode is instructive also in cautioning us to distinguish between the combination which is outlawed specifically because it is subversive and the combination which is banned merely by application of the ordinary rules of criminal conspiracy. It is from examples of the former type that we can evaluate the legal restrictions imposed upon subversive associations,

16 See the later case of United States v. Hudson, 11 U.S. (7 Cranch) 32, 33 (1812).

17 See McLaughlin, A Constitutional History of the United States, Chs. 19, 20 (New York, 1935).

18 See Preston, Documents Illustrative of American History, 1606–1863, 283 et seq. (New York, 1907); American Historical Documents (Syrett ed.) (New York, 1960).

19 See Smith, Freedom's Fetters, Ch. 8 (Ithaca, 1956) for discussion of the Congressional debates.

20 Id. at 150.

21 Ibid.

22 See McLaughlin, A Constitutional History of the United States 267 et seq. (New York, 1935), asserting that the breadth of the prohibitions of speech and expression in the act, and the undue discretion enjoyed by its administrators, rendered it consitutionally invalid; see also Rogge, The First & the Fifth 23–26 (New York, 1960). See Sweezy v. New Hampshire, 354 U.S. 234 (1957).

which restrictions differ in the scope and definition of the forbidden object from the prohibitions of ordinary criminal conspiracy.[23]

C. SUBVERSIVE ASSOCIATIONS IN THE CIVIL WAR

From the Alien and Sedition Laws we turn to the Civil War, which presented the next major test of the power of the government to repress combinations which it deemed subversive.[24] Unlike the Democratic-Republican societies, however, the allegedly subversive groups in the North during the Civil War were quite obviously hostile to the interests, and even the existence, of the Government of the United States.[25] For example, the various Copperhead societies, such as the Knights of the Golden Circle and the Order of American Knights, entertained notions ranging from "peace at any price" to outright Confederate partisanship and active opposition to the government.[26] Their more extremist elements verged into the Northwest Conspiracy, which was basically a Confederate underground military operation in the Middle West.[27] It is not necessary for us to examine in detail the various subversive associations of the Civil War. It is more important to note the legal and semilegal weapons employed against them, and the virtual absence of effective judicial supervision.

Among those weapons was the suspension of the writ of habeas corpus, initially effected by a Presidential proclamation of April 27, 1861, which suspended the writ between Philadelphia and Washington.[28] This action, taken while Congress was not in session, was flatly condemned by Chief Justice Taney, on circuit, in *Ex parte Merryman.*[29] But the Chief Justice's assertion that only Congress had the

[23] See Carroll, Freedom of Speech and of the Press in the Federalist Period: The Sedition Act, 18 Mich. L. Rev. 615 (1920).

[24] In the interim, there were other conflicts, especially those arising from the nativist and abolitionist movements, but they are of only passing interest as far as the development of the right of association is concerned. See Whipple, The Story of Civil Liberty in the United States 49–83 (New York, 1960); Horn, Groups and the Constitution 155 (Stanford, 1956); Eaton, Censorship of the Southern Mails, 48 Am. Hist. Rev. 266 (1943).

[25] See Hicks & Mowry, A Short History of American Democracy 371 (Boston, 1956); 1 Chitwood & Owsley, A Short History of the American People 770 (New York, 1951).

[26] Weyl, The Battle Against Disloyalty 54 et seq. (New York, 1951); Hicks & Mowry, id. at 771.

[27] See Weyl, id. at Ch. 5, for details of the Conspiracy and how it was smashed by counterespionage and military trials.

[28] Randall, Constitutional Problems under Lincoln 149 (New York, 1926).

[29] 17 Fed. Cas. No. 9, 487 (1861).

suspending power was generally disregarded,[30] and was flatly challenged by Attorney General Bates.[31] The suspension was extended throughout the country by the President on September 24, 1862.[32] In 1863, Congress ratified the suspension of the writ by the President throughout the United States.[33] Note President Lincoln's defense of the constitutionality of his suspension of the writ:

> The whole of the laws which were required to be faithfully executed were being resisted . . . in nearly one third of the States. Must they be allowed to finally fail of execution, even had it been perfectly clear that by the use of the means necessary to their execution some single law, made in such extreme tenderness of the citizen's liberty that, practically, it relieves more of the guilty than of the innocent should to a very limited extent be violated? . . . But it was not believed . . . that any law was violated. . . . But . . . it cannot be believed the framers of the instrument intended that in every case the danger should run its course until Congress could be gotten together.[34]

The Supreme Court in 1866 assumed that the Act of March 3, 1863 was valid.[35] Since the constitutional provision authorizing the suspension of the writ of habeas corpus does so only "when in cases of rebellion or invasion the public safety may require it," [36] this repressive device is of little practical consequence in relation to the peculiar subversive problems of the present day, which do not involve actual insurrection or invasion. However, the possibility of suspension of the writ as a weapon against subversion and subversive associations when insurrection or invasion are present should be noted, as well as the unpleasant fact that the suspension in the Civil War was followed by numerous arbitrary confinements of suspected persons.[37] After the war was safely over, the Supreme Court denied the right of military authorities to arrest and try civilians as long as the civil courts were functioning.[38]

[30] See Randall, Constitutional Problems under Lincoln, Ch. 8 (New York, 1926).

[31] 10 Op. Atty. Gen. 74 (1861–1863); see Ex parte Bollman, 8 U.S. (4 Cranch) 75 (1807).

[32] Rossiter, Constitutional Dictatorship 225 et seq. (Princeton, 1948).

[33] Act of March 3, 1863; 12 Stat. 755 (1863); see also 12 Stat. 326 (1861).

[34] Message to Congress, July 4, 1861; 2 Nicolay and Hay, Lincoln, Complete Works 55 (1894).

[35] Ex parte Milligan, 71 U.S. 2 (1866).

[36] Art. I, Sec. 9, cl. 2.

[37] The number of such confinements has been variously estimated, from 13,000 to 38,000. Hall, Free Speech in Wartime, 21 Colum. L. Rev. 526, 527 (1921).

[38] Ex parte Milligan, 71 U.S. 2 (1866); see Ex parte Vallandigham, 68 U.S. 243 (1864); see also The Constitution of the United States of America (Read ed.) 399–401 (Washington, Government Printing Office, 1953).

As an incident of the government's policy of confining undesirables, treason prosecutions were also employed. Numerous charges were brought, and confinements thereby imposed, but in no case was any sentence carried out in a treason prosecution arising out of the Civil War.[39] Akin to the treason statute was the Conspiracies Act of July 31, 1861, which provided in part:

> . . . if two or more persons . . . shall conspire together to overthrow, or to put down, or to destroy by force, the Government of the United States, or to levy war against the United States, or to oppose by force the authority of the Government of the United States, or by force to prevent, hinder, or delay the execution of any law of the United States . . . each and every person so offending . . . shall be punished by a fine . . . or by imprisonment. . . .[40]

This statute does not punish mere association with a conspiring group, but rather active conspiracy on the part of the individual defendant. It is, nevertheless, an acknowledgment that subversion is usually effected by a combination, and that criminal legislation must take account of that fact.[41] Theretofore, the law had punished any forcible opposition to the execution of a Federal law, but the Act of July 31, 1861 was the first since the expiration of the Sedition Act to penalize a mere conspiracy for that purpose.[42] It was the first Federal statute ever to punish such a conspiracy which was not consummated by an overt act.[43] Since 1861 such conspiracy legislation has remained in force, and it constituted a primary weapon for the punishment of subversive combinations in World War I.[44]

Another Civil War restraint on subversive activity was the imposition of loyalty oaths as a condition of voting, holding public office or engaging in certain occupations.[45] In two leading cases, the Supreme Court struck down test oaths, as applied to clergymen and attorneys, as bills of attainder and *ex post facto* laws because some of the acts, which the affiant must swear that he did not commit,

[39] Randall, Constitutional Problems under Lincoln 91–94 (New York, 1926); see the Treason Act of 1862, 12 Stat. 589.

[40] 12 Stat. 284; constitutionality upheld in In re Impaneling, etc., 26 Fed. 749 (D.C., Ore., 1886).

[41] See Presidential Proclamation of April 15, 1861; 6 Richardson, Messages and Papers of the Presidents, 13 (Washington, 1897).

[42] Charge to Grand Jury, Treason, 30 Fed. Cas. No. 18,272 (C.C., Ohio, 1861).

[43] Grand Jury, Treason and Piracy, 30 Fed. Cas. No. 18,277 (C.C., Mass., 1861).

[44] Chafee, Free Speech in the United States 40–41 (Cambridge, 1941).

[45] Emerson & Haber, Political and Civil Rights in the United States 283 (Buffalo, 1958).

"have never been classed as offences in the laws of any State, and some of the acts, under many circumstances, would not even be blameworthy."[46] The test oaths of the Civil War and Reconstruction, directed against participation in a subversive conspiracy, foreshadowed similar techniques of the present time.

D. WORLD WAR I

In contrast to the sweeping assumption of executive power over dangerous persons by President Lincoln, involving neither the enforcement of legislation nor prosecution in the courts, the anti-subversion measures of the First World War were based upon a full and elaborate statutory foundation.[47] The government utilized the conspiracy legislation, enacted prior to World War I, to suppress individual and combined action obstructive to the Selective Service Act[48] and other aspects of the war effort.[49] When the existing legislation proved inadequate to cope with the novel problems of the War,[50] Congress enacted the Espionage Act of 1917,[51] punishing the dissemination of false statements with intent to interfere with the war effort, and the obstruction of recruitment or military discipline, in addition to punishing conventional espionage. The 1918 amendment[52] to the Espionage Act added nine new prohibited acts, including abusive language toward the government, the military uniform or flag, urging curtailment of war production, disloyally obstructing the sale of war bonds, or opposing in any way, by word or act, the cause of the United States.[53] Section Four of the Espionage Act, applicable also to the 1918 amendment, punished conspiracy to violate the act.[54] Convictions under this conspiracy section were upheld in several

[46] Cummings v. Missouri, 71 U.S. (4 Wall.) 277, 316–17 (1867); see also Ex parte Garland, 71 U.S. (4 Wall.) 333 (1867); Russ, The Lawyer's Test Oath during Reconstruction, 10 Miss. L.J. 154 (1938).

[47] Randall, Constitutional Problems under Lincoln 525 (New York, 1926).

[48] 40 Stat. 76, C. 15.

[49] Goldman v. United States, 245 U.S. 474 (1918); Wells v. United States, 257 Fed. 605 (9th Cir., 1919); Bryant v. United States, 257 Fed. 378 (5th Cir., 1919); Orear v. United States, 261 Fed. 257 (5th Cir., 1919).

[50] Randall, Constitutional Problems under Lincoln 526–27 (New York, 1926).

[51] 40 Stat. 217.

[52] 40 Stat. 553.

[53] The Espionage Act, as amended, was repealed in 1921. 41 Stat. 1359.

[54] "If two or more persons conspire to violate the provisions . . . of this title, and one or more of such persons does any act to effect the object of the conspiracy, each of the parties to such conspiracy shall be punished. . . ." 40 Stat. 219.

cases by the Supreme Court.[55] The associational issue was ignored in the decisions, which generally turned upon issues of freedom of speech. Many states enacted statutes modeled upon the Espionage Act, and most contained similar conspiracy provisions.[56] Enforcement of both the state and Federal statutes was thoroughgoing and strict.[57]

E. CRIMINAL ANARCHISM AND CRIMINAL SYNDICALISM

The conspiracy statutes of the Civil War and World War I did not in themselves depart radically from prior conceptions of conspiracy which required full personal intent, on the part of the individual defendant, to effect the unlawful object.[58] Toward the end of the nineteenth century, however, anarchistic and socialistic organizations attained strength, real or apparent, which was alarming to some state legislatures.[59] The first of the restrictive state laws which resulted was the New York Criminal Anarchy Act of 1902.[60] With the end of World War I, there were thirty-two states with such legislation.[61] These state laws represent a break with the past and a definite stage in the development of freedom of association. They not only forbade the advocacy of criminal anarchy[62] or criminal syndicalism,[63] but also

[55] Schenck v. United States, 249 U.S. 47 (1919) (In Schenck, Mr. Justice Holmes, for a unanimous court, first enunciated the clear-and-present-danger test. "The question in every case is whether the words used are used in such a nature as to create a clear and present danger that they will bring about the substantive evils that Congress has a right to prevent.") 249 U.S. at 52; Frohwerk v. United States, 249 U.S. 204 (1919); Abrams v. United States, 250 U.S. 616 (1919) (Holmes, joined by Brandeis, dissented because there was no sufficient showing of intent or of "immediate danger"), 250 U.S. at 628; Schaefer v. United States, 251 U.S. 466 (1920) (Brandeis, joined by Holmes, dissented); Pierce v. United States, 252 U.S. 239 (1920) (Brandeis, joined by Holmes, dissented); Stilson v. United States, 250 U.S. 583 (1919) (Holmes and Brandeis dissented); O'Connell v. United States, 253 U.S. 142 (1920).

[56] See Chafee, Free Speech in the United States, Appendix III (Cambridge 1941); the Minnesota statute was sustained in Gilbert v. Minnesota, 254 U.S. 325 (1920) (Brandeis dissented).

[57] See Emerson and Haber, Political and Civil Rights in the United States 284–90 (Buffalo, 1958).

[58] See Phipps v. United States, 251 Fed. 879 (4th Cir., 1918).

[59] See generally, Dowell, A History of Criminal Syndicalism Legislation in the United States (Baltimore, 1939).

[60] L. 1902, C. 371, Sec. 1; New York Penal Law, Sec. 161.

[61] See Chafee, Free Speech in the United States, Appendix III (Cambridge, 1941).

[62] "Criminal anarchy is the doctrine that organized government should be overthrown by force or violence, or by assassination of . . . any of the executive officials of government, or by any unlawful means. . . ." New York Penal Law, Sec. 160.

[63] ". . . any doctrine . . . advocating . . . the commission of crime, sabotage

prohibited association with any group formed to espouse the prohibited doctrines.[64] The New York statute was sustained in *Gitlow v. New York,*[65] a case which is well remembered as the first in which the court assumed that the First Amendment freedoms of speech and of the press are among the "liberties" protected by the due-process clause of the Fourteenth Amendment,[66] and because the court limited the clear-and-present-danger doctrine by holding that it had no application to a state statute which specifically prescribes "that utterances of a certain kind involve such danger of substantive evil that they may be punished."[67] However, the membership prohibition of New York Penal Law, Sec. 161(4) was not at issue in Gitlow; nor was the following provision:

> Whenever two or more persons assemble for the purpose of advocating or teaching the doctrines of criminal anarchy . . . such an assembly is unlawful, and every person voluntarily participating therein by his presence and/or instigation, is guilty of a felony. . . .[68]

There have been no cases directly construing or applying section 161(4) or section 162.[69] The associational issue was raised, however, with reference to a similar California statute,[70] in *Whitney v. California,*[71] where the court sustained the enactment against objections based upon the rights of free speech, assembly, and association.[72] Mr. Justice Brandeis, in his concurrence, emphasized the novel character

. . . , or unlawful acts of force and violence . . . as a means of accomplishing a change in industrial ownership or control, or effecting any political change." California Statutes 1919, Ch. 188, at 281, Sec. 1; now contained in California Penal Code, Secs. 11400 et seq.

[64] See New York Penal Law, Sec. 161(4); California Penal Code, Sec. 11401(4).

[65] 268 U.S. 652 (1925) (Holmes, joined by Brandeis, dissented).

[66] 268 U.S. at 666; this position had been suggested in United States v. Hall, 26 Fed. Cas. No. 15,282 (C.C.S.D., Ala., 1871).

[67] 268 U.S. at 670.

[68] New York Penal Law, Sec. 162.

[69] But see Application of Cassidy, 288 App. Div. 282, 51 N.Y.S. 2d 202, 204–205 (2d Dept., 1944), indicating that the maintenance of a private militia, for the purpose of suppressing a feared imminent Communist insurrection, would violate Secs. 161 and 162.

[70] "Any person who: . . . (4) Organizes or assists in organizing, or is or knowingly becomes a member of, any organization, society, group or assemblage of persons organized or assembled to advocate, teach or aid and abet criminal syndicalism . . . is guilty of a felony. . . ." California Statutes, 1919, Ch. 188 at 281, now California Penal Code, Sec. 11401(4).

[71] 274 U.S. 357 (1927) (Brandeis, joined by Holmes, concurred). Accord: Burns v. United States, 274 U.S. 328 (1927) (Brandeis dissented).

[72] 274 U.S. at 371.

of the state laws which proscribed mere association [73] rather than the usual criminal conspiracy:

> The felony which the statute created is a crime very unlike the old felony of conspiracy or the old misdemeanor of unlawful assembly. The mere act of assisting in forming a society for teaching syndicalism, or becoming a member of it, or of assembling with others for that purpose is given the dynamic quality of crime. There is guilt although the society may not contemplate immediate promulgation of the doctrine. . . . The novelty in the prohibition introduced is that the statute aims, not at the practice of criminal syndicalism, nor even directly at the preaching of it, but at association with those who propose to preach it.[74]

Mr. Justice Brandeis even intimated in his *Whitney* opinion that there is a fundamental right of subversive association, an intimation which was to find some judicial support in later years:

> I am unable to assent to the suggestion in the opinion of the court that assembling with a political party, formed to advocate the desirability of a proletarian revolution by mass action at some date necessarily far in the future, is not a right within the protection of the Fourteenth Amendment.[75]

On the same day as the *Whitney* decision, the court reversed a conviction under the Kansas statute, on the grounds that there was insufficient proof that the Industrial Workers of the World, the association to which defendant belonged, advocated criminal syndicalism.[76] It was the first such case in which a defendant was successful in the Supreme Court.

It is significant, in view of the introduction by the state anarchism and syndicalism statutes of a new concept which may be described as "guilt by knowing association," that those laws were consistently upheld. The state court decisions sustained them against objections principally based on the rights of assembly and association,[77] due

[73] But the defendant in Whitney had knowledge of the nature and purposes of the organization she joined; in apparent reliance upon that fact, the majority upheld the act against objections based upon free speech, assembly, and association. 274 U.S. at 371.

[74] 274 U.S. at 372–73.

[75] 274 U.S. at 379; compare Yates v. United States, 350 U.S. 860 (1956).

[76] Fiske v. Kansas, 274 U.S. 380 (1927).

[77] People v. Taylor, 187 Calif. 378, 203 Pac. 85 (1921); State v. Dingman, 37 Idaho 253, 219 Pac. 760 (1923); State v. Laundy, 103 Ore. 443, 204 Pac. 958 (1922).

process,[78] freedom of speech,[79] and the alleged vagueness of the prohibitions.[80] In fact, it was generally held in the state courts that mere membership in an organization advocating the proscribed doctrine—in each case either the Communist Party or the Industrial Workers of the World—was sufficient by itself for a conviction under the statutes, without proof of personal adherence by the defendant to the doctrines.[81] However, the Supreme Court of the United States cast doubt upon these cases by its decision in *DeJonge v. Oregon,*[82] where the court reversed a conviction based upon the mere fact that defendant participated in a meeting called by the Communist Party. There was no evidence that anything unlawful was done or advocated at the meeting, and the state court relied upon the alleged purposes of the Communist Party. The court unanimously said:

> The holding of meetings for peaceable political action cannot be proscribed. Those who assist in the conduct of such meetings cannot be branded as criminals on that score. The question . . . is not as to the auspices under which the meeting is held but as to its purpose; not as to the relations of the speakers, but whether their utterances transcend the bounds of the freedom of speech. . . . If the persons assembling have committed crimes elsewhere, if they have formed or are engaged in a conspiracy . . . they may be prosecuted for their conspiracy or other violation of valid laws. But it is a different matter when the State, instead of prosecuting them for such offenses, seizes upon mere participation in a peaceable assembly and a lawful public discussion as the basis for a criminal charge.[83]

The effect of mere participation in an association is an issue which will be central to our later discussion of the restrictive measures aimed specifically at the Communist Party. It is significant here to note that *DeJonge* was the culmination of a process by which the court, in handling the anarchist and syndicalist legislation, moved

[78] State v. Sinchuk, 96 Conn. 605, 115 Atl. 33 (1921); People v. Wagner, 65 Cal. App. 704, 225 Pac. 464 (1924).

[79] State v. Kassay, 126 Ohio St. 177, 184 N.E. 521 (1932); Commonwealth v. Widovich, 295 Pa. 311, 145 Atl. 295 (1929).

[80] People v. Lloyd, 304 Ill. 23, 136 N.E. 505 (1922); People v. Ruthenberg, 229 Mich. 315, 201 N.W. 358 (1925).

[81] People v. McClennegen, 195 Cal. 445, 234 Pac. 91 (1925); State v. Dingman, 37 Idaho 253, 219 Pac. 760 (1923); State v. Berquist, 109 Kan. 382, 199 Pac. 101 (1921).

[82] 299 U.S. 353 (1937).

[83] 299 U.S. at 365.

from simple concepts of freedom of speech [84] through a specific reliance upon the right to associate,[85] to the recognition, in *DeJonge*, that the act of associating is unpunishable without some further element of personal culpability.[86]

F. THE KU KLUX KLAN

Even though the act of association was thus considered by the court immune to criminal punishment without personal guilt, there was a parallel development which recognized a liability to lesser penalties and disabilities. Since 1871, the Ku-Klux Klan had been the object of restrictive legislation.[87] In the 1920's, Klan agitation was even stronger than that of the anarchists and syndicalists.[88] Although its constitution and creed proclaim freedom for all and full adherence to the Constitution of the United States, the Klan urges white supremacy, bitter antagonism toward its opponents, and a virulent prejudice against Negroes, Catholics, and Jews.[89] Since its avowed purposes are not illegal, the Klan has not been outlawed as such, nor has membership in it been made in itself illegal.[90] Rather, regulatory devices have been employed to inhibit its undesirable activities. New York took the lead in regulating the Klan in the 1920's, with a statute [91] requiring that all oath-bound societies, except labor unions and benevolent orders recognized under state law, must file a membership list and other information with the Secretary of State. It further provided that "any person who becomes a member of any such . . . association, or remains a member thereof, or attends a meeting thereof, with knowledge that such . . . association has failed to comply . . . shall be guilty of a misdemeanor."

[84] See Gitlow v. New York, 268 U.S. 652 (1925).

[85] See concurring opinion of Mr. Justice Brandeis in Whitney v. California 274 U.S. 357 (1927); see also Stromberg v. California, 283 U.S. 359 (1931).

[86] See note, The Supreme Court as Protector of Political Minorities, 46 Yale L.J. 862 (1937).

[87] In that year, Congress, by the so-called Ku-Klux Act (Act of April 20, 1871; 17 Stat. 14–15), authorized the President to suspend the writ of habeas corpus in nine designated counties of South Carolina. President Grant then suspended the writ in an effort to quell the rising Klan activity in the area. See Randall, Constitutional Problems under Lincoln 135 (New York, 1926).

[88] Horn, Groups and the Constitution 128 (Stanford, 1956).

[89] See note, Constitutional Law; Fourteenth Amendment; Discriminating Legislation, 13 Marq. L. Rev. 242 (1929).

[90] Abernathy, The Right of Association, 6 S.C.L.Q. 32, 73–74 (1953).

[91] New York Civil Rights Law, Art. 5A.

The Klan refused to abide by the statute. Bryant, who was a member, was arrested, and he sought habeas corpus, alleging that the statute was violative of the Fourteenth Amendment. The Supreme Court unanimously sustained the statute.[92] The court denied that the privilege "to be and remain a member of a secret, oath-bound association within a state" is a privilege of United States citizenship.[93] Also rejected was the relator's contention that the statute "deprives him of liberty in that it prevents him from exercising his right of membership in the association." [94] The regulation was held to be reasonable.[95] In requiring knowledge of the default before subjection of the individual to criminal penalties, the statute and the court are fully consistent with the later rationale of *DeJonge v. Oregon*.[96] Significantly, however, the requirement that the individual member's name be made a matter of public record is not conditioned upon any knowledge on his part of the nature of the association or of the statutory requirement. Indeed, such a requirement would probably stultify the operation of the statute in its inception. It appears, rather, that an individual acts at his peril in joining an association, to the extent that his participation may be made a matter of public record if the requisite public purpose is served by such disclosure. On this latter point, the character of the group is determinative. The National Association for the Advancement of Colored People [97] is placed in a different class from the concededly invidious Ku Klux Klan.[98] Perhaps most importantly, the court may judicially notice the nature of the association, in assessing the reasonableness of the classification which singles it out for regulation. In the *Zimmerman* case, the court took notice of the readily available public information about the Klan's odious activities, and assumed that the legislature had that information before it; therefore, the classification, be-

[92] People ex rel. Bryant v. Zimmerman, 278 U.S. 63 (1928) (Mr. Justice McReynolds concurred on procedural grounds).

[93] 278 U.S. at 71.

[94] 278 U.S. at 72.

[95] ". . . the state within whose territory and under whose protection the association exists is entitled to be informed of its nature and purpose, of whom it is composed and by whom its activities are conducted. . . . Of course, power to require the disclosure includes authority to prevent individual members of an association which has failed to comply from attending meetings or retaining membership with knowledge of its default. . . ." 278 U.S. at 72–73.

[96] Supra pp. 46, 109.

[97] Supra pp. 112 et seq.

[98] See discussion in NAACP v. Alabama, 357 U.S. 449, 465 (1958).

cause it was based on reasonable and relevant factual criteria, was permissible.[99]

G. NAZI AND FASCIST ORGANIZATIONS

The principles theretofore evolved, that an individual is immune from criminal punishment for associating with an allegedly subversive group unless he himself is culpable through actual knowledge or personal activity, and that lesser disabilities may be imposed on members of such associations without direct personal culpability, found application in the measures directed against the domestic Nazi and Fascist associations prior to and during World War II. There were prosecutions under the then-existing Espionage Act,[100] including prosecutions for conspiracy to violate the act.[101] But the peculiar nature of those associations, and of the active Communist apparatus, required legislation to fit the situation. The Smith Act[102] imposed criminal penalties for advocating the forceful overthrow of the government or for organizing, or affiliating with, any association so advocating. But the penalty imposed on membership was conditioned upon knowledge, on the part of the member, of the purposes of the association.[103]

[99] 278 U.S. at 76–77.

[100] 50 U.S.C. Secs. 33, 34.

[101] See Hartzel v. United States, 322 U.S. 680 (1944) (conviction reversed for insufficiency of evidence); see also Application of Cassidy, 268 App. Div. 282, 51 N.Y.S.2d 202 (2d Dept., 1944) (New York Criminal Anarchy Act); Weyl, The Battle Against Disloyalty 158–59 (New York, 1951).

[102] Act of June 28, 1940; 54 Stat. 670, 671; see 18 U.S.C. Sec. 2385.

[103] "Sec. 2.(a) It shall be unlawful . . .

"(1) to knowingly or willfully advocate, abet, advise, or teach the duty, necessity, desirability, or propriety of overthrowing or destroying any government in the United States by force or violence . . . ;

"(2) with the intent to cause the overthrow . . . of any government in the United States, to print, publish, edit, issue, circulate, sell, distribute, or publicly display any written or printed matter advocating . . . the duty, necessity, desirability, or propriety of overthrowing or destroying any government in the United States by force or violence;

"(3) to organize or help to organize any society, group, or assembly of persons who teach, advocate, or encourage the overthrow or destruction of any government in the United States by force or violence; or to be or become a member of, or affiliate with, any such society, group, or assembly of persons, knowing the purpose thereof.

. . . . .

"Sec. 3. It shall be unlawful for any person to attempt to commit, or to conspire to commit, any of the acts prohibited by the provisions of this title." 54 Stat. 670, 671.

Effective September 1, 1948 the Smith Act was repealed, and substantially re-

This enactment was upheld against the contention that it imposed an unconstitutional guilt by association in *Dunne v. United States,*[104] where the Circuit Court of Appeals clarified a member's liability to punishment under the Smith Act:

> . . . the statute does not cover . . . members unless they have knowledge of the unlawful purpose of the group. If they have that knowledge, they are adding their weight to the accomplishment of such unlawful purposes, whether those purposes are approved by them or not and whether any of such purposes were or were not the incentive for their becoming or remaining members. . . .
>
> Finally, it is argued that every member of a group or party is penally responsible for the conduct of every other member and "for every phrase in the statements and documents which are adjudged to reflect party views." . . . Such responsibility is not indefinitely sweeping. It attaches only to authoritative statements of which the member has knowledge; and it depends upon what he does or does not do or say, as manifesting his approval or disapproval, after he has such knowledge.[105]

The Smith Act will be discussed in detail below in connection with the later prosecutions of alleged Communists. It is only in recent years that it has received full elucidation by the courts. We note it here to show its genesis as a restriction of Nazi and Fascist, as well as Communist, associations, the nature of its restraint upon the right of association, and the attitude of the courts in upholding its constitutionality.[106]

In addition to their liability to criminal penalty, if they were possessed of the requisite knowledge, the members of Nazi and Fascist associations were confronted with other disabilities which were, in some situations, imposed irrespective of their personal knowledge or culpability.[107] For example, government employment was soon foreclosed to members of organizations advocating the "overthrow of our

enacted as 18 U.S.C. Sec. 2385, 62 Stat. 808. This recodification did not carry into Sec. 2385 the conspiracy provisions of Sec. 3 of the Smith Act. They were covered by the general conspiracy statute (18 U.S.C. Sec. 371) until the conspiracy provisions were inserted in Sec. 2385, as of July 24, 1956. 70 Stat. 623.

[104] 138 F.2d 137 (8th Cir., 1943), cert. den. 320 U.S. 790 (1943), reh. den. 320 U.S. 814 (1943), reh. den. 320 U.S. 815 (1944) (convictions of members of Socialist Workers Party upheld).

[105] 138 F.2d at 144.

[106] See also Pelley v. Botkin, 152 F.2d 12 (Dist. Col., 1945); United States v. McWilliams, 163 F.2d 695 (Dist. Col., 1947).

[107] See note, Recent Legislative Attempts to Curb Subversive Activities in the U.S., 10 Geo. Wash. L. Rev. 104, 117–25 (1941).

constitutional form of government in the United States."[108] The 1940 appropriation for the Works Projects Administration was explicit:

No alien, no Communist, and no member of any Nazi Bund Organization shall be given employment or continued in employment on any work project prosecuted under the appropriations contained in this joint resolution.[109]

The Voorhis Act, effective January 15, 1941, required registration with the Attorney General, and the filing of detailed information including membership lists, by political organizations subject to foreign control, political or foreign-controlled organizations engaged also in military activity, and organizations which aim to forcibly overthrow the government.[110] Alien members of Nazi, Fascist, or Communist associations were subject to exclusion from the country[111] and, if they were naturalized, they were liable, in some instances, to denaturalization.[112]

The experience gained in the restriction of the Nazi and Fascist associations, and of the right to join them, proved helpful in dealing with the later, and more formidable, threat to constitutional liberty posed by the Communist Party and its adherents.

H. THE COMMUNIST PARTY

In our discussion heretofore, we have sought to discern and analyze the constituent principles of the freedom of association, which,

[108] Sec. 9A of the Hatch Act; 53 Stat. 1148 (1939); 18 U.S.C. Secs. 61, 61(f) (1939). See also 54 Stat. 592 (National Youth Administration appropriation denying compensation "to any person who advocates, or who is a member of an organization that advocates, the overthrow of the Government of the United States through force or violence.") See also 53 Stat. 935 (WPA appropriation).

[109] 54 Stat. 620.

[110] Act of October 17, 1940; 54 Stat. 1201; U.S.C. Sec. 2386. This provision was held constitutional; see Pelley v. Botkin, 152 F.2d 12 (Dist. Col., 1945); Dunne v. United States 138 F.2d 137 (8th Cir., 1943), cert. den. 320 U.S. 790 (1943), reh. den. 320 U.S. 814 (1943), reh. den. 320 U.S. 815 (1944).

At its convention in November, 1940, the Communist Party, U.S.A., resolved: "That the Communist Party of the U.S.A., in convention assembled, does hereby cancel and dissolve its organizational affiliation to the Communist International . . . for the specific purpose of removing itself from the terms of the so-called Voorhis Act." The Subversive Activities Control Board found, however, that this tactic did not alter the domination of the Communist Party, U.S.A., by the Communist International. See Internal Security Subcommittee, Senate Committee on the Judiciary, Report, The Communist Party of the United States of America 2 (84th Cong., 1st Sess., 1955).

[111] 8 U.S.C. Sec. 137; 54 Stat. 673.

[112] See Baumgarten v. United States, 322 U.S. 665 (1944).

it is submitted, had been present in a latent form long before its explicit recognition as a fundamental right. In the story of the Communist Party in the United States, one can see the culmination of those emergent principles. We have seen that seditious combinations were restricted, prior to World War I, by the orthodox rules of criminal conspiracy, embodying a requirement of some personal culpability in the unlawful enterprise. Even during that war, the departures from the orthodox treatment were hardly significant. However, the different problem presented by the anarchist, syndicalist, and similar groups dictated the employment of repressive measures differing in kind, and not merely in degree, from those that had gone before. The mere act of knowledgeable association with a proscribed group took on "the dynamic quality of crime," [113] irrespective of the individual's personal implication in actual subversion. Also, the member incurred some noncriminal disabilities, even without a showing that he knew of the nature and purposes of the association. Parallel developments, we have noted, affected the members of the Ku Klux Klan.

When the nation was confronted with the Nazi and Fascist associations of the 1930's and early 1940's, the menace was materially different from the preceding ones. In terms of conspiratorial organization and antagonism to the basic requirements of national security, the Nazi and Fascist groups were more advanced than the anarchists and syndicalists. There was added, moreover, the element of disciplined and efficient foreign direction, an element which had been rather haphazard in the earlier groups. Against the danger presented by the Nazi and Fascist associations, the weapons employed were those which had evolved from the earlier experience. Adherence to a subversive group entailed criminal penalties, but only if the member were aware of its nature; some noncriminal disabilities, however, continued to be imposed without such full personal knowledge.

With the Communist Party, subversive activity reached its apex in organization, tactical amorality, and foreign domination. In determining the right of the individual to associate with the Party, the principles developed in relation to the other subversive groups apply. Relevant also are the principles of freedom of association developed in connection with other, nonsubversive, types of associations. The claim of the Party to be a bona fide political party, for example, requires analysis in terms of the right to associate for po-

[113] Concurring opinion of Mr. Justice Brandeis in Whitney v. California, 274 U.S. 357, 372–73 (1927).

litical purposes. Perhaps the central feature of the Communist movement is its domination by the Union of Soviet Socialist Republics. The revulsion generated by this hostile foreign control calls to mind the advice of Locke, in another connection, that one type of religious association not entitled to toleration is one in which "all those who enter into it do thereby *ipso facto* deliver themselves up to the protection and service of another prince." [114] Because the Communist movement has sought to permeate every aspect of American society, calling into play a wide variety of restrictive measures against it, its experience affords us an opportunity to see the attributes and limitations of the right of subversive association, if such there be, etched in a detail and clarity which would otherwise be unobtainable.

1. Liability of Members of Communist Party to Criminal Penalties

In the leading case of *Dennis v. United States,*[115] the Supreme Court upheld the convictions of eleven leading members of the Communist Party on a charge of conspiring to violate the substantive provisions of the Smith Act.[116] The question of freedom of association was not raised by counsel for either side, and the five opinions emphasized the freedoms of speech and press and the issue of a clear and present danger.[117] The plurality opinion (Chief Justice Vinson, with concurrence of Justices Reed, Burton, and Minton) held that the trial court had properly ruled that there was a clear and present danger of the forceful overthrow of the government, an evil which Congress was empowered to prevent. The Chief Justice accepted Chief Judge Learned Hand's formulation of the clear-and-present-danger test in the Court of Appeals, that the test is "whether the gravity of the 'evil,' discounted by its improbability, justifies such invasion of free speech as is necessary to avoid the danger." [118] Those four justices rejected the contention that the power of Congress to regulate the unlawful advocacy depends upon the "success or probability of success" of the subversive movement.[119] They distinguished the broad formulations of Holmes and Brandeis on the ground that

[114] See above p. 11.
[115] 341 U.S. 494 (1951).
[116] Act of June 28, 1940; 54 Stat. 670, 671; 18 U.S.C. Sec. 2385; supra note 102, p. 135.
[117] See Corwin, Bowing Out "Clear and Present Danger," 27 Notre Dame Law. 325 (1952).
[118] 341 U.S. at 510.
[119] Ibid.

"they were not confronted with any situation comparable to the instant one—the development of an apparatus designed and dedicated to the overthrow of the Government, in the context of world crisis after crisis." [120] Mr. Justice Frankfurter, in his concurring opinion, upheld the enactment as a product of a valid legislative balancing of the competing interests of national security and free speech. It is relevant to our inquiry whether there is a constitutional right to associate for subversive purposes that Mr. Justice Frankfurter noted that "no government can recognize a 'right' of revolution, or a 'right' to incite revolution if the incitement has no other purpose or effect." [121] Mr. Justice Jackson, in his concurrence, alluded most clearly to the fact that the principal danger is presented, not by the acts of mere individual Communists, but from the coordinated activities of "an aggressive international Communist apparatus," the strength of which is in "selected, dedicated, indoctrinated, and rigidly disciplined members." [122] Limiting the clear-and-present-danger test to the sort of case where "the issue is criminality of a hot-headed speech on a street corner, or circulation of a few incendiary pamphlets, or parading by some zealots behind a red flag, or refusal of a handful of school children to salute our flag," [123] Mr. Justice Jackson upheld the self-preserving power of Congress to employ the tool of criminal conspiracy against the cohesive and secret activities of the Communist apparatus. Justices Black and Douglas dissented separately, finding no sufficient clear-and-present danger to justify the restriction on free speech involved in the act.

While the Dennis case did not involve a prosecution for membership in the Communist Party, and therefore treated the associational issues only obliquely, it is instructive as a modern example of the use of a criminal conspiracy statute to restrain subversive association. The court abided by accepted rules of construction in requiring proof of intent, on the part of the individual conspirators, to overthrow the government by force or violence.[124] Furthermore, the conspiracy itself is the statutory crime, and no overt act seems to be required.[125] Of importance also is the fact that what was punished in

[120] Ibid.
[121] 341 U.S. at 549.
[122] 341 U.S. at 563, 564.
[123] 341 U.S. at 568.
[124] 341 U.S. at 499–500; see United States v. Foster 9 F.R.D. 367 (D.C., New York, 1949).
[125] See discussion in concurring opinion of Mr. Justice Jackson, 341 U.S. at 575; see also Yates v. United States, 354 U.S. 298, 322–25 (1957).

Dennis was not advocacy itself, but conspiracy to advocate.[126] Arguably, in this respect the case is not materially different from the conspiracy cases arising from the World War I Espionage Act.[127] However, the comparison fails in view of the court's later narrow construction of the Smith Act's prohibition of advocacy.[128]

In the years between 1951 and 1957, the government obtained 96 other convictions under the Smith Act; four were on grounds of membership in the Communist Party, and the rest, as in *Dennis*, were for conspiracy.[129] In two of those conspiracy convictions, the Supreme Court denied *certiorari*.[130] To resolve ambiguities arising from the *Dennis* opinions, the court granted *certiorari*, in 1956, on convictions of fourteen California defendants on a single-count indictment charging them with conspiring to advocate the forceful overthrow of the government and conspiring to organize the Communist Party as an organization so advocating.[131] The majority of the court, through Mr. Justice Harlan, reversed the convictions, holding that Congress intended to punish the advocacy only of concrete action for the forcible overthrow of the government and not mere advocacy of forcible overthrow as an abstract doctrine.[132] On the charge that the defendants conspired to "organize" the Communist Party, the court held that Congress intended to limit the meaning of "organize" to acts involved in "creating a new organization," and did not intend thereby "to embrace the activities of those concerned with carrying on the affairs of an already existing organization."[133] Since the Party was "organized" in 1945 and the indictment was not returned until 1951, it was held that the charge was barred by the three-year statute of limitations.[134] Against five of the defendants, "the sole evidence . . . was that they had long been members, of-

[126] See note, Constitutional Law-Civil Rights-First Amendment Freedoms–Reformulation of the Clear-and-Present-Danger Doctrine, 50 Mich. L. Rev. 451, 461 (1952).

[127] See above p. 128.

[128] See Yates v. United States, 354 U.S. 298 (1957).

[129] Emerson and Haber, Political & Civil Rights in the United States 371 (Buffalo, 1958); see also Annual Report of the Attorney General of the United States 65 (1956).

[130] United States v. Frankfeld, 198 F.2d 679 (4th Cir., 1952), cert. den. 344 U.S. 922 (1953); United States v. Flynn, 216 F.2d 354 (2d Cir., 1954), cert. den. 348 U.S. 909 (1955); see note, Post-Dennis Prosecutions under the Smith Act, 31 Ind. L.J. 104 (1955).

[131] Yates v. United States, 350 U.S. 860 (1956).

[132] See 354 U.S. at 320.

[133] 354 U.S. at 308.

[134] 354 U.S. at 312.

ficers or functionaries of the Communist Party of California. . . ." Applying Section 4(f) of the Internal Security Act of 1950,[135] the court held that their membership, of itself, "makes out no case against them."[136] Since the prosecution was laid, for the period after September 1, 1948, under the general conspiracy statute[137] rather than the conspiracy provisions of the original Smith Act,[138] an overt act was held necessary to a conviction.[139] Significantly for our purpose, the court ruled that attendance by some defendants at otherwise lawful and orderly meetings of the Communist Party constituted, as to them, a sufficient "overt Act" to warrant a conspiracy conviction.[140] Mr. Justice Black hinted at the problem of association involved when he noted[141] the apparent contradiction between this ruling, attaching a species of criminal liability to mere attendance at a lawful meeting, and *DeJonge v. Oregon.*[142]

The *Yates* decision, coupled with that in *Jencks v. United States,*[143] effectively halted prosecutions under the conspiracy provisions of the Smith Act.[144] However, there were pending at that time eight cases[145] charging violations of the membership provisions of the Smith Act, which rendered it unlawful "to be, or become a member of, or affiliate with, any such society, group, or assembly of persons, knowing the purposes thereof."[146] Two of those finally did receive a definitive treatment by the Supreme Court. From them, if we bear in mind the developments already discussed, we can gain a fair understanding of the role of freedom of association as an instrument

[135] "Neither the holding of office nor membership in any Communist organization by any person shall constitute per se a violation of . . . this section or of any other criminal statute." 64 Stat. 987, 50 U.S.C. Sec. 783(f).

[136] 354 U.S. at 330.

[137] 18 U.S.C. Sec. 371.

[138] See 354 U.S. at 301.

[139] 354 U.S. at 334.

[140] 354 U.S. at 333–34.

[141] 354 U.S. at 342–43.

[142] 299 U.S. 353, 364, 365 (1937); supra p. 132.

[143] 353 U.S. 657 (1957) (holding that defendant has a right to inspect and use, on cross-examination of prosecution witnesses, statements made by those witnesses to the FBI concerning matters about which the witnesses had testified at the trial). See 71 Stat. 595 (1957), limiting the Jencks decision; 18 U.S.C. Sec. 3500; for legislative history, see 1957 U.S. Cong. & Ad. News, 1861.

[144] For enumeration and disposition of cases pending at time of Yates see Emerson and Haber, Political and Civil Rights in the United States 390–92 (Buffalo, 1958).

[145] For enumeration and disposition see Emerson and Haber, Political and Civil Rights in the United States 391–92 (Buffalo, 1958).

[146] 18 U.S.C. Sec. 2385.

for the evaluation of the right to join the Communist Party. In *Scales v. United States,*[147] the court first rejected the contention that section 4(f) of the Internal Security Act of 1950[148] repealed the membership clause of the Smith Act. Rather, the purpose of Section 4(f) is purely "clarifying,"[149] emphasizing that mere Communist Party membership is not of itself a crime. The Smith Act thereby requires "not only knowing membership, but active and purposive membership, purposive that is as to the organization's criminal ends."[150]

The defendant in Scales next assailed the membership provision as simply invalid on its face, since it offends:

> . . . (1) the Fifth Amendment [Defendant relied upon the due process clause of the Fifth Amendment], in that it impermissibly imputes guilt to an individual merely on the basis of his associations and sympathies, rather than because of some concrete personal involvement in criminal conduct; and (2) the First Amendment, in that it infringes on free political expression and association."[151]

Defendant further asserted that the statute failed to require a specific intent to accomplish violent overthrow, failed to require that membership be "active," and was impermissibly vague in punishing the act of being a "member."[152] The court rejected these contentions as a matter of statutory interpretation, advancing the *Dennis* decision[153] as an additional ground for the requirement of specific intent.[154]

The majority of the court, through Mr. Justice Harlan, also rejected the assertions that the restriction by the statute on freedom of association violated the First Amendment or the due-process clause of the Fifth Amendment. The distinction between the associational problems involved in the Smith Act and the similar elements in the law of criminal conspiracy was strongly emphasized by the court:

> Any thought that due process puts beyond the reach of the criminal law all individual associational relationships, unless accompanied by

[147] 367 U.S. 203 (1961).
[148] "Neither the holding of office nor membership in any Communist organization by any person shall constitute per se a violation of . . . this section or of any other criminal statute. . . ." 64 Stat. 987, 50 U.S.C. Sec. 783(f).
[149] 367 U.S. at 217.
[150] 367 U.S. at 209. See similar holding in Yates v. United States, supra p. 141.
[151] 367 U.S. at 220.
[152] 367 U.S. at 220–21.
[153] Supra p. 139.
[154] 367 U.S. at 221–22.

the commission of specific acts of criminality, is dispelled by familiar concepts of the law of conspiracy and complicity. . . . The fact that Congress has not resorted to either of these familiar concepts means only that the enquiry here must direct itself to an analysis of the relationship between the fact of membership and the underlying substantive illegal conduct. . . . In this instance it is an organization which engages in criminal activity, and we can perceive no reason why one who actively and knowingly works in the ranks of that organization, intending to contribute to the success of those specifically illegal activities, should be any more immune from prosecution than he to whom the organization has assigned the task of carrying out the substantive criminal act. Nor should the fact that Congress has focused here on "membership" . . . of itself require the conclusion that the legislature has traveled outside the familiar and permissible bounds of criminal imputability. In truth, the specificity of the proscribed relationship is not necessarily a vice; it provides instruction and warning.[155]

In short, the court upheld the proscription of "membership" because it reached "only 'active' members having also a guilty knowledge and intent," thereby preventing "a conviction on what otherwise might be regarded as merely an expression of sympathy with the alleged criminal enterprise, unaccompanied by any significant action in its support or any commitment to undertake such action."[156] But there is a deeper associational issue, arising from the fact that a subversive association such as the Communist Party usually engages in some activities which are not in themselves unlawful,[157] whereas the traditional criminal conspiracy does not. What, then, is to be done with the individual who knows of the unlawful purpose of the Party, but does not himself intend to effect that purpose and desires only to engage in activities of the Party which are not unlawful as such? The court attempted to answer this question:

It is, of course, true that quasi-political parties or other groups that may embrace both legal and illegal aims differ from a technical conspiracy, which is defined by its criminal purpose, so that all knowing association with the conspiracy is a proper subject for criminal proscription as far as First Amendment liberties are concerned. If there were a

[155] 367 U.S. at 225–27.

[156] 367 U.S. at 228.

[157] The Party, for example, sometimes conducts social activities for its members. See, Internal Security Subcommittee of Senate Committee on the Judiciary, Report, The Communist Party of the United States of America 46 (84th Cong., 1st Sess., 1955).

similar blanket prohibition of association with a group having both legal and illegal aims, there would indeed be a real danger that legitimate political expression or association would be impaired, but the membership clause, as here construed, does not cut deeper into the freedom of association than is necessary to deal with "the substantive evils that Congress has a right to prevent." *Schenck v. United States*, 249 U.S. 47, 52. The clause does not make criminal all association with an organization, which has been shown to engage in illegal advocacy. There must be clear proof that a defendant "specifically intend(s) to accomplish [the aims of the organization] by resort to violence." *Noto v. United States*. . . . Thus the member for whom the organization is a vehicle for the advancement of legitimate aims and policies does not fall within the ban of the statute: he lacks the requisite specific intent "to bring about the overthrow of the government as speedily as circumstances would permit." Such a person may be foolish, deluded, or perhaps merely optimistic, but he is not by this statute made a criminal.[158]

Seemingly, this test would exculpate one who, though aware of the invidious purpose and activities of the Party, believed that it worked also to alleviate harmful social imbalances, believed that its activity in this regard was good and separable from its harmful work, and intended to promote only that good end by his membership. The problem of proof in this connection is formidable. The court's analysis and the explicit language of Section 4(f) of the Internal Security Act of 1950 [159] would prevent a deduction, from the mere fact of membership, that such a member possessed the requisite guilty knowledge and intent. In *Scales* and the companion case of *Noto v. United States*,[160] the court reviewed the evidence on the record to determine what proof would suffice to justify a finding of that knowledge and intent. This problem has two aspects. First, it must be shown that the Party as such advocates the unlawful, forcible overthrow of the government. Secondly, it must be shown that the defendant is implicated therein by having the necessary knowledge and intent. The first question involves the ascertainment of the component parts of the proscribed advocacy, whether such advocacy has been made, and whether the advocacy is imputable to the Party. Building upon the preceding cases, the court in *Scales* discussed the nature of the forbidden advocacy:

[158] 367 U.S. at 229–30.
[159] Supra p. 142.
[160] 367 U.S. at 290 (1961).

Dennis and Yates have definitely laid at rest any doubt but that present advocacy of future action for violent overthrow satisfies statutory and constitutional requirements equally with advocacy of immediate action to that end. 341 U.S., at 509; 354 U.S., at 321. Hence this record cannot be considered deficient because it contains no evidence of advocacy for immediate overthrow.[161]

As to the actual ingredients of the proscribed advocacy, the *Scales* court, again building upon *Yates*, held that at least two concrete types of advocacy are punishable:

. . . (a) the teaching of forceful overthrow, accompanied by directions as to the type of illegal action which must be taken when the time for the revolution is reached; and (b) the teaching of forceful overthrow, accompanied by a contemporary, though legal, course of conduct clearly undertaken for the specific purpose of rendering effective the later illegal activity which is advocated.[162]

The court then upheld the finding that there was in the case before it such advocacy of "the doctrine of violent revolution . . . as a guide to future action. . . ." [163] The imputability of the advocacy to the Party was established through "the testimony of the witnesses . . . indicating a sufficiently systematic and substantial course of utterances and conduct on the part of those high in the councils of the Party, including the petitioner himself. . . ." Such was sufficient "to entitle the jury to infer that these activities reflected tenets of the Party." [164]

Having upheld the findings of illegal advocacy, and of Party responsibility therefor, the *Scales* court went on to affirm the findings that the defendant had the requisite knowledge and specific intent, apparently basing the conclusion upon the active and pervasive character of defendant's participation as a member of the Party.[165]

One significant thing about the *Noto* decision is the insistence by a unanimous court that the determination of whether the Party engages in illegal advocacy of action must be made only on the basis of the evidence in the record of the instant case, "and not upon the evidence in some other record or upon what may be supposed to be the tenets of the Communist Party." [166] This result seems to accord with the *Dennis* [167] and *Yates* decisions.[168] It does, however,

[161] 367 U.S. at 251.
[162] 367 U.S. at 234.
[163] 367 U.S. at 253.
[164] 367 U.S. at 254.
[165] 367 U.S. at 254–55.
[166] 367 U.S. at 299.
[167] 341 U.S. at 512–13.
[168] 354 U.S. at 329–30.

overlook the technique of judicial notice, which was employed in *People ex rel. Bryant v. Zimmerman*[169] to support the legislative determination that the Ku Klux Klan ought to be required to disclose its membership. Where the *Zimmerman* court stood ready to notice, without formal proof, the nature and purposes of the Ku Klux Klan, the court today has regularly required that the nature and purposes of the Communist Party must be proved in each case. The result is that if two members of the Communist Party are prosecuted under the Smith Act in separate trials, and the evidence in each case clearly shows that each defendant is possessed of the necessary knowledge and intent, one may be convicted and one may be acquitted because of variances in the proofs on the common issue of whether the Party as such is engaged in unlawful advocacy. Such a situation was nearly presented in the *Scales* and *Noto* cases. The conviction of Noto was reversed because the Party was not shown, on the record, to be engaged in illegal advocacy.[170] In fact, the proof of his own knowledge and intent was also lacking, so that there could have been no conviction even if the Party's advocacy had been proven.[171] But if Noto's knowledge and intent had been sufficiently shown, Scales would have been punished while Noto would have been freed, because of a variance in proof of a common issue. This analysis, of course, assumes that the different units of the Party in which the defendants were members were both engaged in unlawful advocacy. (Scales was active in the Party in North Carolina; Noto in New York.) It may be undesirable on this last point to notice judicially the nature and purpose of, say, the North Carolina branch of the Party, even though it may be feasible to notice the nature and purpose of the Party as a whole. Even if the national character of the Party should, in some future case, be judicially noticed, it would seem necessary to have some actual proof on the record as to the "conspiratorial-nexus"[172] between the local branch and the national Party. If such connecting proof were lacking, then judicial notice of the illegal advocacy of the local branch would come close to the proscription by name alone which was properly rejected in *Communist Party v. Peek*.[173] With this qualification, it would not appear unreasonable for the court to notice judicially the general nature and purpose of the

[169] 278 U.S. 63 (1928).
[170] 367 U.S. at 299.
[171] Ibid.
[172] 367 U.S. at 231.
[173] 20 Calif. 2d 536, 127 P.2d 889 (1942).

Communist Party of the United States of America. The Supreme Court has often judicially noticed facts of historical, political and general notoriety.[174] As long as the notice is not conclusive, and may be rebutted by proof that the Party is not engaged in illegal advocacy, the rights of the defendant would be preserved and the result would be a conservation of much time otherwise involved in the presentation of the prosecution's case.[175] The fact that the Communist Party nationally advocates, as a rule of action, the overthrow of the government by force and violence ought to be at least as evident as the fact that the Ku Klux Klan promotes hateful activities.[176] This conclusion draws support from the Congressional declarations as to the nature of Communism and the Party.[177]

In view of the complex associational problems presented by the membership clause of the Smith Act, it is regrettable that the latitudinarian opinions of Justices Black, Douglas, and Brennan [178] in the *Scales* and *Noto* cases did not advert to them with great particularity. Mr. Justice Douglas, however, in his *Scales* dissent, did touch upon the perplexity of punishing a man for his associations, however active they may be:

[174] See Sweezy v. New Hampshire, 354 U.S. 234, 266 (1957) (Separate opinion of Justices Frankfurter and Harlan; Court may take notice of historical facts in deciding whether it is reasonable to regard a political party as not a conventional party); Ohio Bell Tel. Co. v. Public Util. Comm'n 301 U.S. 292 (1937) (general economic depression); Daniels v. Tearney, 102 U.S. 415 (1880) (circumstances surrounding adoption of secession ordinance); Neely v. Henkel, 180 U.S. 109 (1901) (United States occupation and control of Cuba in 1900).

[175] "That a matter is judicially noticed means merely that it is taken as true without the offering of evidence by the party who should ordinarily have done so. This is because the court assumes that the matter is so notorious that it will not be disputed. But the opponent is not prevented from disputing the matter by evidence, if he believes it disputable." Wigmore, Evidence, Sec. 2567 (Boston, 1940); see also Morgan, Judicial Notice, 57 Harv. L. Rev. 269, 279–80 (1944); United States v. Aluminum Co. of America, 148 F.2d 416, 446 (2d Cir., 1945).

[176] The literature published by the United States Government itself on the nature and purposes of the Communist movement and the Communist Party is voluminous. See, e.g., United States Department of State, Soviet World Outlook—a Handbook of Communist Statements (Washington, D.C., Govt. Printing Office, 1959); Internal Security Subcommittee, Senate Committee on the Judiciary, The Communist Party of the United States of America (84th Cong., 1st Sess., 1955); Committee on Un-American Activities, House of Representatives, The Communist Conspiracy: Marxist Classics (84th Cong., 2d Sess., 1956).

[177] See Sec. 2 of the Internal Security Act of 1950, 64 Stat. 987, 50 U.S.C., Sec. 781 et seq.; Sec. 2 of the Communist Control Act of 1954, 68 Stat. 775, 50 U.S.C., Sec. 841 ("The Congress hereby finds and declares that the Communist Party of the United States, although purportedly a political party, is in fact an instrumentality of a conspiracy to overthrow the Government of the United States.")

[178] The Chief Justice joined in Mr. Justice Brennan's dissent in Scales and joined in the latter's concurring statement in Noto.

We legalize today guilt by association, sending a man to prison when he committed no unlawful[179] act. Today's break with tradition is a serious one. It borrows from the totalitarian philosophy. . . .

The case is not saved by showing that petitioner was an active member. None of the activity constitutes a crime. . . .

Not one single illegal act is charged to petitioner. That is why the essence of the crime covered by the indictment is merely belief—belief in the proletarian revolution, belief in Communist creed.[180]

In this extract, Mr. Justice Douglas has adverted to a critical reality of our day. In the face of a massive conspiratorial, foreign-directed, Communist drive, employing the guise of legitimate association, the traditional concepts of individual substantive guilt are no longer adequate. Even the idea of ordinary conspiracy, with its meticulous emphasis upon the overt act and individual complicity, cannot entirely deal with a "conspiracy" which works, for the time being, at advocacy and planning only, and which would really act overtly only at a time when the hour for normal legal sanctions had, by definition, passed irrevocably. It is to fill this void and to deal with this novel problem that the concept of culpable association has been developed. Some, such as Justice Douglas, have sought to adhere strictly to the traditional measures of guilt. Their reluctance is a measure of their adherence to their conceptions of free expression and free association. Others have resisted the Smith Act and similar statutes by invoking a blanket interdiction against "guilt by association."[181] But these solutions appear to avoid the question whether the act of association has indeed taken on a quality which it heretofore lacked, wherein, although it cannot be the sole component of guilt, it may, in the context of Communism, further the unlawful combination so greatly that it merits punishment as fully as does the traditional act of conspiracy. At least this is credible where the necessary knowledge and intent are present, as outlined in the *Scales* majority opinion.

In addition to the membership prohibition of the Smith Act, there

[179] Mr. Justice Douglas does not consider the defendant's act of associating to be unlawful. The majority of the court considers this in itself to be an unlawful act if performed with the requisite knowledge and intent.

[180] 367 U.S. at 263–65.

[181] See O'Brian, National Security and Individual Freedom 27–28 (Cambridge, 1955).

are other Federal and state laws [182] which purport to punish membership in Communist associations. Some are striking in the amplitude of their proscriptions and terminology. For example, Section 4(a) of the Internal Security Act of 1950 provides:

> It shall be unlawful for any person knowingly to combine, conspire, or agree with any other person to perform any act which would substantially contribute to the establishment within the United States of a totalitarian dictatorship . . . the direction and control of which is to be vested in, or exercised by or under the domination or control of, any foreign government, foreign organization, or foreign individual: Provided, however, that this subsection shall not apply to the proposal of a constitutional amendment.[183]

The "totalitarian dictatorship" mentioned in this section is defined in section 3(15) of the act as a system of government:

> . . . not representative in fact, characterized by (A) the existence of a single political party, organized on a dictatorial basis, with so close an identity between such party and its policies and the governmental policies of the country in which it exists, that the party and the government constitute an indistinguishable unit, and (B) the forcible suppression of opposition to such party.[184]

There have been no prosecutions under section 4(a),[185] and the judicial reluctance, discussed above, to interfere with the right of association (whether it is a constitutional right or not), except insofar as absolutely necessary, renders it doubtful that such a prosecution would be attended with success upon review by the Supreme Court. Nor would the reservation in section 1(b) of the act, that nothing therein shall be construed "in any way to limit or infringe upon freedom of the press or of speech as guaranteed by the Constitution of the United States . . ." [186] insure the validity of the broad statutory standard.[187]

[182] For the state laws, see Fund for the Republic, Digest of the Public Record of Communism in the United States (New York, 1955). On the issue of Federal preemption, see Pennsylvania v. Nelson, 350 U.S. 497 (1956); Uphaus v. Wyman, 360 U.S. 72 (1959).

[183] 50 U.S.C. Sec. 783(a).

[184] 50 U.S.C. Sec. 782(15).

[185] See Emerson and Haber, Political and Civil Rights in the United States 414 (Buffalo, 1958). In Cramp v. Board of Public Instruction, 368 U.S. 278 (1961), the Court invalidated for vagueness a Florida statute requiring every state employee to swear that, among other things, he has never lent his "aid, support, advice, counsel, or influence to the Communist Party."

[186] 50 U.S.C. Sec. 798.

[187] See note, The Internal Security Act of 1950, 51 Colum. L. Rev. 606 (1951).

It may safely be said that any statute which imposes criminal penalties upon the act of associating with the Communist Party will be subject to the qualifications as to knowledge and specific intent which have evolved out of the many cases from the post-World War I period to the *Scales* and *Noto* decisions. These qualifications would seem to apply where the penalty is for failing to disclose membership as well as where it is upon the act of membership itself.[188]

2. *Civil and Quasicriminal Penalties Imposed upon Members of the Communist Party*

In addition to his liability to criminal penalty, we must be interested, in a chronicle of freedom of association, in a member's susceptibility to civil or quasi-criminal disabilities as a result of his membership in an association stigmatized as subversive. No such association has drawn upon its members more potential and actual disabilities than the Communist Party. Indeed, the restrictions are so extensive and so varied that it is difficult to formulate any workable general rule as to the necessity of knowledge or intent on the part of the member. One device which has been employed is that of compulsory registration of the association with a public official, and an attendant publicity of its membership lists. Immediately, this evokes a recollection of the Ku Klux Klan [189] and the National Association for the Advancement of Colored People, two prominent targets of such legislation.[190] The Communist Party, however, requires a somewhat novel analysis.[191]

Section 7(a) of the Internal Security Act of 1950 [192] requires registration with the Attorney General of all "Communist-action" organi-

[188] Sec. 5 of the Internal Security Act of 1950 (50 U.S.C. Sec. 784), penalizing such nondisclosure by public or defense employees, requires knowledge or notice that the association is registered as a Communist organization, and it has been upheld. Communist Party of the U.S.A. v. SACB, 223 F.2d 531 (Dist. Col., 1955), rev'd. on other grounds, 351 U.S. 115 (1956); see Communist Party v. SACB, 367 U.S. 1 (1961).

[189] Supra pp. 133 et seq.

[190] Supra pp. 112 et seq.

[191] Congress, in the Internal Security Act of 1950, made an extensive declaration of the nature and purposes of the Communist movement. 50 U.S.C., Sec. 782. A similar declaration about the Communist Party itself was made in the Communist Control Act of 1954. 50 U.S.C. Sec. 841.

[192] 50 U.S.C. Sec. 786, as amended by the Communist Control Act of 1954, 68 Stat. 775.

zations.[193] Such an organization must divulge, among other things, the identity of each person who was a member at any time during the preceding twelve months.[194] "Communist-front" organizations [195] are also required to register, but need not divulge the names of non-officer members. The Subversive Activities Control Board is authorized to determine which organizations are "Communist-action" or "Communist-front" and therefore required to register, and whether an individual is a member of a "Communist-action organization." [196] By the Communist Control Act of 1954,[197] the board was also empowered to determine "whether any organization is a Communist-infiltrated organization." [198] Such "infiltrated" associations are not required to register, but must label appropriately their mail and broadcasts, and are denied some tax exemptions, privileges under the National Labor Relations Act, and other privileges.[199]

This arsenal of legal weapons was brought to bear upon the Communist Party when the Attorney General, on November 22, 1950, filed a petition with the Subversive Activities Control Board to compel the Party to register as a "Communist-action organization." [200]

[193] A "Communist-action organization" is one, other than a diplomatic mission, "(a) . . . which (i) is substantially directed, dominated, or controlled by the foreign government or foreign organization controlling the world Communist movement . . . , and (ii) operates primarily to advance the objectives of such world Communist movement . . . ; and (b) any section, branch, fraction, or cell of any organization defined in subparagraph (a) . . . which has not complied with the registration requirements of this subchapter." 50 U.S.C. Sec. 782(3).

[194] 50 U.S.C. Sec. 786(d)(4).

[195] Defined as "any organization in the United States (other than a Communist-action organization) which (A) is substantially directed, dominated, or controlled by a Communist-action organization, and (B) is primarily operated for the purpose of giving aid and support to a Communist-action organization, a Communist foreign government, or the world Communist movement. . . ." 50 U.S.C. Sec. 782(4).

[196] 50 U.S.C. Sec. 791(e).

[197] 68 Stat. 778.

[198] 50 U.S.C. Sec. 791(e)(3).

[199] See 50 U.S.C. Secs. 789, 790. A "Communist-infiltrated organization" is broadly defined as: ". . . any organization in the United States (other than a Communist-action organization or a Communist-front organization) which (A) is substantially directed, dominated, or controlled by an individual or individuals who are, or who within three years have been actively engaged in, giving aid or support to a Communist-action organization, a Communist foreign government, or the world Communist movement . . . , and (B) is serving, or within three years has served, as a means for (i) the giving of aid or support to any such organization, government, or movement, or (ii) the impairment of the military strength of the United States or its industrial capacity to furnish logistical or other material support required by its armed forces. . . ." 50 U.S.C. Sec. 782.

[200] New York Times, Nov. 23, 1950.

After exhaustive procedural maneuvering,[201] the board's order directing the Party to register was upheld on the merits by the Supreme Court.[202] The only question before the court was the obligation of the Party to register. The various disabilities imposed by the Internal Security Act and other statutes [203] on the association and its members were not at issue.[204] (The constitutionality of those strictures may be determined at a later date.) The Party was not prevented, however, from asserting the rights of its members, such as anonymity, which it alleged were infringed by the very act of registration by the Party.[205] Likening the registration provisions of the act to the registration requirements of the Public Utility Holding Company Act of 1935,[206] the court rejected numerous constitutional objections, including ones based upon the First Amendment freedoms of expression and association.

Significantly for the distinction we have intimated hereinbefore, that nonpenal disabilities may be imposed upon members of a subversive association without such rigorous standards of knowledge and intent as are needed for the imposition of penal sanctions, the court emphasized the merely regulatory nature of the registration requirements.[207] Mr. Justice Frankfurter, for the five-member majority, said that an organization may be found to advance the unlawful objectives defined by the act, and therefore may be required to register ". . . although it does not incite the present use of force. Nor does the First Amendment compel any other construction. The Subversive Activities Control Act is a regulatory, not a prohibitory statute. It does not make unlawful pursuit of the objectives" which

[201] See Communist Party v. SACB, 351 U.S. 115 (1956); Emerson & Haber, Political and Civil Rights in the United States 415–19 (Buffalo, 1958).

[202] Communist Party v. SACB, 367 U.S. 1 (1961).

[203] See, for example, 8 U.S.C. Secs. 1182, 1251, 1424, 1451 (immigration and naturalization restrictions); 42 U.S.C. Sec. 410 (ineligibility of employees of association for Social Security); 50 U.S.C. Secs. 811 et seq. (possible detention during "internal security emergency.")

[204] 367 U.S. at 77–79, 103–104.

[205] Accord: NAACP v. Alabama, 357 U.S. 449 (1958); Bates v. Little Rock, 361 U.S. 516 (1960).

[206] 49 Stat. 803; Electric Bond & Share Co. v. Securities & Exch. Comm'n, 303 U.S. 419 (1938).

[207] The assertion by the majority that the registration requirement is merely regulatory and not penal was flatly challenged by the Chief Justice, who argued therefrom in his dissent that a stricter standard should govern the question of whether the Party is engaged in illegal advocacy. 367 U.S. at 132–33. The same challenge was made at least inferentially by the other dissenters.

it defines.[208] Since the issue of a member's personal liability to further civil disabilities, upon disclosure of his membership, was not before the court, this holding is not authority for the proposition that such disabilities can be imposed regardless of the member's knowledge or intent. It is, however, a holding that the member may be subjected to the disability, if it be such, of having his membership disclosed, irrespective of his knowledge or intent. The act requires that a Communist-action organization disclose the names of all members, and not merely those with specified knowledge or intent.[209]

The court upheld the finding by the board that the Party is under the substantial direction, domination, or control of the foreign Communist apparatus.[210] Rejecting the Party's contention that the foreign control required by section 3(3) of the act [211] must be no less than the fact that the foreign government or foreign organization controlling the world Communist movement exercises over the Party in this country "an enforceable, coercive power to exact compliance with its demands," [212] the court held:

> The subjection to foreign direction, domination, or control . . . is a disposition unerringly to follow the dictates of a designated foreign country or foreign organization, not by the exercise of independent judgment on the intrinsic appeal that those dictates carry, but for the reason that they emanate from that country or organization.[213]

In addition to thus finding foreign control through "voluntary compliance as well as through compulsion," [214] the court held that the second requirement of the definition of a "Communist-action organization," namely that the organization "operates primarily to advance the objectives of [the] world Communist movement," [215] was satisfied by the Party's advocacy of forcible overthrow of the government, "although it does not incite the present use of force." [216] This conclusion was reinforced by the regulatory and nonprohibitory nature of the act.

The First Amendment issues of free expression and association were among those raised by the Party. Declaring that "to preserve its independence, and give security against foreign aggression and encroachment, is the highest duty of every nation," [217] Mr. Justice

[208] 367 U.S. at 56. The Subversive Activities Control Act is Title I of the Internal Security Act of 1950.
[209] 50 U.S.C. Sec. 786.
[210] 367 U.S. at 36–55.
[211] Supra note 193, at 152.
[212] 367 U.S. at 36.
[213] 367 U.S. at 39–40.
[214] 367 U.S. at 42.
[215] 50 U.S.C., Sec. 782(3).
[216] 367 U.S. at 56.
[217] 367 U.S. at 96.

Frankfurter, for the majority, sought to balance that public interest against the individual interest:

> Against the impediments which particular governmental regulation causes to entire freedom of individual action, there must be weighed the value to the public of the ends which the regulation may achieve.[218]

The court distinguished the impermissible registration requirements imposed by some states upon the National Association for the Advancement of Colored People,[219] by reference to the "magnitude of the public interests which the registration and disclosure provisions are designed to protect, and . . . the pertinence which registration and disclosure bear to the protection of those interests."[220] As in the New York regulation of the Ku Klux Klan[221] and the Federal lobbying and corrupt practices legislation,[222] "secrecy of associations and organizations, even among groups concerned exclusively with political processes, may under some circumstances constitute a danger which legislatures do not lack constitutional power to curb."[223] In upholding the forfeiture of the Party member's right to privacy of association, the court epitomized the inherent vulnerability of the putative freedom of subversive association:

> Where the mask of anonymity which an organization's members wear serves the double purpose of protecting them from popular prejudice and of enabling them to cover over a foreign-directed conspiracy, infiltrate into other groups, and enlist the support of persons who would not, if the truth were revealed, lend their support . . . it would be a distortion of the First Amendment to hold that it prohibits Congress from removing the mask.[224]

Two of the dissenting opinions in *Communist Party v. Subversive Activities Control Board* are especially significant from the standpoint of freedom of association. Mr. Justice Black emphasized that: "The freedom to advocate ideas about public matters through associations of the nature of political parties and societies was con-

[218] 367 U.S. at 91.
[219] Supra pp. 113 et seq.
[220] 367 U.S. at 93.
[221] People ex rel. Bryant v. Zimmerman, supra note 92, p. 134.
[222] United States v. Harriss, 347 U.S. 612 (1954); Burroughs v. United States, 290 U.S. 534 (1934).
[223] 367 U.S. at 101.
[224] 367 U.S. at 102–103.

templated and protected by the First Amendment."[225] Drawing a parallel between the Internal Security Act of 1950 and the Alien and Sedition Laws of 1798, Mr. Justice Black went on to find the 1950 Act, and the Smith Act as well, even more oppressive than the latter.[226] The Black opinion characteristically rejected the "balancing" technique employed by the majority[227] and offered, as an alternative to repression of associations advocating subversive doctrines, an unqualified reliance upon the efficacy of free discussion and persuasion:

> Talk about the desirability of revolution has a long and honorable history, not only in other parts of the world, but in our own country. This kind of talk, like any other, can be used at the wrong time and for the wrong purpose. But under our system of Government, the remedy for this danger must be the same remedy that is applied to the danger that comes from any other erroneous talk—education and contrary argument. If that remedy is not sufficient, the only meaning of free speech must be that the revolutionary ideas will be allowed to prevail.[228]

The last quoted sentence conjures up an image of a society helpless, but for the force of persuasion, before the attacks of the Communist conspiracy. But it is essential to remember Mr. Justice Black's unspoken premise that the act is a regulation only of persuasion and advocacy, that is, only of speech.[229] If we grant that assumption, he may well be logically correct in denying the government the power to compel registration by a group which, by the assumed premise, is merely a sort of debating society[230] composed of "governmental critics."[231] The basic premise, however, is unrealistic in today's world. A preferable analysis, it would appear, is that of Mr. Justice Douglas, who, in his dissent, found that the advocacy by the Party was more than merely speech and that, as in the case of picketing, it was not totally immune from infringement. The collateral aspect here, which justifies the restriction, is foreign control:

> If lobbyists can be required to register, if political parties can be required to make disclosure of the sources of their funds, if the owners

[225] 367 U.S. at 148; see also dissenting opinion of Mr. Justice Douglas, 367 U.S. at 171.

[226] 367 U.S. at 159–60.

[227] 367 U.S. at 164.

[228] 367 U.S. at 147–48.

[229] See 367 U.S. at 147–49.

[230] See 367 U.S. at 153.

[231] See 367 U.S. at 164.

of newspapers and periodicals must disclose their affiliates, so may a group operating under the control of a foreign power.[232]

In this passage, Mr. Justice Douglas is touching upon one of the unifying principles of freedom of association as applied to the various types of groups we have discussed. It is not an absolute freedom, even if it is considered to be of constitutional rank. It is properly amenable to necessary and rational restriction based upon a judicious balancing of interests. Nor can the act of associating be insulated from regulation by the fact that the association engages in speech. In each case, it cannot be said to be beyond the power of the legislature to impose a necessary and reasonable regulation tailored to the underlying nature, purpose and activity of the association. Whether the group is a lobby, a labor union, a religious organization,[233] a political party or a subversive group, the particular interests of the partial association and its members do not enjoy an infrangible primacy over the general interests of society. Therefore, in dealing with a subversive association, the government is not limited by freedom of association to the noncoercive weapons of counterargument and persuasion.

The four dissenters (Mr. Justice Brennan, joined by the Chief Justice, and Justices Black and Douglas) all were of the opinion that the registration provisions violated the privilege against self-incrimination. It is not within the scope of this work to examine this aspect of the matter. Our concern is with the newly recognized freedom of association. It need hardly be said that the individual, in exercising his right to associate, does not thereby abandon the rights, some at least as fundamental as freedom of association, which are similarly protected by the Constitution. But it would be an undue extension of the scope of this inquiry to examine whether, in the case of the Communist Party, the registration device is being invalidly "used as a mechanism for compulsory disclosure of criminal activities." [234]

[232] 367 U.S. at 174. Mr. Justice Brennan, joined by the Chief Justice, agreed with the court and Mr. Justice Douglas that the registration requirement "is not constitutionally invalid as an invasion of the rights of freedom of advocacy and association guaranteed by the First Amendment to Communists as well as to all others." 367 U.S. at 191.

[233] The regulatory power here is narrower due to the express dictates of the First Amendment.

[234] Dissent of Mr. Justice Douglas, 367 U.S. at 183–84.

From the various opinions in the *Dennis, Yates, Scales,* and *Noto* cases, we have gained an idea of why the Communist Party is considered a subversive association[235] and what kind of participation therein will subject a member to criminal sanctions. In the opinions in *Communist Party v. Subversive Activities Control Board,* the necessary characteristics of a subversive association were more sharply delineated, and the court affirmed that Congress possesses a greater latitude in prescribing merely regulatory, and not prohibitory, restrictions. There was, of course, a sharp divergence[236] as to whether the registration requirement at issue was regulatory or penal. But we may still draw the conclusion that some nonpenal disabilities, at least the disability of having his membership disclosed, may be imposed upon a member by a statute with a reasonable relation to a valid legislative purpose, without a showing that the member possesses any knowledge of the unlawful purpose of the association or intent to effectuate it. That such imposition of civil disabilities without culpable knowledge and intent was the purpose of Congress may be seen from other provisions of the Internal Security Act of 1950. A member of an association which is registered or ordered to register need only have knowledge of that fact in order to be barred from government or defense employment and from obtaining a passport.[237] An attempt to obtain such employment or passport by a member with such knowledge is punishable as a crime.[238] It remains to be seen whether any criminal intent beyond this mere knowledge will be necessary for such a conviction.[239]

The Communist Party was, in effect, legislatively declared to be a "Communist-action organization" by the Communist Control Act of 1954:

> (a) Whoever knowingly and willfully becomes or remains a member of (1) the Communist Party, or (2) any other organization having for one of its purposes the . . . overthrow of the Government . . . by the use of force or violence, with knowledge of the purpose or objective

[235] Within our narrow definition; see above, p. 121.

[236] For example, between Mr. Justice Frankfurter and the Chief Justice. On the philosophical differences among the members of the court, see Lewis, A New Line-up on the Supreme Court, The Reporter, August 17, 1961; but see the Letter to the Editor by Mr. Justice Douglas in The Reporter, Sept. 14, 1961.

[237] 50 U.S.C. Secs. 784, 785.

[238] 50 U.S.C. Sec. 794(c).

[239] Compare 50 U.S.C. Sec. 794(b), punishing the making of a false registration statement, if made "willfully."

of such organization shall be subject to all the provisions and penalties of the Internal Security Act of 1950, as amended as a member of a "Communist-action" organization.

(b) For the purposes of this section, the term "Communist Party" means the organization now known as the Communist Party of the United States of America, the Communist Party of any State or subdivision thereof, and any unit or subdivision of any such organization, whether or not any change is hereafter made in the name thereof.[240]

While the bill of attainder problem involved here is notable,[241] this provision arguably does require the elements of knowledge, intent and even willfulness before the member may be subjected to even the civil penalties of the Internal Security Act. However, this section effectively sidesteps the declaratory function of the Subversive Activities Control Board and legislatively subjects the member to penal and civil sanctions without recourse to the registration machinery. This factor may explain the apparent requirement of willful personal participation.

There are other areas in which an individual's membership in a subversive association may subject him to disabilities irrespective of his personal culpability. From the unlimited power of Congress to exclude aliens,[242] it follows that Congress can exclude an alien on the basis of his subversive activities or associations.[243] By the Immigration and Nationality Act of 1952,[244] members or affiliates of any American or foreign Communist or totalitarian party are among those excluded.[245] The same classes are also made liable to deportation.[246] Exemption from exclusion or deportation is conferred if the alien shows that his membership was involuntary, or while he was less than sixteen years of age, or by operation of law, or that the membership has been terminated for five years and the alien has, throughout that time, opposed the tenets of the proscribed organization, and that his admission is in the public interest.[247] Unlike earlier sta-

[240] 50 U.S.C. Sec. 843.

[241] See United States v. Lovett, 328 U.S. 303 (1946).

[242] Head Money Cases, 112 U.S. 580 (1884).

[243] See Turner v. Williams, 194 U.S. 279 (1904).

[244] 66 Stat. 163; 8 U.S.C. Sec. 1101–1503.

[245] 8 U.S.C. Sec. 1182(A)(28); the visa restrictions are similar, 8 U.S.C. Sec. 1182(a).

[246] 8 U.S.C. Sec. 1251; The power of Congress to exclude aliens is subject to fewer limitations than the power to deport. See Ng Fung Ho v. White, 259 U.S. 276 (1922); United States ex Rel. Knauff v. Shaughnessy, 338 U.S. 537, 544 (1950); Yamataya v. Fisher, 189 U.S. 86 (1903).

[247] 8 U.S.C. Sec. 1182(A)(28)(I).

tutes,[248] the present law does not require that the alleged membership exist at the time of exclusion or arrest. In view of Congress' plenary power in the premises, this is constitutional.[249] Furthermore, the statute does not require, on the part of the member, "support, or even demonstrated knowledge, of the Communist Party's advocacy of violence. . . . It is enough that the alien joined the Party, aware that he was joining an organization known as the Communist Party, which operates as a distinct and active political organization, and that he did so of his own free will." [250] There is room, however, for a showing by the alien that his membership was so innocent, nominal, and lacking in "meaningful association" that he ought not to be subjected to deportation.[251] The protection afforded to the alien by this judicial exception is slight and of uncertain extent, since the burden of establishing the innocence of his membership appears to be a heavy one.[252]

An individual's membership in a subversive association may constitute a bar to naturalization [253] or a ground for denaturalization.[254] But where the issue is citizenship, and not merely admission or exclusion, it appears that the membership requirement will be strictly construed, so that the member will not be penalized unless he were aware of, and supported, the objectionable tenets of the subversive group to which he belonged. At least the cases to date, which have arisen under the similar provisions of the Nationality Act of 1940,[255] so indicate.[256]

Freedom of association does not appear to protect a member of a subversive association from being denied a passport because of that membership, as long as the basic requirements of due process,

[248] Act of October 16, 1918; 40 Stat. 1012; Kessler v. Strecker, 307 U.S. 22 (1939).

[249] See Harisiades v. Shaughnessy, 342 U.S. 580 (1952).

[250] Galvan v. Press, 347 U.S. 522, 528 (1954).

[251] Rowoldt v. Perfetto, 355 U.S. 115, 120 (1957).

[252] See Niukkanen v. McAlexander, 362 U.S. 390 (1960). The Immigration and Nationality Act broadly defines affiliation: "The giving, loaning, or promising of support or of money or any other thing of value for any purpose to any organization shall be presumed to constitute affiliation therewith; but nothing in this paragraph shall be construed as an exclusive definition of affiliation." 8 U.S.C. Sec. 1101(e)(2). Contrast the former narrow interpretation in Bridges v. Wixon, 326 U.S. 135 (1945).

[253] 8 U.S.C. Sec. 1424 (membership within ten years preceding naturalization).

[254] 8 U.S.C. Sec. 1451 (membership within five years after naturalization is prima facie evidence that citizen was not, at time of naturalization, "attached to the principles of the Constitution," and will suffice for denaturalization, in the absence of countervailing evidence).

[255] 54 Stat. 1137.

[256] Polites v. United States, 364 U.S. 426 (1960); Maisenberg v. United States, 356 U.S. 670 (1958); Nowak v. United States, 356 U.S. 660 (1958).

such as notice and hearing, are met.[257] However, since the freedom of movement is a fundamental constitutional right,[258] restrictions upon it will not be loosely implied. A denial of passports by the Secretary of State, on the basis of the applicants' subversive activities and associations, was therefore invalidated where the Congressional intent to delegate that power to the Secretary was not clearly shown.[259] In the *Kent* and *Dayton* cases, the court was interpreting Section 215 of the Immigration and Nationality Act of 1952[260] and the Act of July 3, 1926.[261] The registration provisions of the Internal Security Act of 1950[262] had not yet come into effect. However, since the Supreme Court has affirmed the registration order directed at the Communist Party,[263] which includes a passport interdiction, the constitutional issue may now be squarely presented. In view of the involvement here of the fundamental right to travel, which has long been recognized within the borders of the nation[264] and which has now been extended by the court to international travel,[265] an applicant's membership in a subversive group ought not to warrant a denial of that right unless the member evinces some knowledge of the purposes of the group and some intent to support them. The main evil to be prevented is support of the Communist movement by American citizens traveling abroad.[266] There obviously ought to be room for a showing by the applicant that his membership is wholly innocent. However, subject to the basic procedural requirements of due process and the necessity of some knowledge and intent, the denial of a passport to an applicant

[257] See Bauer v. Acheson, 106 F. Supp. 445 (Dist. Col., 1952); Dulles v. Nathan, 225 F.2d 29 (Dist. Col., 1955).

[258] Kent v. Dulles, 357 U.S. 116, 125–26 (1958).

[259] Kent v. Dulles, ibid.; Dayton v. Dulles, 357 U.S. 144 (1958).

[260] 8 U.S.C. Sec. 1185.

[261] 22 U.S.C. Sec. 211(a).

[262] Providing that it shall be unlawful, when a Communist organization is registered under the act, or when "there is in effect a final order of the Board requiring an organization to register," for any member having knowledge of such registry and order to apply for a passport. 50 U.S.C. Secs. 781, 785.

[263] Communist Party v. SACB, supra p. 153.

[264] See Edwards v. California, 314 U.S. 160 (1941).

[265] Kent v. Dulles, 357 U.S. 116, 125–26 (1958).

[266] See 22 C.F.R., Secs. 51–135 (State Department Regulations). On January 12, 1962, the Department of State issued revised regulations providing for disclosure to the applicant of confidential information used by the department in denying him a passport. Representative Francis E. Walter has introduced a bill (H.R. 9754, 87th Congress, 2d Session, 1962) to prevent the disclosure of confidential information affecting the national security or tending to compromise investigative sources and methods.

due to his subversive associations would not seem to infringe unduly upon freedom of association. To hold otherwise would convert freedom of association into a virtual absolute at the very outset of its open constitutional career, and would prostulate a fundamental freedom of subversive association, as well as exalting the right to travel to a practically absolute position.[267]

Although the Congress in 1954 rejected the proposal by Senator Humphrey that mere membership in the Communist Party be made a crime,[268] it did enact, in Section 3 of the Communist Control Act, a practical proscription of the Party itself:

> The Communist Party of the United States, or any successors . . . whose object or purpose is to overthrow the Government of the United States . . . are not entitled to any of the rights, privileges, and immunities attendant upon legal bodies . . . and whatever rights, privileges, and immunities which have heretofore been granted to said party or any subsidiary organization by reason of the laws . . . are terminated. . . .[269]

The Supreme Court has not directly ruled on the constitutionality of this provision. It has been upheld in New Jersey as a basis for exclusion of a Communist Party candidate from the ballot.[270] But the court has construed the section so as not to require a denial to an employee of the Party of benefits under New York's unemployment compensation system.[271] A statute like section 3 could be used as a repressive instrument in ways which would fall short of criminal punishment but would effectively subject members of the Party to considerable disability.[272] Indeed, pushed to its verbal limit, section 3 could even withdraw from the Party the right to use the courts. Where Senator Humphrey's explicit punishment of membership was criticized because it would make the privilege against self-incrimination a defense to a registration order under the Internal Security Act of 1950,[273] section 3 may avoid that difficulty because it threatens no prosecution. In effect, however, it may, if energet-

[267] On the relative nature of the right to a passport, see dissent of Mr. Justice Clark in Kent v. Dulles, 357 U.S. 116 (1958).

[268] 100 Cong. Rec. 14208.

[269] 68 Stat. 776, 50 U.S.C. Sec. 842.

[270] Salwen v. Rees, 16 N.J. 216, 108 A.2d 265 (1954).

[271] Communist Party v. Catherwood, 367 U.S. 389 (1961).

[272] Several states already bar the Party and members from the ballot; see Gellhorn, The States and Subversion, Appendix A (Ithaca, 1952).

[273] See 100 Cong. Rec., 14211, 14212, 14217, 14565, 14643, 14644.

ically enforced, impose substantial, though indirect, civil disabilities upon members of the Party, apparently irrespective of their personal knowledge or intent. Thereby, it may amount in practice to a legislative judgment of outlawry as long as the Party persists in its obvious purposes. If so, and if it is valid, any possible right of subversive association, as a constitutional protection against civil disability, evaporates into nothingness as long as the association in question is engaged in conduct which may be validly proscribed by Congress. Necessarily, there must be a clear justification for the imposition of the civil sanctions contemplated by section 3. A mountain of evidence has been advanced as to the nature, purpose and threat of the Communist Party. But the uniquely susceptible character of the Party belies the notion that Congress can use section 3 as a precedent for the imposition of similar disabilities upon lesser organizations. If the Constitution does not invalidate section 3, the imperatives of due process ought to prevent the operation of such a stricture against associations which aim at relatively innocuous ends or pose an insignificant threat to the national safety.

Of all the nonpenal disabilities which can be imposed upon a member of a subversive association, none is more personally catastrophic than loss of employment. It is not surprising, therefore, that although the Supreme Court has upheld the right of the states [274] and the Federal Government [275] to dismiss an employee for disloyalty, of which membership in a subversive association is evidence, the court has emphasized the necessity that the employee must have been aware of the purposes and activities of the subversive organization to which he belonged.[276]

This limitation is observed in the regulations governing security in Federal employment. Prior to 1947, there was no unifying directive controlling the Federal security program. In that year, President Truman issued Executive Order 9835,[277] which provided

[274] Garner v. Board of Public Works, 341 U.S. 716 (1951); Adler v. Board of Educ., 342 U.S. 485 (1952) ("One's associates, past and present, as well as one's conduct, may properly be considered in determining fitness and loyalty. From time immemorial, one's reputation has been determined in part by the company he keeps. In the employment of officials and teachers in the school system, the state may . . . inquire into the company they keep, and we know of no rule . . . that prevents the state, when determining the fitness and loyalty of such persons, from considering the associations and persons with whom they associate.") 342 U.S. at 493.

[275] Bailey v. Richardson, 182 F.2d 46 (Dist. Col., 1950), aff'd. per curiam by equally divided court, 341 U.S. 918 (1951).

[276] Wieman v. Updegraff, 344 U.S. 183 (1952).

[277] 12 Fed. Reg. 1935; Mar. 21, 1947.

for "a loyalty investigation of every person entering the civilian employment . . . of the executive branch of the Federal Government."[278] The standard for the refusal of, or dismissal from, employment "on grounds relating to loyalty" was that on all the evidence, reasonable grounds exist for belief that the person involved is disloyal to the Government of the United States."[279] By Executive Order 10241,[280] this standard was tightened so that the question became whether, "on all the evidence, there is a reasonable doubt as to the loyalty of the person involved. . . ." Under the Truman loyalty program, the individual's associations were relevant but not conclusive, including:

> Membership in, affiliation with or sympathetic association with any foreign or domestic organization, association, movement, group or combination of persons, designated by the Attorney General as totalitarian, fascist, communist, or subversive, or as having adopted a policy of advocating or approving the commission of acts of force or violence to deny other persons their rights under the Constitution of the United States, or as seeking to alter the form of government of the United States by unconstitutional means.[281]

The criterion was changed from loyalty to national security by Executive Order 10450,[282] issued by President Eisenhower. It provided that the question is "whether the employment or retention in employment in the Federal Service of the person being investigated is clearly consistent with the interests of the national security."[283] Among the relevant, but not conclusive, factors was membership in the same general kinds of associations enumerated in Executive Order 9835. Executive Order 10450 is still in effect.[284] The fact that membership in a subversive association[285] does not automatically and conclusively exclude an employee is further evidenced by the administrative practices of the agencies involved. For example, a

[278] Pt. 1, para. 1.
[279] Pt. 5, para. 1.
[280] 16 Fed. Reg. 3690, Apr. 28, 1951.
[281] Pt. 5, para. 2(f).
[282] 18 Fed. Reg. 2489, April 27, 1953.
[283] Sec. 8(a).
[284] See Bureau of National Affairs, Inc., Government Security and Loyalty 11:1 (Washington, Govt. Printing Office, 1955).
[285] Executive Order 9835, Pt. 3, Sec. 3, required the Department of Justice to furnish the Loyalty Review Board with a list of subversive organizations. On this "Attorney General's List," see Joint Anti-Fascist Refugee Comm. v. McGrath, 341 U.S. 123 (1951); note, The Legal Status of the "Attorney General's List," 44 Calif. L. Rev. 748 (1956).

Civil Service Commission Handbook, "Guides for Members of Security Hearing Boards Under Executive Order 10450," provides that:

In evaluating memberships, affiliations, or associations the . . . board will give consideration to the employee's statement of his reason for joining and his knowledge of the purposes of the organization.[286]

It is clear, therefore, that the Federal security regulations do not impose an automatic penalty upon membership in subversive associations. What is not so obvious, but is nonetheless true, is that a regulation attempting to bar from employment on the basis of associations without some element of *scienter* would be unconstitutional. The language of the Supreme Court in *Wieman v. Updegraff* [287] is uncompromising:

Indiscriminate classification of innocent with knowing activity must fall as an assertion of arbitrary power. The oath offends due process.

While the court has not squarely decided the issue in a case involving the Federal security program,[288] the court's emphatic reliance upon due process in *Wieman v. Updegraff*, which involved a state security program, indicates that the Federal employee will be protected against arbitrary dismissal to the same extent as the state employee. The Court of Appeals of the District of Columbia has intimated as much in interpreting the provision of the Internal Security Act of 1950 [289] which denied nonelective government or defense employment to members of an organization ordered to register as subversive. There the Court of Appeals held that "the requirement . . . that a member have knowledge or notice of the registration of the organization, which means that he has knowledge of the nature of the organization, before these sanctions apply to him, satisfies the due-process clause. . . ." [290] The same result is required by the Hatch Act, as amended, prohibiting employment of a "knowing" member of an organization advocating the overthrow of

[286] Bureau of National Affairs, Inc., Government Security and Loyalty 15:582 (Washington, Govt. Printing Office, 1955).

[287] 344 U.S. 183, 191 (1952).

[288] Several decisions have reversed dismissals of Federal employees, but on non-constitutional grounds. See Peters v. Hobby, 349 U.S. 331 (1955); Cole v. Young, 351 U.S. 536 (1956); Service v. Dulles, 354 U.S. 363 (1957).

[289] 50 U.S.C. Sec. 784.

[290] Communist Party v. Subversive Activities Control Board, 223 F.2d 531, 552 (Dist. Col., 1954), reversed on other grounds, 351 U.S. 115 (1956).

the government.[291] It is tenable to say that the right of association is an ingredient of the due process relied upon by the courts to prevent discharge for membership without knowledge of the nature of the association. This is true even in the absence of a fundamental right to associate for subversive purposes.

An indirect way of eroding the strict requirement of *scienter* was opened in *Beilan v. Board of Public Education* [292] and *Lerner v. Casey*,[293] where a teacher in *Beilan* and a transit employee in *Lerner* were discharged for unfitness and incompetence when they refused, on self-incrimination grounds, to answer their superiors' questions relating to their alleged membership in subversive associations. The Supreme Court upheld the discharges, with the majority in each case distinguishing *Slochower v. Board of Education*,[294] where a discharge was invalidated which was based upon the employee's refusal to testify before a Congressional committee, rather than upon an inference of unfitness drawn from a refusal to discuss the alleged associations with the employer. But the distinction between questions asked by an employer and questions asked by a committee is not workable, as shown by *Nelson v. Los Angeles County*,[295] where the majority of the court upheld the discharge of public employees for refusing to answer questions about their associations asked by a Congressional committee. The employees were ordered by their superiors to answer the questions, and a statute [296] made it the duty of a public employee to answer questions about his subversive activity on pain of discharge. The contention of the majority in *Nelson* that the *Slochower* decision was based simply on the exercise of the privilege against self-incrimination, while in *Nelson* the act which precipitated the discharge was not the invocation of the privilege but the failure to answer, is unrealistic at best.[297] Nor is a solid distinction to be found in the fact that the employees in *Nelson* were ordered by the statute and their superiors to give the testimony. It seems, rather, that *Nelson*, like *Beilan* and *Lerner*, signifies a departure from the spirit of the *Slochower* case. These later cases appear to recognize the inherent

[291] 5 U.S.C., Sec. 118(p); see Housing Authority v. Cordova, 130 Cal. App. 2d 883, 279 P.2d 215 (1955), 350 U.S. 969.

[292] 357 U.S. 399 (1958).

[293] 357 U.S. 468 (1958).

[294] 350 U.S. 551 (1956).

[295] 362 U.S. 1 (1960).

[296] California Government Code, Sec. 1028.1.

[297] See dissent by Mr. Justice Brennan in the Nelson case, 362 U.S. at 14–15.

vulnerability of the supposed right to associate for subversive ends, and at the same time they tend to limit the privilege against self-incrimination to its traditional function as a protection only against criminal penalties.[298] The freedom of association in this area, whether as a constitutional freedom or as merely an indirect creature of due process, remains operative as a shield against criminal penalty for the innocent, unknowing member. But it does not insulate him against disclosure of his membership and, indeed, the details of his activity in the association.[299]

In fact, by the very act of asserting the unknowing character of his membership, so as to prevent his discharge, the employee himself would nullify whatever right he has to keep silent about his associations. Since there must be at least a minimal standard of candor in public employment, and since an individual's knowing subversive association may warrant even criminal punishment, it would seem that the employee who is faced with evidence of, or questions concerning, an alleged knowing subversive association on his part ought not to be privileged to remain silent and yet retain his employment. At least the freedom of association, which does not protect him against criminal penalty for a knowing membership, would not seem to protect him against the civil disability of loss of employment. The right to join the Communist Party is, naturally, far more limited than the right to join the Elks or the National Association for the Advancement of Colored People. The employee in this situation must, therefore, put his trust in the privilege against self-incrimination, and the *Beilan, Lerner,* and *Nelson* cases indicate that this is a slender bulwark.

A related problem was presented in *Cramp v. Board of Public Instruction*[300] where the Supreme Court invalidated an oath for a public employee which required him not only to deny membership in the Communist Party but also to swear "that I have not and will not lend my aid, support, advice, counsel or influence to the Communist Party. . . ." The decision was rested upon the vagueness of the standard. The impediment to free association could have been argued as an alternative ground. For example, one might be discouraged by such an oath requirement from joining the American Civil Liberties Union which has lent its "advice" and "counsel" to

[298] See Brown v. Walker, 161 U.S. 591 (1896).
[299] See Nelson v. Los Angeles County, 362 U.S. 1 (1960).
[300] 368 U.S. 278 (1961).

persons accused of Communist Party membership in cases involving what the Union considers important civil liberties. However, the Florida court had ruled that "the element of scienter was implicit in each of the requirements of the statute."[301] Perhaps if the Florida court had particularized this requirement of *scienter,* so that the employee must have rendered the assistance to the Party in order specifically and willfully to promote its unlawful purposes and not for any innocent purpose such as the protection of constitutional rights by provision of legal counsel to accused Party members, the oath provision might have been saved.[302] The *Cramp* case illustrates the incongruity of treating the Party as a criminal conspiracy for some purposes and as a valid political association for others. Such ambivalence accentuates the uncertainty of the extent to which one may deal with the Party while at the same time it fails to extirpate the Communist conspiracy.[303]

It appears, from the material discussed above, that freedom of association does not protect a deliberate member of a Communist association from deprivation of government or defense employment, even if the freedom of subversive association be accorded constitutional rank.[304] The problem of security in public and defense employment is too complex to permit examination in detail here.[305] But it may safely be said that deprivation of government employment for an innocent membership in a subversive association is irrevocably unconstitutional as a violation of due process.[306]

[301] Cramp v. Board of Public Instruction, 125 So. 2d 554, 557 (Fla., 1960).

[302] Compare Wieman v. Updegraff, 344 U.S. 183 (1952).

[303] Note the advocacy by Tocqueville of simple proscription of dangerous associations, above, p. 41. See also von Schmertzing, ed., Outlawing the Communist Party (A Case History) (Bookmailer, New York, 1957), describing the outlawry of the Communist Party in the German Federal Republic. The 1962 report of the official Radcliffe Committee on the internal security problem in Great Britain noted that effective counter-subversive action is hindered because the British government does not exclude Communists from its service, and the Communist Party is treated there as a political party. See New York Times, April 6, 1962, p. 1.

[304] Nor would the concept of freedom of association change the result in American Communications Ass'n v. Douds, 339 U.S. 382 (1950), upholding the non-Communist affidavit requirement of Section 9(h) of the Taft-Hartley Act as a condition of a labor union's access to the NLRB. But see Cramp v. Board of Public Instruction, 368 US 278 (1961) and the opinion in the lower court in the Cramp case, 125 So. 2d 554 (Fla., 1961).

[305] See, for example, Newman, Control of Information Relating to Atomic Energy, 56 Yale L.J. 769 (1947); Brown & Fassett, Security Tests for Maritime Workers: Due Process under the Port Security Program, 62 Yale L.J. 1163 (1953); Greene v. McElroy, 360 U.S. 474 (1959).

[306] Wieman v. Updegraff, supra p. 165 and discussion following.

Although it has not been so employed, it would seem that freedom of association, at least as a product of due process, if not as an independent constitutional freedom, would be a helpful tool for clarifying such cases, particularly where the privilege against self-incrimination is not involved. The standards implicit in this freedom would require, first, that only a knowledgeable association may occasion the civil sanction of loss of public employment, and second, that the character of the association labeled as subversive must bear some relation to the employment in question. Deliberate membership in the German-American Bund or the Communist Party readily disqualifies one from any employment by the government which those associations sought or seek to subvert. But from these precedents Congress cannot extract a power to penalize with loss of public or defense employment the members of every minority or radical group, however innocuous in doctrine or insignificant in numbers and power, which Congress or the Attorney General may decide to stigmatize as subversive.

The spirit of freedom of association would seem to apply to private as well as public employment. Prospective loss of employment in a private school because of one's associations is as heavy a restraint upon the inclination to associate as it is in a public school or government position. Nevertheless, the constitutional concept of freedom of association is relevant to private employment only insofar as it is government action which provides the challenge.[307] There have been efforts by major private employers and by professional associations to protect the right of association against what they consider undue infringement by antisubversive restrictions.[308] But these private activities are only collateral to the constitutional issue.

One area of private endeavor in which the rights of association do benefit from constitutional protection is that of the professions. Here the requisite state action is found in the state's control over

[307] See Greene v. McElroy, 360 U.S. 474 (1959), where the court held that the right to hold specific private employment free from unreasonable government interference is within the liberty and property protected by the due-process clause of the Fifth Amendment.

[308] See note, Loyalty and Private Employment: The Right of Employers to Discharge Suspected Subversives, 62 Yale L.J. 954 (1953); American Association of University Professors, Report: Academic Freedom and Tenure in the Quest for National Security, 42 A.A.U.P. Bull. 49 (1956); Statement of the Association of American Law Schools Regarding Loyalty Oaths and Related Matters, A.A.L.S. 1951 Proceedings, 98–101, approved, 8–13, 61–62; Brown, Loyalty and Security 120–31 (New Haven, 1958).

admission and expulsion. Naturally, the legal profession has been the most fertile source of litigation in this connection. All states require newly admitted attorneys to swear to support the Constitution, and several additionally provide, by statute or judicial rule, for the exclusion or expulsion of persons who advocate the forcible overthrow of the government or belong to associations which do so.[309] All states require satisfactory moral character as a condition for admission to the practice of law.[310] It seems clear that the requirements of due process prevent exclusion from the bar solely on the basis of an innocent past or present membership in a subversive association.[311] Moreover, the court has held that a good-faith refusal, in reliance upon constitutional claims, to answer questions posed by a bar-examining committee as to membership in a subversive association, does not necessarily show bad moral character.[312] This is so even though the burden of proving good moral character rests upon the applicant.[313] However, since an applicant's adherence to the Constitution is a legitimate subject for inquiry by bar examiners,[314] the applicant is under a duty to cooperate with the examiners and not to frustrate their investigation of his qualifications. The court has held, therefore, that a deliberate refusal to answer questions about one's allegedly subversive associations may justify exclusion as an entirely independent ground and not merely as evidence of bad moral character.[315] Indeed, there is an obligation to answer such questions even though they are purely exploratory and the examiners have no evidence of any subversive associations on the part of the petitioner.[316] That the underlying constitutional principle here is freedom of association was recognized in the 1961 *Konigsberg* and *Anastaplo* decisions. The majority in each case applied the familiar "balancing" test[317] and held that the state's "interest in having lawyers who are devoted to the law in its broadest sense"[318] outweighed "the interest in not subjecting

309 See Brown & Fassett, Loyalty Tests for Admission to the Bar, 20 U. Chi. L. Rev. 480 (1953).

310 See West Publishing Company, Rules for Admission to the Bar (1957).

311 Schware v. Board of Bar Examiners, 353 U.S. 232, 243–46 (1957); Konigsberg v. State Bar of California, 366 U.S. 36 (1961).

312 Konigsberg v. State Bar of California, 353 U.S. 252 (1957).

313 Konigsberg v. State Bar of California, 366 U.S. 36 (1961).

314 In re Summers, 325 U.S. 561 (1945).

315 Konigsberg v. State Bar of California, 366 U.S. 36 (1961).

316 Re Anastaplo, 366 U.S. 82 (1961).

317 See Bates v. Little Rock, 361 U.S. 516, 524 (1960).

318 366 U.S. at 52.

speech and association to the deterrence of subsequent disclosure."[319] Therefore, the exclusion of the petitioner from practice was not unconstitutional. Mr. Justice Black, in dissent, rejected the "balancing" test in principle,[320] as a reduction of the fundamental freedoms of speech and association to a "conditional" rank.[321] Furthermore, assuming *arguendo* the pertinency of "balancing," Mr. Justice Black found that the deterrent effect upon association was greater than the "interest of the Committee in satisfying its curiosity with respect to Konigsberg's 'possible' membership in the Communist Party two decades ago."[322]

The parallel between these bar-admission cases and the *Beilan, Lerner,* and *Nelson* decisions[323] is apparent and was relied upon by the majority in *Konigsberg* and *Anastaplo.* In both types of cases, the protection afforded by freedom of association against the imposition of a criminal or civil penalty for innocent membership is evaded by the requirement of answering questions. This requirement, justified by "balancing," subjects even a wholly innocent member to the disability of making a full revelation of his relevant associational record. However, in view of the evident state power over admission to the bar, and the public interest in maintaining the integrity of that bar, it seems that the restrictions upon association embodied in *Konigsberg* and *Anastaplo* are constitutionally permissible, at least so far as the Communist Party is the subversive association in question.[324] The bar-admission cases, and the similar restrictions on eligibility for other professions,[325] therefore, reinforce the conclusion that the freedom of subversive association, if such there be, is peculiarly vulnerable. In liability to criminal penalty, general civil disability and disclosure of his membership, the member of the group validly stigmatized as subversive occupies a position vastly inferior to that of the member of a religious, labor or truly political association. Indeed, but for the efforts of the Supreme Court to retain for it some minimal degree of protection, the right to join a subversive association would long ago have ceased to exist

[319] Ibid.

[320] Mr. Justice Black has consistently expressed his opposition to "balancing." See his dissent in American Communications Ass'n v. Douds, 339 U.S. 382, 445–53 (1950).

[321] 366 U.S. at 68.

[322] 366 U.S. at 74.

[323] Supra p. 166.

[324] See discussion of the Beilan, Lerner, and Nelson cases, supra pp. 166 et seq.

[325] See Barsky v. Board of Regents, 347 U.S. 442 (1954) (physician); Barnett, Public Licenses and Public Rights, 33 Ore. L. Rev. I (1953).

even in theory. As it is, the vulnerability of that right, even under the generally liberalizing influence of freedom of association, is perhaps its salient characteristic.

The especially precarious position of the Communist Party in this respect has been emphasized by the court in upholding the constitutionality of contempt convictions for refusal to answer a Congressional committee's questions about the witness's suspected membership in the Party.[326] Indeed, the court, in the *Barenblatt* majority opinion, explicitly recognized the distinctive position of the Party:

> . . . this Court . . . has consistently refused to view the Communist Party as an ordinary political party, and has upheld federal legislation aimed at the Communist problem which in a different context would certainly have raised constitutional issues of the gravest character. . . . To suggest that because the Communist Party may also sponsor peaceable political reforms the constitutional issues before us should now be judged as if that Party were just an ordinary political party from the standpoint of national security, is to ask this Court to blind itself to world affairs. . . .[327]

Of course, the questions asked must be pertinent to a reasonable object of legislative investigation, and the witness has a right to have that pertinency explained to him.[328] However, the court appears to hold that the mere disclosure of the witness's associational tie with the Party is itself a valid object of the questioning, or at least an object which is beyond judicial scrutiny.[329] These, and other decisions [330] which admit the Federal and state legislative power of investigation of the Communist Party and its membership, afford but another example of the inferior status of that Party, and, inferentially, of all validly declared subversive groups, in the catalogue of freedom of association.[331]

[326] Barenblatt v. United States, 360 U.S., 109 (1959); Wilkinson v. United States, 365 U.S. 399 (1961); Braden v. United States, 365 U.S. 431 (1961).

[327] 360 U.S. at 128–29; see also, Wilkinson v. United States, id., 365 U.S. at 414.

[328] Watkins v. United States, 354 U.S. 178 (1957).

[329] See Barenblatt v. United States, 360 U.S. at 131, 132; Wilkinson v. United States, 365 U.S. at 409–13; but see dissents of Mr. Justice Black in Barenblatt and of Mr. Justice Brennan in Wilkinson.

[330] See, for example, Uphaus v. Wyman, 360 U.S. 72 (1959).

[331] Contrast, for example, the treatment of pressure groups as targets of legislative inquiry. See United States v. Rumely, 345 U.S. 41 (1953).

I. GENERAL CONCLUSIONS CONCERNING FREEDOM OF ASSOCIATION AND SUBVERSIVE ASSOCIATIONS

1. Logically, there can be no constitutional freedom of subversive association. That is, there can be no constitutionally protected right to join or support a subversive association. At least, this is true where the association is "subversive" because it levels a fundamental attack at the government itself. The Constitution cannot consistently contain within itself provisions in detail for its permanent endurance and adjustment to the requirements of generations unborn, and at the same time legitimize the efforts of those who would disregard those provisions and overturn it from its foundations. As Mr. Justice Frankfurter said in the *Dennis* case: ". . . no government can recognize a 'right' of revolution, or a 'right' to incite revolution if the incitement has no other purpose or effect."[332] Even the right of revolution posited by Locke became operative only in the face of a governmental attempt "to take away and destroy the property of the people, or to reduce them to slavery under arbitrary power." Only then are the people "absolved from any farther obedience."[333] Such oppression by the exercise of arbitrary power would in itself be contrary to the Constitution of the United States. That instrument provides for measures, such as judicial review and frequent elections, to forestall usurpation and abuse. It sanctifies neither a despotism imposed in its name, nor the efforts of those who, to right a wrong they perceive, would destroy the Constitution itself.

2. While there can be no constitutional freedom of subversive association, there is a semblance of it. There are, as we have seen, areas and ways in which the government is constitutionally prevented from interfering with subversive associations and their members. But these inhibitions arise, not from a substantive guarantee of the right of subversive association, but rather from general constitutional guarantees. Thus, the concept of due process of law insures that the Federal Government, and the states, shall not label an association as subversive without substantial evidence to support the determination. Also operative in this connection are the First Amendment freedoms of speech and press, the prohibition of

[332] Dennis v. United States, 341 U.S. 494, 549 (1951).
[333] Locke, Of Civil Government 229 (Everyman's Library, London, 1924).

bills of attainder, the privilege against self-incrimination, and other constitutional protections of individual liberty. Together, these guarantees circumscribe the efforts of government to stigmatize the association and punish the members.[334] But they are not translatable into a fundamental right of subversive association. Rather, the right to associate for subversive ends sometimes appears to exist on a fundamental plane only because such basic constitutional restrictions on government activity have determined that the member of a subversive group may be burdened only under the circumstances and conditions dictated by those basic guarantees. The supposed freedom of subversive association is, therefore, analytically but a function of those fundamental provisions. It is, it may be said, a reflected right and not an independent constitutional right. Therefore, it is of a subconstitutional order.

3. The reflected right of subversive association, because it is of a lower constitutional order than the right of association for genuine purposes of religion, political activity or livelihood, is subject to greater restrictions than those other and fundamental associational rights. The government may infringe upon the right of subversive association in any way, and to whatever extent, it sees fit, subject only to the requirements of due process and the other constitutional guarantees of individual liberty. Unlike the other types of associations, there is no additional fundamental right of subversive association which independently restrains the government.

4. Criminal penalties may be imposed upon members of a subversive association only if they are: ". . . 'active' members having also a guilty knowledge and intent." [335] But this restriction is referable to the guarantee of due process rather than to any fundamental right to join a subversive association. Indeed, such a right, if it existed, would be stultified by this rule, which in effect immunizes it from punishment only when it is exercised in a meaningless and unconscious manner.

5. The intent required, by due process of law, to subject a member of a subversive association to criminal penalty must be an intent to effectuate specifically the illegal aims of the association and

[334] It was arguably these protections which Mr. Justice Brandeis had in mind when he suggested that "assembling with a political party, formed to advocate the desirability of a proletarian revolution by mass action at some date necessarily far in the future, is . . . a right within the protection of the Fourteenth Amendment." Whitney v. California, 274 U.S. 357, 379 (1927); supra p. 131.

[335] Scales v. United States, 367 U.S. 203, 228 (1961).

cannot be merely an intent to achieve some good or harmless end which the group also seeks.[336]

6. Civil disabilities may be imposed upon a member of a subversive association who has a lesser knowledge and intent than would be required to make him liable to criminal penalty. The varied restrictions imposed upon the Communist Party have resulted in a refinement of this principle. Thus, there are today few, if any, civil disabilities which can be imposed upon the member without some culpable knowledge and intent on his part.[337] Practically all require some *scienter*, including even, to a limited extent, immigration and naturalization restrictions. This result is properly attributable to the command of due process of law.

7. The regulatory power of government over subversive activity is broadened when that activity is in the form of a combination. In such cases the individual member of the combination may be criminally punished for his culpable association with it, even though there is lacking the personal intent or activity which would be necessary for a conviction of merely individual subversive activity or of ordinary criminal conspiracy. This development has been accelerated by the experience with the Communist Party. The deduction cannot be made, however, that whatever restrictions may be imposed upon the Communist Party may be inflicted upon other subversive associations which may lack the foreign domination and other peculiarly pernicious characteristics of the Communist Party.

[336] Supra pp. 144, 145.
[337] For example, publicity of his membership through registration.

VII. Basic Principles of Freedom of Association in the United States

1. Freedom of association, as described hereinbefore, is a fundamental constitutional right, at least so far as association for the advancement of beliefs and ideas is concerned. Religious, political, subversive, and even labor associations all engage to a substantial extent in the propagation of ideas. It is in connection with these groups that the emergence of the constitutional right of association can be seen.

2. Freedom of association, protecting as it does the individual's right to join with others in a common enterprise, is distinct from the usual individual civil liberties, such as freedom of speech and of religion. As a fundamental constitutional right, freedom of association is independent of, and not merely ancillary to, those individual freedoms.

3. The exercise of the freedom of association in some cases expands the individual rights of the members of the association, and in other cases contracts those rights. Thus, for example, the individual's freedom of religious exercise may broaden when he becomes a member of a bona fide religious association.[1] Conversely, when an individual becomes a member of a subversive association, he may be liable to criminal and civil penalties for conduct which would not so subject him if he were not affiliated with the subversive association.[2]

[1] See above, pp. 58 et seq.

[2] See above, pp. 263 et seq., 151 et seq., 175.

4. Freedom of association is newly recognized but, although not considered by the framers and not expressed in the Constitution, it has been latent in that charter and may be said to have been a tacit, though unrecognized, basis for some past conclusions generally ascribed to the application of other freedoms.[3]

5. The fundamental freedom to join and support associations, and to practice their precepts, can be qualified in the interest of public order, to prevent breach of the peace and impairment of public morality. The various restrictions on political campaign activity and expenditures,[4] and upon the outward practices of religious sects,[5] illustrate this proposition.

6. The freedom not to join or support associations, and not to practice their precepts, can be qualified for sufficient reasons of public interest. The union shop,[6] the rendering of public aid to religious associations,[7] and sumptuary laws,[8] provide examples in support of this principle.

7. Although there is a fundamental general freedom of association, there is no constitutional freedom of subversive association. There is, however, a reflected right of subversive association which is of a subconstitutional order. This reflected right appears to exist only because the fundamental guarantees of liberty in the Constitution, especially due process and the freedoms of speech and press and from self-incrimination, prevent the government from interfering arbitrarily with the members of subversive groups. The government may restrict or penalize the members of subversive associations, at least those which seek to overthrow the government, in any way it sees fit, subject only to the restrictions imposed on it by those fundamental constitutional guarantees. In dealing with subversive associations and their members, therefore, the government is not further restrained by the fundamental freedom of association. It must be remembered, however, that the fundamental guarantees of individual liberty which do inhibit the government in its dealings with subversive associations and their members work genuine and substantial restraints upon the exercise of official power. Often they are as effective in restricting the government as would be a fundamental freedom of subversive association.[9]

[3] See, for example, above, pp. 48 et seq., 84 et seq., 112 et seq., 131 et seq.

[4] See above, pp. 107–108, 110 et seq.

[5] See above, pp. 48 et seq.

[6] See above, pp. 82 et seq.

[7] See above, pp. 63 et seq.

[8] See above, pp. 66 et seq.

[9] See generally, above pp. 173 et seq.

Bibliography

*Abernathy. The Right of Assembly and Association. Columbia, South Carolina, 1961.
———. The Right of Association, 6 S.C.L.Q. 32 (1953). **71, 101ff., 108, 110ff., 133**
Adams, G. B. and Schuyler. Constitutional History of England. New York, 1921. **109**
Adams, J. T. The Epic of America. New York, 1931. **21, 22, 28, 32**
America. Golden Jubilee of the NAACP (August 1, 1959). **110**
American Federation of Labor. The Right to Wreck! Washington, D.C., 1954. **90**
American Association of University Professors. Report: Academic Freedom and Tenure in the Quest for National Security, 42 A.A.U.P. Bull. 49 (1956). **169**
*AFL–CIO. Union Security. Washington, D.C., AFL–CIO, 1958.
Ames. The Proposed Amendments to the Constitution of the United States During the First Century of Its History (H.R. Doc. No. 353, Pt. 2, 54th Cong., 2d Sess.). **65**
Annotation. Constitutionality of Federal and State Regulation of Obscene Literature, Federal Cases, 4 L.Ed. 2d 1821 (1959). **66**
Aquinas. Selected Political Writings. Dawson transl. Oxford, 1948. **5**
Aristotle. The Nicomachean Ethics. Thomson transl. London, 1953. **3**
*———. The Works of, translated into English. Oxford, 1921.
Association of American Law Schools. Loyalty Oaths and Related Matters, A.A.L.S. 1951 proceedings. **169**
Attorney General of the United States. Annual Report. 1956. **141**
St. Augustine. The City of God. Marcus Dods transl. New York, Modern Library, 1950. **3, 4**

* Used for general reference.

Bacon. Of Seditions and Troubles. Eliot ed. New York, The Harvard Classics, 1909. **13**

*Bancroft. History of the United States of America. 6 vols. New York, 1891.

Barker. Greek Political Theory. London, 1951. **2, 14**

Barnett. Public Licenses and Public Rights, 33 Ore. L. Rev. 1 (1953). **171**

Barr. Voltaire in America, 1744–1800. Baltimore, 1941. **15**

Beard, Charles A. and Mary R. The Rise of American Civilization. New York, 1930. **21, 33**

Becker. Heavenly City of the Eighteenth-Century Philosophers. New Haven, 1932. **13**

Berger. The New York State Law Against Discrimination: Operation and Administration, 35 Cornell L.Q. 747 (1950). **80**

*Berns. Freedom, Virtue and the First Amendment. Baton Rouge, Louisiana, 1957.

Beth. The American Theory of Church and State. Gainesville, Florida, 1958. **21ff., 30**

Bicks and Friedman. Regulation of Federal Election Finance: A Case of Misguided Morality, 28 N.Y.U.L. Rev. (1953). **93**

Blackstone. Commentaries on the Laws of England. (Chase ed.) New York, 1936. **12**

Blaisdell. American Democracy Under Pressure. New York, 1957. **108ff.**

*Blitzer. An Immortal Commonwealth. New Haven, 1960.

*Bluck. Plato's Life and Thought. London, 1949.

Blum. Religious Liberty and Religious Garb, 22 U. Chi. L. Rev. (1955). **65**

Bone. American Politics and the Party System. New York, 1955. **101, 110, 111, 113**

*Boorstin. The Lost World of Thomas Jefferson. New York, 1948.

Boudin. State Poll Taxes and the Federal Constitution, 28 Va. L. Rev. (1941). **105**

Bradley. Involuntary Participation in Unionism. Washington, D.C., American Enterprise Association, Inc., 1956. **90**

Brant. Madison: On the Separation of Church and State, 8 William & Mary Q. 1 (1951). **15**

———. James Madison, the Virginia Revolutionist. Indianapolis, 1941. **29**

Brissenden. The I.W.W. New York, 1919. **17**

Brooklyn Tablet. President's Committee to Study the United States Military Assistance Program, Nov. 21, 1959. **69**

*Brown. Charles Beard and the Constitution. Princeton, 1956.

———. Loyalty and Security. New Haven, 1958. **169**

———. State Regulation of Union Political Action, 6 Lab. L.J. (1955). **93**

Brown and Fassett. Loyalty Tests for Admission to the Bar, 20 U. Chi. L. Rev. (1953). **170**

———. Security Tests for Maritime Workers: Due Process under the Port Security Program 62 Yale L.J. 1163 (1953). **168**

Brundel. Zoning Out Religious Institutions, 32 Notre Dame Law. (1957). **54**

Bryce. The American Commonwealth. 2 vols. London, 1907. **24**

Bureau of National Affairs, Inc. Government Security and Loyalty. Washington, D.C., 1955. **164**

Burke. Thoughts on the Cause of the Present Discontents. London, 1770. **13**

Cahn. The "Establishment of Religion" Puzzle, 36 N.Y.U.L. Rev. 1274 (1961). **10ff., 16**

———. The Predicament of Democratic Man. New York, 1961. **3, 13, 16**

*Carlton. Organized Labor in American History. New York, 1920.

Carroll. Freedom of Speech and of the Press in the Federalist Period: The Sedition Act, 18 Mich. L. Rev. (1920). **125**

*Castberg. Freedom of Speech in the West. New York, 1960.

Chafee. Free Speech in the United States. Cambridge, 1941. **67, 127, 129ff.**

———. Government and Mass Communications. Chicago, 1947. **110.**

Chamber of Commerce of the United States. The Right of the Right to Work. Washington, D.C., 1962. **90**

*Chandler, ed. Genesis and Birth of the Federal Constitution. New York, 1924.

Chitwood and Owsley. A Short History of the American People. 2 vols. New York, 1951. **20ff., 25ff., 30ff., 122, 125**

CIO. Economic Outlook, January, 1955. **90**

Coker. Recent Political Thought. New York, 1934. **18**

*Comment: Criminal Syndicalism and the Civil Liberties, 36 Ill. L. Rev. 357 (1941).

———. 50 Mich. L. Rev. 576 (1952). **51**

*———. The "Right" to Work–Euphemism or Constitutional Guarantee? 50 Nw. U.L. Rev. 773 (1956).

———. Group Action in the Fight for Civil Liberties, 58 Yale L.J. 574 (1949). **113**

Committee on Un-American Activities, House of Representatives. The Communist Conspiracy: Marxist Classics (84th Cong., 2d Sess., 1956). **148**

Commons et al., eds. A Documentary History of American Industrial Society. Cleveland, 1910–1911. **76ff.**

Commerce Clearing House. Labor Law Course. Chicago, 1957. **74ff.**

———. Labor Law Reporter. New York, 1960. **85, 87**

*Cooley. Principles of Constitutional Law. Boston, 1898.
Corwin. Bowing Out "Clear and Present Danger," 27 Notre Dame Law. 325 (1952). **139**
———. The Constitution and What It Means Today. Princeton, 1958. **62**
———, ed. The Constitution of the United States of America. Washington, D.C., Government Printing Office, 1953. **27, 30, 36ff., 109ff., 126ff.**
Council of State Governments. The Book of the States, 1958–1959. Chicago, 1958. **106, 112**
*Cox. The Duty of Fair Representation, 2 Vill. L. Rev. 151 (1957).
Davis. Essays in the Earlier History of American Corporations. Cambridge, 1917. **xix**
Dawson. The Sons of Liberty in New York. Poughkeepsie, 1859. **27**
Del Vecchio. Philosophy of Law. Thomas O. Martin transl. Washington, 1953. **3, 15, 17**
Dicey. Law and Public Opinion in England. London, 1926. **1, 16, 88**
Documents Illustrative of the Formation of the Union of the American States. Washington, D.C., Government Printing Office, 1927. **34**
Dowell. A History of Criminal Syndicalism Legislation in the United States. Baltimore, 1939. **129**
*Drost. Human Rights as Legal Rights. Leiden, 1951.
Duguit. Law in the Modern State. Frida & Harold Laski, transl. New York, 1919. **16, 17**
*———. The Law and the State. Frederick J. deSloovere, transl. 31 Harv. L. Rev. 1 (1917).
Dulles, Foster R. Labor in America. New York, 1949. **76**
Dumbauld. The Bill of Rights and What It Means Today. Norman, Okla., 1957. **28, 35ff.**
———. The Declaration of Independence and What It Means Today. Norman, Okla., 1950. **2, 4, 11, 36**
———. Thomas Jefferson and American Constitutional Law, 2 J. Pub. L. 381 (1953). **35**
Durant. The Story of Philosophy. New York, 1938. **15**
Dwight. Harrington and His Influence Upon American Political Institutions. 2 Pol. Sci. Q. (1887). **71**
Eaton. Censorship of the Southern Mails, 48 Am. Hist. Rev. 266 (1943) **125**
Eckenrode. Separation of Church and State in Virginia. 1910. **29**
Elias. The Jehovah's Witnesses Cases, 16 Kan. L. Rev. 140 (1948), **54**
Emerson and Haber. Political and Civil Rights in the United States. 2 vols. Buffalo, 1958. **123ff., 127, 129, 141, 142, 150, 153**
*Evans. Jacques Maritain and the Problem of Pluralism in Political Life, 22 The Review of Politics 307 (July, 1960).

Fagley. The Population Explosion and Christian Responsibility. New York, 1960. **68**

*Fairman. The Supreme Court, 1955 Term, 70 Harv. L. Rev. 83 (1956).

Farrand, ed. Records of the Federal Convention of 1787. New Haven, 1937. **34**

Faulkner. American Economic History. New York, 1949. **23, 31ff.**

Fennell. The "Reconstructed Court" and Religious Freedom: The Gobitis Case in Retrospect, 19 N.Y.U.L. Rev. 31 (1941). **53**

Ferguson. Fifty Million Brothers. New York, 1937. **xix**

Field. The Philosophy of Plato. Oxford, 1949. **2**

Figgis. The Political Aspects of St. Augustine's "City of God." London, 1921. **4**

———. Political Thought from Gerson to Grotius, 1414–1625. New York, 1960. **4ff.**

*Forkosch. A Treatise on Labor Law. Indianapolis, 1953.

*Fraenkel. The Supreme Court and Civil Liberties. New York, 1960.

Friedman. The Parents' Right to Control the Religious Education of a Child, 29 Harv. L. Rev. 485 (1916). **71**

———. Reflections Upon the Law of Political Parties, 44 Calif. L. Rev. 65 (1956). **101**

Fund for the Republic. Digest of the Public Record of Communism in the United States. New York, 1955. **150**

Gale Research Co. Encyclopedia of American Associations. Detroit, 1959. **110**

*Gassman. Election Law. New York, 1951.

Gellhorn. The States and Subversion. Ithaca, 1952. **162**

Greenberg. Race Relations and American Law. New York, 1959. **113ff.**

Greene. Religion and the State. New York, 1941. **121**

Gregory. Labor and the Law. New York, 1958. **22ff., 74, 76ff., 82**

Gurvitch. La Déclaration des Droits Sociaux. New York, 1944.

Hall. Free Speech in Wartime, 21 Colum. L. Rev. 526 (1921). **126**

Hamburger. Morals and Law, the Growth of Aristotle's Legal Theory. New Haven, 1951. **3ff.**

Hamilton, Madison, Jay. The Federalist. New York, Modern Library, 1937. **15, 34ff., 37ff.**

Hamlin. Legal Education in Colonial New York. New York, 1940. **23**

Hammond. Banks and Politics in America. Princeton, 1957. **xix**

Harlow. The Growth of the United States. 2 vols. New York, 1943. **20ff., 25ff., 31ff., 36, 122ff.**

Harrington. Oceana. 1656. **12**

Hart. Epochs of American History: Formation of the Union, 1750–1829. New York, 1925. **26, 32**

Harvard University, Center for the Study of the History of Liberty in America. The Dimensions of Liberty (Cambridge, prepublication draft, March 15, 1961). **21, 26, 28**

Hawkins. A Treatise of the Pleas of the Crown. London, 1716. **22**

Hayes, Baldwin, and Cole. History of Europe. New York, 1949. **20, 40**

Hazard. The Organization of the Boot and Shoe Industry in Massachusetts Before 1875. Cambridge, 1921. **23**

Heisler. The Law Versus the Conscientious Objector, 20 U. Chi. L. Rev. 441 (1953). **59**

Heller. A Turning Point for Religious Liberty, 29 Va. L. Rev. 440 (1943). **53**

Hicks and Mowry. A Short History of American Democracy. Boston, 1956. **20ff., 25ff., 33, 74, 123, 125**

*Hoar. Subversive Activities against Government—Two Conflicting Doctrines, 27 Marq. L. Rev. 72 (1942).

Hobbes. Leviathan. Ernest Rhys, ed. London. **6ff., 10**

Horn. Groups and the Constitution. Stanford, 1956. **6, 9ff., 17, 76, 78, 105, 122, 125, 133**

Howerton. Jehovah's Witnesses and the Federal Constitution, 17 Miss. L.J. 347 (1946). **54**

Hoxie. Trade Unionism in the United States. New York, 1936. **74ff.**

Hsiao. Political Pluralism. New York, 1927. **1, 17**

Internal Security Subcommittee, Senate Committee on the Judiciary. Report: The Communist Party of the United States of America (84th Cong., 1st Sess., 1955). **144, 148**

*Jacobs. Political Parties. New York, 1951.

Jaffe. Law Making by Private Groups, 51 Harv. L. Rev. 201 (1938). **91**

Jefferson. Writings. Washington, 1861. **61**

Jensen. The Articles of Confederation: An Interpretation of Social-Constitutional History of the American Revolution, 1774–1781. Madison, Wis., 1940. **31**

Jones. Trade Associations and the Law. New York, 1922. **xix**

Kauper. Church, State and Freedom: A Review, 52 Mich. L. Rev. 829 (1954). **62**

Keller. The Case for Right-to-Work Laws. Chicago, 1956. **90**

Key. Politics, Parties, and Pressure Groups. New York, 1948. **110**

Kilpatrick. The Sovereign States. Chicago, 1957. **123**

*Klement. The Copperheads in the Middle West. Chicago, 1960.

Kovarsky. A Review of State FEPC Laws, 9 Lab. L.J. 478 (1958). **80**

Kropotkin. Mutual Aid. New York, 1919. **17**

Labaree. Royal Instructions to Colonial Governors. New York, 1935. **23**

Landis and Manoff. Cases on Labor Law. Chicago, 1942. **78**

Laski. Authority in the Modern State. New Haven, 1919. **17ff.**
———. The Foundations of Sovereignty. New York, 1921. **17ff.**
———. Morris Cohen's Approach to Legal Philosophy, 15 U. Chi. L. Rev. 575 (1948). **88**
Legislative Drafting Research Fund. Index Digest of State Constitutions. New York, 1959. **43**
*Lenhoff. A Century of American Unionism, 22 B.U.L. Rev. 357 (1942).
Lewis. The Genossenschaft-Theory of Otto von Gierke, Madison, Wis., 1935. **5, 17**
———. A New Line-up on the Supreme Court, The Reporter, August 17, 1961. **158**
Lincoln. Complete Works. Nicolay and Hay eds. 1894. **126**
Link. Democratic-Republican Societies, 1790–1800. New York, 1942. **122**
Locke. Letter on Toleration. New York, 1957. **9ff., 49**
———. Of Civil Government. London, Everyman ed., 1924. **11, 173**
Lockhart & McClure. Censorship of Obscenity: The Developing Constitutional Standard, 45 Minn. L. Rev. 5 (1960). **67**
———. Literature, the Law of Obscenity, and the Constitution, 38 Minn. L. Rev. 295 (1954). **67**
———. Obscenity Censorship: The Constitutional Issue—What is Obscene? 7 Utah L. Rev. 289 (1961). **67**
MacIver. European Doctrine and the Constitution, in The Constitution Reconsidered. Read ed. New York, 1938. **11, 13**
Malick. Terry v. Adams: Governmental Responsibility for the Protection of Civil Rights, 7 Western Pol. Q. 51 (1954). **106**
Manning. Aid to Education—Federal Fashion; Aid to Education—State Style, 29 Fordham L. Rev. 495 (1961). **65**
Maritain. Man and the State. Chicago, 1951. **16**
Martin. French Liberal Thought in the Eighteenth Century. London, 1929. **4, 13, 16**
Mason. The Corporation in Modern Society. Cambridge, 1959. **xix**
Matthews, ed. Labor Relations and the Law. Boston, advance printing, 1953. **78**
*Mayers. Right to Work in Practice. New York, Fund for the Republic, 1959.
McKay. Book Review, 15 Rutgers L. Rev. 145 (1960). **47**
———. The Repression of Civil Rights as an Aftermath of the School Segregation Decisions, 4 How. L.J. 9 (1958). **113**
McKean. Party and Pressure Politics. Boston, 1949. **110**
McLaughlin. A Constitutional History of the United States. New York, 1935. **5, 124ff.**
Metz. Labor Policy of the Federal Government. Washington, 1945. **79**

*Million. Political Crimes, 5 Mo. L. Rev. 164, 293 (1940).
———. Validity of Compulsory Flag Salutes in Public Schools, 28 Ky. L.J. 306 (1940). **53**
Millis & Brown. From the Wagner Act to Taft-Hartley. Chicago, 1960. **79**
Milton. Areopagitica. Eliot, ed. New York, The Harvard Classics, 1909. **13**
*Mitau. Judicial Determination of Political Party Organizational Autonomy, 42 Minn. L. Rev. 245 (1957).
*Montesquieu. The Spirit of Laws. Nugent transl. Cincinnati, 1873.
Morgan. Judicial Notice, 57 Harv. L. Rev. 269 (1944). **148**
Morley, ed. Ideal Commonwealths. London, 1901. **12**
Morris. Criminal Conspiracy and Early Labor Organizations, Pol. Sci. Q. (1937). **22**
———. Government and Labor in Early America. New York, 1946. **22ff., 27ff., 31ff., 76ff.**
———, ed. The Great Legal Philosophers. Philadelphia, 1959. **3, 5ff., 14**
Morse. Parties and Party Leaders. Boston, 1923. **26**
*Murray. Red Scare. Minneapolis, 1955.
NAACP. An American Organization. New York, 1960. **113, 116**
———. NAACP, Its Program and Objectives. New York, 1960. **113**
———. This Is the NAACP. New York, 1960. **113**
National Right-to-Work Committee. Do Right-to-Work Laws Help or Hurt the Economy? (1955). **90**
Nelles. The First American Labor Case, 41 Yale L.J. 165 (1931). **76**
Nelson. Public Employees and the Right to Engage in Political Activity, 9 Vand. L. Rev. 27 (1955). **108**
Newman. Control of Information Relating to Atomic Energy, 56 Yale L.J. 769 (1947). **168**
———. The Law of Labor Relations. Buffalo, 1953. **74ff.**
New York Gazeteer. Feb. 16, 1775. **26**
New York Times. Sept. 21, 1947. **64**
———. Nov. 23, 1950. **152**
———. Nov. 26, 1959. **69**
Nicolay and Hay, eds. Complete Works of Lincoln. 1894. **126**
Niebank. In Defense of Right-to-Work Laws, 8 Lab. L.J. 459 (1953). **91**
Norton. The Constitution of the United States. New York, 1956. **36**
*Note. Constitutional Law–Freedom of Speech–Under Neutrality Act of 1940–Under Espionage Act of 1917, 24 B.U.L. Rev. 266 (1944).
*———. Criminal Law–Espionage Act Specific Intent–Clear and Present Danger, 44 Colum. L. Rev. 930 (1944).
———. The Legal Status of the "Attorney General's List," 44 Calif. L. Rev. 748 (1956). **164**
———. Birth Control Legislation, 9 Clev.-Mar. L. Rev. 245 (1960). **68**

Note. Limitations on Access to the General Election Ballot, 37 Colum. L. Rev. 86 (1937). **102**

*———. Recent Federal Legislation against Subversive Influences, 41 Colum. L. Rev. 159 (1941).

———. Denial of Equal Voting Facilities to Minor Parties, 50 Colum. L. Rev. 712 (1950). **103**

———. The Internal Security Act of 1950, 51 Colum. L. Rev. 606 (1951). **150**

———. Labor Law—Agency Shop Lawful Form of Union Security Under Labor Management Relations Act, 30 Fordham L. Rev. 530 (1962). **86**

———. Recent Legislative Attempts to Curb Subversive Activities in the United States, 10 Geo. Wash. L. Rev. 104 (1941). **136**

———. Churches and Zoning, 70 Harv. L. Rev. 1428 (1957). **54**

———. The Right to Form a Political Party, 43 Ill. L. Rev. 832 (1949). **101**

———. The Lobbying Act: An Effective Guardian of the Representative System, 28 Ind. L.J. 78 (1952). **111**

———. Anonymity: An Emerging Fundamental Right, 36 Ind. L.J. 306 (1961). **115**

———. Post-Dennis Prosecutions under the Smith Act, 31 Ind. L.J. 104 (1955). **141**

———. Constitutional Law; Fourteenth Amendment; Discriminating Legislation; Classification, 13 Marq. L. Rev. 242 (1929). **133**

———. Constitutional Law–Civil Rights–First Amendment Freedoms—Reformulation of the Clear-and-Present Danger Doctrine, 50 Mich. L. Rev. 451 (1952). **141**

———. Constitutional Law—Freedom of Press—Validity of Motion Picture Licensing Statute, 58 Mich. L. Rev. 134 (1959). **67**

———. Regulation of Lobbying, 30 N.Y.U.L. Rev. 1249 (1955). **111**

———. Federal Regulation of Lobbying Act—Constitutionality and Future Application, 49 Nw. U.L. Rev. 807 (1955). **111**

———. Use of Literacy Tests to Restrict the Right to Vote, 31 Notre Dame Law. 251 (1956). **106**

*———. Voting Rights, 3 Race Rel. L. Rep. 371 (1958).

———. Constitutional Law–Religious Liberty—Fluoridation of Municipal Water Supply, 3 St. Louis U.L.J. 284 (1955). **57**

*———. Sunday Laws—Application to Persons Observing a Different Sabbath, 25 So. Cal. L. Rev. 131 (1951).

———. Federal Aid to Education—For Some or for All? 23 Temple L.Q. 227 (1950). **65**

———. Legal Barriers Confronting Third Parties: The Progressive Party in Illinois, 16 U. Chi. L. Rev. 499 (1949). **102**

———. Constitutional Law—Freedom of Religion—Statute Outlawing Snake Handling, 2 Vand. L. Rev. 694 (1949). **57**

Note. Constitutional Law—State Appropriation for Education of War Orphans Held Unconstitutional Insofar as It Could Be Used to Finance Attendance at Private or Sectarian Schools, 42 Va. L. Rev. 437 (1956). **65**

———. Freedom of Association: Constitutional Right or Judicial Technique? 46 Va. L. Rev. 730 (1960). **xviii**

———. The Supreme Court as Protector of Political Minorities, 46 Yale L.J. 862 (1937). **133**

———. Enforceability of Ante-Nuptial Contracts in Mixed Marriages, 50 Yale L.J. 1286 (1941). **71**

———. Legal Obstacles to Minority Party Success, 57 Yale L.J. 1276 (1948). **102ff.**

———. Loyalty and Private Employment: The Right of Employers to Discharge Suspected Subversives, 62 Yale L.J. 954 (1953). **169**

———. Connecticut's Birth Control Law: Reviewing a State Statute Under the Fourteenth Amendment, 70 Yale L.J. 322 (1960). **68**

———. The Constitutional Right to Anonymity, 70 Yale L.J. 1084 (1961). **116**

O'Brian. National Security and Individual Freedom. Cambridge, 1955. **149**

Odegard and Helms. American Politics. New York, 1947. **102**

O'Neill. Religion and Education Under the Constitution. New York, 1949. **62, 63**

Ovington. How the National Association for the Advancement of Colored People Began. New York, 1914. **113**

Packard. History of Medicine in the United States. New York, 1931. **146**

Palmer. A History of the Modern World. New York, 1959. **20, 22**

Pargellis. The Theory of Balanced Government, in The Constitution Reconsidered. Read ed. New York, 1938. **12, 13**

Patterson. The Forgotten Ninth Amendment. Indianapolis, 1955. **47**

Penniman. Sait's American Parties and Elections. New York, 1952. **102**

Perry. Sources of Our Liberties. Chicago, 1959. **10, 109**

Peterman. Municipal Control of Peddlers, Solicitors and Distributors, 22 Tul. L. Rev. 284 (1947). **51**

Petro. The Labor Policy of the Free Society. New York, 1957. **76, 78ff., 83, 89**

Pfeffer. Church, State and Freedom. Boston, 1953. **21, 30, 65**

———. Church and State: Something Less Than Separation, 19 U. Chi. L. Rev. (1951). **64**

———. Religion in the Upbringing of Children, 35 B.U.L. Rev. 333 (1955). **71**

Pierson. Tocqueville and Beaumont in America. New York, 1938. **38ff.**

Pius XI. Encyclical on Christian Marriage, in Five Great Encyclicals. New York, 1939. **68**

Planned Parenthood Federation of America. The Anatomy of a Victory. New York, 1959. **69**

Plato. Works. Jowett transl. 5 vols. Oxford, 1892. **2, 3**

Plucknett. A Concise History of the Common Law. Boston, 1956. **8**

Pollock and Maitland. The History of English Law. Cambridge, 1923. **22**

President's Committee to Study the U.S. Military Assistance Program. Third Interim Report, Economic Assistance Programs and Administration (1959). **69**

Preston. Documents Illustrative of American History, 1606–1863. New York, 1907. **124**

Randall, Henry. The Life of Thomas Jefferson. New York, 1858. **29**

Randall, James. Constitutional Problems Under Lincoln. New York, 1926. **125, 127, 128, 133**

Rayback. A History of American Labor. New York, 1959. **24, 31, 74ff.**

Read, ed. The Constitution Reconsidered. New York, 1938. **11ff.**

Reed. Church, State and the Zorach Case, 27 Notre Dame Law. 529 (1952). **64**

Religious Liberty Association. American State Papers on Freedom in Religion. Washington, D.C., 1949. **21**

*Reppy. Civil Rights in the United States. New York, 1951.

*Reuschlein. Jurisprudence—Its American Prophets. Indianapolis, 1951.

Rice. Collective Labor Agreements in the American Law, 44 Harv. L. Rev. 572 (1931). **82**

Richardson. Messages and Papers of the Presidents. Washington, 1897. **127**

Robertson. The Trial of James Robertson Callender. Petersburg, Va., 1804. **123**

Rogge. The First and the Fifth. New York, 1960. **12ff., 46, 47, 124ff.**

Rossiter. Constitutional Dictatorship. Princeton, 1948. **126**

Rothenberg. Labor Relations. Buffalo, 1949. **74ff.**

Rousseau. Social Contract, and Other Works. Cole transl. Oxford, 1913. **13ff.**

Russ. The Lawyer's Test Oath During Reconstruction, 10 Miss. L.J. 154 (1938). **128**

Schapiro. Condorcet and the Rise of Liberalism. New York, 1934. **15**

Schlesinger. Biography of a Nation of Joiners, 50 Am. Hist. Rev. 1 (1944). **xviii, 25ff**

Schmertzing, ed. Outlawing the Communist Party (A Case History). Bookmailer, New York, 1957. **168**

Schneider. Philosophical Differences between the Constitution and the Bill of Rights, in The Constitution Reconsidered. Read ed. New York, 1938. **12, 13**

Schroeder. Constitutional Free Speech. New York, 1919. **67**

Scott. The Slave Insurrection in New York in 1712, 45 N.Y. Hist. Soc. Q. 43 (1961). **26**

Shafer. The American Medical Profession, 1783–1850. New York, 1936. **23**

*Shientag. From Seditious Libel to Freedom of the Press, 11 Brooklyn L. Rev. 125 (1942).

Shister. Economics of the Labor Market. New York, 1956. **91**

Smith, James M. Freedom's Fetters. Ithaca, 1956. **123, 124**

Smith, Russell. Harrington and His Oceana. Cambridge, 1914. **12**

*Snyder. Preface to Jurisprudence. Indianapolis, 1954.

Sorel. Reflections on Violence. New York, 1914. **17**

Starr. The Legal Status of American Political Parties, 34 Am. Pol. Sci. Rev. 439 (1940). **101, 102**

Stephen. Hobbes. London, 1904. **6ff.**

Stokes. Church and State in the United States. 3 vols. New York, 1950. **11, 20ff., 67, 68, 70**

Stone and Pilpel. The Social and Legal Status of Contraception, 22 N.C.L. Rev. 212 (1944). **68**

Story. Commentaries. 2 vols. Boston, 1833. **61**

Sulloway. The Legal and Political Aspects of Population Control in the United States, 25 Law & Contemp. Prob. 593 (1960). **68, 69**

Sultan. Historical Antecedents to the Right-to-Work Controversy, 31 So. Cal. L. Rev. 221 (1958). **85**

*———. Right-to-Work Laws: A Study in Conflict. Los Angeles, 1958.

Sutherland. Due Process and Disestablishment, 62 Harv. L. Rev. 1306 (1949). **64**

———. Private Government and Public Policy, 41 Yale Rev. 407 (1952). **1**

Swarthout and Bartley. Principles and Problems of American National Government. New York, 1955. **31, 32**

Symposium. Equality before the Law: A Symposium on Civil Rights, 54 Nev. U.L. Rev. 330 (1959). **113, 117**

———. Religion and the State, 14 Law and Contemp. Prob. 3 (1949). **64**

*Syrett, ed. American Historical Documents. New York, 1960.

Taylor. Thomas Hobbes. London, 1908. **8**

Teller. Labor Disputes and Collective Bargaining. 3 vols. New York, 1940. **82, 85, 91**

Thorpe, ed. The Federal and State Constitutions, Colonial Charters, and Other Organic Laws. Washington, 1909. **10**

Tocqueville. Democracy in America. 2 vols. Reeve transl. New York, 1904. **68ff.**

Toner. The Closed Shop in the American Labor Movement. Catholic University of America Studies in Economics. 1941. **85**

———. Right-to-Work Laws: Public Frauds, 8 Lab. L.J. 193 (1957). **90**

Torff. Collective Bargaining. New York, 1953. **84, 90**
Turner. Party and Constituency: Pressures on Congress. Baltimore, 1951. **111**
United States Congressional and Administrative News (1957). **142**
United States Department of Commerce. Statistical Abstract of the United States. Washington, 1961. **75**
———. Historical Statistics of the United States. Washington, 1960. **75**
United States Department of Labor. Brief History of the American Labor Movement. Washington, 1957. **74**
United States Department of State. Soviet World Outlook—A Handbook of Communist Statements. Washington, 1959. **148**
United Nations. Universal Declaration of Human Rights. **xvii**
Van Tyne. The Causes of the War of Independence. New York, 1951. **27, 28**
Versfeld. A Guide to "The City of God." New York, 1958. **3, 4**
Waite. The Debt of Constitutional Law to Jehovah's Witnesses, 26 Minn. L. Rev. 409 (1944). **54**
Walsh. A History of Anglo-American Law. Indianapolis, 1932. **5**
———. The Political Science of John Adams. New York, 1915. **34**
Warren. The New "Liberty" Under the Fourteenth Amendment, 39 Harv. L. Rev. 431 (1926). **45**
*Warrender. The Political Philosophy of Hobbes. Oxford, 1957.
Webster's New International Dictionary, Unabridged. Springfield, 1949. **120**
West Publishing Co. Rules of Admission to the Bar, 1957. **170**
Weyl. The Battle against Disloyalty. New York, 1951. **125, 135**
Whipple. The Story of Civil Liberty in the United States. New York, 1927. **125**
Wigmore. Evidence. Boston, 1940. **148**
Williston. Contracts. 1938. **70**
*Wilson. The State. Boston, 1918.
*Wirtz. Government by Private Groups, 13 La. L. Rev. 440 (1953).
Witte. Early American Labor Cases, 41 Yale L.J. 825 (1926). **76ff.**
Wolman. Ebb and Flow in Trade Unionism. New York, 1936. **85**
Woodburn. Political Parties and Party Problems in the United States. New York & London, 1924. **24, 31**
Wright. The Battles of Labor. Philadelphia, 1906. **31**
———. The Meaning of Rousseau. Oxford, 1929. **15**
Zeller. The Federal Regulation of Lobbying Act, 42 Am. Pol. Sci. Rev 239 (1948). **111**

INDEX OF CASES CITED

INDEX OF CONSTITUTIONS AND STATUTES

England

GENERAL INDEX